Roth after Eighty

Roth after Eighty

Philip Roth and the American Literary Imagination

Edited by
David Gooblar
Aimee Pozorski

LEXINGTON BOOKS
Lanham • Boulder • New York • London

Published by Lexington Books
An imprint of The Rowman & Littlefield Publishing Group, Inc.
4501 Forbes Boulevard, Suite 200, Lanham, Maryland 20706
www.rowman.com

Unit A, Whitacre Mews, 26-34 Stannary Street, London SE11 4AB

British Library Cataloguing in Publication Information Available

Library of Congress Cataloging-in-Publication Data

ISBN 978-1-4985-1465-1 (cloth: alk. paper)
ISBN 978-1-4985-1466-8 (electronic)

♾️™ The paper used in this publication meets the minimum requirements of American National Standard for Information Sciences—Permanence of Paper for Printed Library Materials, ANSI/NISO Z39.48-1992.

Printed in the United States of America

For Mark Shechner, 1940–2015

Permissions

Chapter 1 is a revised version of Shostak, Debra. "Roth's Graveyards, Narrative Desire, and 'Professional Competition with Death.'" *CLCWeb: Comparative Literature and Culture* 16.2 (2014): http://dx.doi.org/10.7771/1481 –4374.2407. Copyright release to the author by Purdue University 2015. All rights reserved.

Contents

Acknowledgments

We would like to thank Philip Roth, with whom this volume begins and ends.

We thank the founding members of the Philip Roth Society—as well as other members past and present—for their ongoing support of our work.

Thank you to all of the contributors to this special volume, a passion project for us both: David Brauner, Claudia Franziska Brühwiler, Alex Calder, Amy Gelbart, Aurélie Guillain, Patrick Hayes, Catherine Morley, Ira Nadel, Adam Zachary Newton, and Debra Shostak.

We thank our families for their continued dedication and shared commitment to our work.

We thank the many departments at Lexington Press who produced this volume: first and last, we thank our commissioning editor Lindsey Porambo, as well as the executive board, designers, copy setters, proofreaders, and marketing team.

Thank you to Central Connecticut State University Honors student, Liz Willett, for sharing her talents with us by contributing the Roth portrait for our cover.

Thank you to Nettie Hansen and Sarah C. Shechner for supporting us in our work to publish the last essay of our friend and mentor, Mark Shechner. This collection is dedicated to Mark.

After Eighty

Philip Roth and the American Literary Imagination

Aimee Pozorski

The Ghost Writer (1979) is the first novel by Philip Roth that I ever read. I was 22 years old and trying to figure out how to be a writer in my own right. I read it in a seminar on representations of the Holocaust in the contemporary American literary imagination, although the novel is not about that as much as it is about the life of a writer and about writers writing. From the very first chapter, entitled "Maestro," I knew Roth to be a maestro himself—a writer who not only changed the landscape of American literature, but who had also sustained two generations (and counting) of fellow writers with his early acknowledgement of the sacrifice the vocation requires.

As *The Ghost Writer's* E. I. Lonoff, an established author, tells Nathan Zuckerman, an emerging writer in search of a mentor: "If your life consists of reading and writing and looking at the snow, you'll wind up like me. Fantasy for thirty years" (30). As it happens, within this early novel, Roth predicted the trajectory of his own life: he would write for over thirty more years, secluded in his farmhouse in Western Connecticut looking at snow, or in his New York City apartment, writing novels about writing, about the sacrifice required, all while reinterpreting American history in the second half of the twentieth century and beyond.

Such a prediction was not difficult to make in 1979, the year *The Ghost Writer* appeared. It was certainly not Roth's first book, but it was his first fully conceived Nathan Zuckerman book, with the character of Zuckerman providing a way to describe what it means to be a writer without Roth having to speak so literally about his own life. As James Atlas wrote for *The New York Times* after visiting Roth that year: "The aura of literary vocation is everywhere: in the lithographs by the Polish writer Bruno Schultz; the framed jackets of Roth's own books, blown up to poster size; the file cabinets and typewriters in every room." Atlas quotes Roth as saying that, in *The Ghost*

Writer, "Zuckerman is in search of 'a way to live as a writer . . . and he sees Lonoff's way and Abravanel's way—and the consequences of each.'" For Roth, *The Ghost Writer* is about the surprises that the vocation of writing brings"—a vocation that allows the writer to work in seclusion only to find that, once a book is out in the world, it takes on a life of its own.

Thirty-three years later, Roth once again opened his home to a journalist, Charles McGrath, who visited after Roth had announced his retirement. McGrath reports finding a post-it note in Roth's New York apartment that reads: "The struggle with writing is over." As Roth tells McGrath: "I look at that note every morning . . . and it gives me such strength." After fifty-three years of turning sentences around, of writing in seclusion and dodging the spotlight after the provocative and perpetual appearances of his masterpieces, Roth seemed deeply at peace with his decision to retire—a decision followed by Roth's rereading of his own *oeuvre*, one that he discovered, not unlike the rest of us, had profoundly changed the trajectory of American literature.

Following his retirement, Philip Roth again made headlines in May of 2014. This time, it was not for any personal or literary scandal—not for some imaginary crime he had committed—but for announcing all that he would continue *not* to do. Robert McCrum reported for the *The Guardian* that Roth's May 2014 interview with Alan Yentob was to be his last. In McCrum's words, it was the "latest episode in Roth's long goodbye," referring to official news of his retirement approximately two years before. In the same month, Jennifer Schuessler, writing for *The New York Times*, reported following his reading at the 92nd Street YMCA in Manhattan that Roth declared, "You can write it down: this was absolutely the last appearance I will make on any public stage, anywhere." The ongoing series of "lasts" ending such a fine career led Andy Borowitz ultimately to satirize them in his *New Yorker* blog: "Philip Roth says he has had his last sandwich."

Rather than simply considering these moments as "lasts"—even the fictionalized "last sandwich"—however, this collection seeks to reposition Roth and his career in light of his retirement, a "post"-career phase that nevertheless has succeeded in perpetuating new and vigorous conversations about his important work. As the Philip Roth Society newsletter editor at the time, Richard Sheehan, observed: "It's quite surprising how much stuff there is considering Roth's retired."

As Roth scholars, it is both surprising and gratifying how much critical work there is to be done as Roth himself enters the retirement phase of his career. Sheehan's statement reminds me of the astute observation at the end of David Gooblar's book, *The Major Phases of Philip Roth*: "It is surely telling that Roth, a longtime student of Freud, conceives of his *oeuvre* as a series of dreams, for, like Freud's dreams, Roth's books, and his career as a whole, invite endless interpretation, but resist any ultimate, definite, explanation" (157). Indeed, for Freud and Roth the preference for interpretation rather than explanation is perhaps the point. Our collection, in keeping with the challenge to shed new light on a career that so self-consciously resists "ultimate, definite, explanation," seeks to raise new questions about Roth's entire body work—a body of work we can now read holistically, retrospectively, retroactively.

Even before the series of "lasts" publicized throughout the month of May 2014, we had a sense that Roth was both simultaneously slipping out of public view and challenging scholars to take up a public conversation about his work. On March 18 and 19, 2013, the executive committee of the Philip Roth Society that I led alongside Gooblar, co-editor of this book and the Programming Chair at the time, hosted an international conference commemorating the 80th birthday of Philip Roth—with Roth's participation. The two-day event culminated in a keynote given by Roth and several of his longtime friends, including Claudia Roth Pierpont, Edna O'Brien, and Hermione Lee. The Library of America later published the transcripts of these lectures in a special edition entitled *Philip Roth at 80: A Celebration.*

A second result of that conference was the reunion of international scholars committed to the study of Roth's past writing and legacy. The conference received international news coverage, but even after the interest of local and international media dissipated, scholars seemed still to be thinking about what it meant for Philip Roth to turn 80, what his retirement one year before would mean for the landscape of American literature, and what his professed disappearance from the public eye in 2014 would mean for the future consideration of his legacy.

This collection seeks to address those questions in a scholarly way. Composed of eleven original essays written by accomplished scholars in the field of Philip Roth Studies, the collection contributes to the current scholarship on Roth on three levels: it is the first of its kind to offer a scholarly retrospective of Roth's works and career; it considers Roth within the American literary imagination; and it speculates on Roth's legacy—particularly the enduring quality of his novels that will continue to resonate long after his retirement.

The project is among the first of its kind to bring together scholars of Philip Roth from all over the world (Velichka Ivanova's 2014 *Philip Roth and World Literature* is also groundbreaking in this way); the remaining collections that do exist contain primarily U.S. American scholars. The other significant aspect of this collection is that it will be only the third to appear after Roth's retirement from writing novels.

While the language of most scholarly introductions would have us consider "competing" books, we see our collection more in conversation with—rather than in direct competition with—many previously published works on Roth. The list of excellent books on the work of Philip Roth is indeed long, and has grown seemingly exponentially in the last several years, but this shows, more than anything, that readers and scholars are insatiable when it comes to reading about Roth's fiction. The scholars who wrote such monographs as *Philip Roth* (Brauner, 2007); *Political Initiation in the Novels of Philip Roth* (Brühwiler, 2013); *The Major Phases of Philip Roth* (Gooblar, 2011); *Philip Roth: Fiction and Power* (Hayes, 2014); *Philip Roth and the Zuckerman Books* (Masiero, 2011); *Critical Companion to Philip Roth* (Nadel, 2011); *Philip Roth's Rude Truth* (Posnock, 2008); *Roth and Trauma* (Pozorski, 2011); *Mocking the Age: The Later Novels of Philip Roth* (Safer, 2006); *Up Society's Ass, Copper* (Shechner, 2003); and *Philip Roth—Countertexts, Counterlives* (Shostak, 2004) have been in conversation with each other for over ten years, since the founding of the Philip Roth Society. Many of them we have consulted for this very collection and they have chapters in these pages. Yet, they all take up specific angles (trauma, comedy, politics, celebrity, career trajectory, narrative form, to name only a few) in their own way, leaving space for our unique contribution of the retrospective following Roth's 80th and quiet retirement and all of the subsequent "lasts" that would begin in 2014.

Furthermore, all of these books—in addition to important essay collections on Roth such as *Turning Up the Flame: Philip Roth's Later Novels* (Halio and Siegel, 2005); *Philip Roth and World Literature* (Ivanova, 2014); *The Cambridge Companion to Philip Roth* (Parrish, 2007); *Roth and Celebrity* (Pozorski, 2012); *Philip Roth: New Perspectives on an American Author* (Royal, 2005); and *Philip Roth: American Pastoral, The Human Stain, The Plot Against America* (Shostak, 2011)—have two strengths in common: a broad knowledge of Roth and Roth Studies, and a strong sense of the context in which Roth was writing since the 1950s. The work of our collection draws on the previous knowledge published in these earlier works—monographs and collections alike—but also recasts it in light of the final stages of Roth's career.

Brauner's and Shostak's monographs are important for situating Roth in terms of his writing contemporaries, just as Safer's work contextualizes Roth in light of his sense of contemporary culture. Brauner and Shostak are also strong readers of Roth's difficult prose. Like Brauner and Shostak, Posnock's work also locates Roth within a community of writers. With this collection, we can only hope to continue this conversation by reconsidering Roth's work not in terms of the influence of his peers, since that has been done so well already, but in terms of the influence of Roth and his works more generally.

In the last few years, Roth studies seems to have taken a turn to much more specific points of focus on Roth—and that seems to have been led by two presses in particular: Cambria Press has put out two books considering

Roth's narrative frame and Roth's context in global literature (by Ivanova and Masiero respectively); and Bloomsbury has published several titles on Roth, most notably Shostak's edited collection focused on *American Pastoral, The Human Stain, and The Plot Against America*, Gooblar's work on the phases of Roth's career, Brühwiler's work on the representation of politics in Roth's career, and Pozorski's work on the representation of trauma in Roth's later works. The chapters in this collection build upon published scholarship by updating a sense of Roth and his legacy for the twenty-first century with a new focus on the future of Roth Studies in the wake of his retirement and radical turn against writing fiction in his later years.

In each of the following chapters, contributors take on this compelling task in various ways. We have organized the chapters chronologically, from essays that take up the beginning of Roth's career to those, at the end, that take up novels published at the end of Roth's career. Such an organization allows for a sense of Roth's career trajectory and, as such, reveals a trajectory of our sense of the American literary landscape. As American history and culture change, so too does Roth's fiction. It is from this retrospective, we hope, that we are able to sense the evolution of Roth's writing as a whole—an evolution that takes place, as he predicted in 1979, from a life of "fantasy for thirty years."

Debra Shostak, in chapter one: "'Every third thought shall be my grave': Roth, *Memento Mori*, and Story," meditates on Roth's graveyard moments, particularly when they function as narrative beginnings and endings. Drawing on psychoanalytic accounts of narrative desire, the article argues that Roth is preoccupied with the graveyard scene as a symbolic incitement to the compulsion that he calls in *The Human Stain* (2000) "professional competition with death" (337–338). The essay takes Roth's early short story "The Day It Snowed" (1954) as a model for his recurrent representation of the gravesite. After briefly situating the discussion within a range of Roth's books—including *Zuckerman Bound* (1985), *The Anatomy Lesson* (1983), *The Counterlife* (1986), *Patrimony* (1991), *Operation Shylock* (1993), *Exit Ghost* (2007), *Indignation* (2008), *The Humbling* (2009), and *Nemesis* (2010)—the article offers a more detailed reading of *Sabbath's Theater* (1995) and *Everyman* (2006), exploring how the cemetery scenes motivate Roth's fictional forms and his conception of storytelling.

Ira Nadel, in chapter two: "Roth @ 25: Publishing *Goodbye, Columbus*," highlights the steps, missteps, and successes of publishing *Goodbye, Columbus,* Philip Roth's first book, which appeared when he was twenty-six. It provides an in-depth look at the editorial decisions and production processes that created the finished volume, plus the surprisingly direct role of Roth in the advertising and promotion of the book. From the dust jacket to the paper and typeface, Roth took control of, or at least tried to direct, the process, establishing a practice for his later texts. Throughout the steps of preparing the book and its distribution, the young Roth constantly advised, chastised, and criticized the publisher's plans to promote the volume. He repeatedly sought to review, if not write, the advertising copy and purchase of ad space, at one point, even drafting an advertisement directed only at Newark readers. Roth's involvement with the promotion and distribution of *Goodbye, Columbus* set a pattern for his involvement with such later texts as *Sabbath's Theatre, The Dying Animal*, and *The Plot Against America*.

Claudia Brühwiler, in chapter three: "'A Human Being Lives Here': Philip Roth on Scandals and the American Presidency," argues that political scandals have not only animated and inspired the media and the general public, but also novelist Philip Roth. A frequent commenter on American culture, politics, and society, he not only captured the mood and atmosphere developing around one of the most notorious presidential scandals of recent years, Bill Clinton's brush with impeachment, but also foretold the public anger and disappointment unleashed by the Watergate affair. Specifically, Roth uses three distinct narrative modes when he approaches presidential and political scandals—satire, counter-history, and the scandal as a mere allegoric foil. Although Roth does not wholly adapt these three modes to his own ostensible scandals, the latter's fictionalization mirrors many themes from the political works and allow further insight into his judgment of American society's "persecuting spirit."

Patrick Hayes, in chapter four, "'With an accomplice no less brilliant than Jean Genet': A Comparative Approach to Roth's Autofiction," argues that, coming at the end of the Clinton era, Philip Roth's *The Human Stain* makes a powerful statement of opposition to the ways in which a disciplinary and at times highly punitive confessional discourse had become an increasingly invasive part of American life. Drawing upon historical and legal studies of the institution of confession, such as Peter Brooks' *Troubling Confessions*, as well as texts on confessional traditions by contemporaries such as J. M. Coetzee, the essay teases out the ramifications of *The Human Stain* by positioning it within Roth's longstanding exploration of what is at stake in discerning the truth of the self. In a series of early texts, including *Portnoy's Complaint* and *My Life as a Man*, Roth began to question, in a distinctively Nietzschean idiom, the *ressentiment* implicit in constructing the self as an object of knowledge. More broadly, the essay explores some of the ways in which Roth's complex handling of authorial persona in the early Zuckerman novels tends to reflect an interest in exploiting and subverting confessional conventions.

David Brauner, in chapter five: "Performance Anxiety: Impotence, Queerness, and the 'Drama of Self-Disgust' in Philip Roth's *The Professor of Desire* and *The Humbling*," provides a close reading of *The Professor of Desire* and The Humbling to suggest that a mythology has grown up around Roth's men that needs to be challenged; that in fact Roth's representation of male sexuality is much queerer than has been generally acknowledged. As Brauner argues, "The Professor of Desire is a relatively neglected text in Roth's *oeuvre*." Contrary to the few readings of the novel that do exist, Brauner's essay provides a "detailed consideration of Kepesh's early infatuation with the theatre or of what I will argue is the novel's emphasis on the performance of the sexual act and sexual performance as an act."

Aurélie Guillain, in chapter six: "Stalkers, Furies, and Comforters: Roth's Grave Comedy of Persecution," considers how the theme of persecution in Roth's novels functions both as a comic motif and the reflection of a radically agonistic view of human existence. It also gives rise to a central paradox: the threat of being humiliated or destroyed at the hands of some omnipresent, often grotesque opponent is also the crucible of a new, regenerated self which authors itself through a powerful, manly act of counter-persecution. Her essay argues, through readings of the Zuckerman books, *Operation Shylock*, and *Nemesis*, that Roth's fiction, like that of Malamud and Bellow, has never lost sight of the haunting figure of the powerless Jewish victim of European persecution, but that Roth constantly foregrounds the poetic process through which this ghostly, ever-present victim can be transformed into the figure of the "counterpuncher": a persecuted man who is able to become a counter-persecutor, a distinctly American figure whose power of speech is never permanently incapacitated. To this "counterpuncher," persecution becomes a paradoxically empowering experience, a *pro-vocation* in the etymological sense: a violent incentive to let one's wrath become vocal.

Alex Calder, in chapter seven, "'I told my wrath, my Roth did grow': Anger in *Operation Shylock*," takes William Blake's poem of experience, "The Poison Tree" ("I told my wrath"), as its starting point. This essay explores some of the implications of telling or not telling one's anger in Philip Roth's *Operation Shylock: A Confession*. Calder argues that anger is an organizing force throughout the novel, propelling the actions of doubles, as well as illustrating Philip Fisher's remark that "Anger is a territorial passion." Anger discloses a perimeter around which any diminishment of the world of "me and mine" meets resistance. The smirk of a war criminal, the Palestinian situation, the misappropriation of one's identity—these are plausible grounds for an anger that speaks for honor and awakens a sense of injustice. Anger works to undo boundaries in Philip Roth's Jerusalem novel. The chapter ultimately shows that a particularly conceived type of anger—expressing a sense of entitlement, bending towards paranoia, conflating private and public, obscuring its own relationship to any ostensible cause—is the carefully fabricated affect of *Operation Shylock*.

Catherine Morley, in chapter eight, "'My Kinsmen, My Precursors': Philip Roth, Epic, Influence, and Bardic Proclivities," examines Roth's deployment of the conventions of the prose epic in his *American Pastoral* trilogy. Roth's contemporary American epic presents the Jewish experience of post-war optimism and "innocence," retrospectively focusing upon three lives, each in various ways enchanted and disappointed by the dream of a self-reliant, self-sufficient American identity. The essay makes the case that Roth has been profoundly influenced not only by great American forebears such as Emerson and Hawthorne, but also by a European tradition that stretches back to Homer, Virgil, and the classical epic. Moreover, Morley goes on to identify affinities between Roth's approach to the epic and that of James Joyce, whose seminal work *Ulysses* recast the epic for the modernist age.

Adam Zachary Newton, in chapter nine, "'I was the prosthesis': Roth and Late Style," investigates two of Roth's final five books, *Indignation* (2008) and *Nemesis* (2010), in response to Ben Jeffrey's critique that they function as prostheses grafted onto Roth's body of work in order to facilitate that body's continued working, while appearing themselves to remain inert, mechanistic, un-living. The essay examines such a judgment, with sideward glances to Adorno and Said on "late style," by returning to Roth's earliest published work—genesis as, thus, the improbable counter-text to "nemesis."

Amy Gelbart, in chapter ten, "Performance, Affective Adaptation, Memory, Pretend Play, and Suicide in Philip Roth's *The Humbling*," begins with an observation that in *The Humbling*'s Simon Axler, Philip Roth constructs a character who performs and pretends under some very odd circumstances. The sudden loss of his acting abilities, followed by his overwhelming desire to commit suicide, launch the ex-skilled performer into uncharted territory. During his recurring attempts to end his life, he revisits semantic memories and finds himself incapable of adapting to his unexpected circumstances, from which he tries to extricate himself over the course of the novel. Exploring a cognitive interpretation of Roth's self-destructive former thespian, Gelbart's essay pursues Axler's trajectory, examining his fictional mind through performance theorists' performers and improvisers, cognitive scientists' affective adaptation and episodic and semantic memory, and developmental psychologists' child pretenders.

Mark Shechner, in chapter eleven, "Newark: The Shtetl," looks back on the Newark of Philip Roth's childhood, and of Shechner's own. Like Faulkner's Yoknapatawpha, like Dickens's London, like Joyce's Dublin, Roth's Newark is a landscape infused with moral designs and social meanings. With recollected details and pointed critical readings, the essay reconstructs a Jewish Newark that now belongs in equal measure to Roth's page-bound imagination as it does to history.

Finally, in his "Afterword: Mark Shechner's Legacy," David Gooblar writes that, "If Mark Shechner hadn't existed, Philip Roth might have had to invent him." Shechner was, like Lonoff to Roth's Zuckerman, the wise writer coaching all of us to be better versions of ourselves, as writers, as scholars, as colleagues and friends. This volume is dedicated to Mark and his legacy. It has been devastating working on the final revisions of this manuscript knowing that Mark will not hold it—as he has the volumes of so many of us—in his hands. But we know that Mark is with us in other ways, speaking through those who loved him, speaking through his own works on Roth and other important writers of our day.

And so it is with these original chapters written in the wake of Roth's "lasts," that we hope to see the field of Roth Studies grow even more vibrant. Perhaps it is this Phase of the Lasts, paradoxically, that will prove to be a new beginning for scholarly work on Roth's novels—and a new model for reading contemporary writers in their retirement overall.

WORKS CITED

Atlas, James. "A Visit with Philip Roth." *New York Times*, 2 Sept. 1979. Web. 6 March 2016.

Borowitz, Andy. "Philip Roth Says He Has Had His Last Sandwich." *New Yorker*. 20 May 2014. Web. 6 March 2016.

Brauner, David. *Philip Roth*. Manchester: Manchester UP, 2007. Print.

Bruhwiler, Claudia. *Political Initiation in the Novels of Philip Roth*. New York: Bloomsbury, 2013. Print.

Gooblar, David. *The Major Phases of Philip Roth*. New York: Continuum, 2011. Print.

Halio, Jay and Ben Siegel, Eds. *Turning Up the Flame: Philip Roth's Later Novels*. Newark: University of Delaware P, 2005. Print.

Hayes, Patrick. *Philip Roth: Fiction and Power*. Oxford: Oxford UP, 2014. Print.

Ivanova, Velichka, Ed. *Philip Roth and World Literature: Transatlantic Perspectives and Uneasy Passages*. Amherst, NY: Cambria, 2014. Print.

The Library of America, Ed. *Philip Roth at 80. A Celebration*. New York: Library of America, 2014.

Masiero, Pia. *Philip Roth and the Zuckerman Books: The Making of a Storyworld*. Amherst: NY: Cambria, 2011. Print.

McCrum, Robert. "Bye, bye . . . Philip Roth Talks of Fame, Sex, and Growing Old in a Last Interview." *The Observer*. Guardian News and Media Ltd., 17 May 2014. Web. 6 March 2016.

McGrath, Charles. "Goodbye, Frustration: Pen Put Aside, Roth Talks." *New York Times*, 17 November 2012. Web. 6 March 2016.

Nadel, Ira. *Critical Companion to Philip Roth*. New York: Facts on File, 2011.

Parrish, Timothy, Ed. *The Cambridge Companion to Philip Roth*. Cambridge: Cambridge UP, 2007. Print.

Posnock, Ross. *Philip Roth's Rude Truth: The Art of Immaturity*. Princeton: Princeton UP, 2008. Print.

Pozorski, Aimee. *Roth and Celebrity*. Lanham, MD: Lexington, 2012. Print.

———. *Roth and Trauma: The Problem of History in the Later Works*. New York: Bloomsbury, 2011. Print.

Roth, Philip. *The Ghost Writer*. New York: Random House, 1979. Print.

Royal, Derek. *Philip Roth: New Perspectives on an American Author*. Westport, CT: Praeger, 2005. Print.

Safer, Elaine B. *Mocking the Age: The Later Novels of Philip Roth*. Albany: SUNY P, 2006. Print.

Schuessler, Jennifer. "Philip Roth Says He Has Given His Last Public Reading." *The New York Times*, 2 May 2014. Web. 6 March 2016.

Shechner, Mark. *Up Society's Ass, Copper: Rereading Philip Roth*. Madison: U of Wisconsin Press, 2003. Print.

Sheehan, Richard. Personal Interview. 27 September 2014.

Shostak, Debra. *Philip Roth—Countertexts, Counterlives*. Columbia: U of South Carolina P, 2004. Print.

———. Ed. *Philip Roth: American Pastoral, The Human Stain, The Plot Against America*. New York: Continuum, 2011. Print.

Chapter One

"Every third thought shall be my grave"

Roth, Memento mori, *and Story*

Debra Shostak

Toward the end of *The Human Stain* (2000), Nathan Zuckerman visits Coleman Silk's grave where, he writes, "I was completely seized by his story, by its end and by its beginning, and, then and there, I began this book. . . . And that is how all this began: by my standing alone in a darkening graveyard and entering into professional competition with death" (337–338). Philip Roth has sent a surprising number of his characters to meditate in graveyards or at funerals, especially at crucial narrative junctures such as beginnings and endings. I propose that Roth deploys the graveyard scene as a symbolic incitement to the narrative impulse focused on "professional competition with death." For Roth, as for Zuckerman, the gravesite serves as a primal scene, if you will—psychoanalytically, a source of repression, repetition, remembering, and telling; narratively, it serves as an initiatory moment. In many of Roth's novels, the absence signified by the grave stimulates narration, either displacing the trauma of death into the energies of erotic or reportorial desire, or rendering the epistemological problem of reckoning with death's utter absence, or gazing unflinchingly upon the chasm in a moment of narrative stasis, while refusing comforting platitudes about what it all means. To compete with death, Roth suggests, requires oppositional and even counterfactual storytelling: contesting reality by way of skepticism, perhaps, or sex, or talking to the dead.

Of course, Roth never quite wins the competition. His efforts are thwarted by the narratological condition described by Peter Brooks: "the realization of the desire for narrative encounters the limits of narrative, that is, the fact that one can tell a life only in terms of its limits or margins. The telling is always *in terms of* the impending end" (*Reading* 52; emphasis in original). And so Roth's scenes recur from book to book, holding in suspension the contraries—that a man stands alone in a darkening graveyard telling stories to keep the living alive.

Such gravesite scenes abound in Roth's *oeuvre*. Consider, for example, the three-thousand-word eulogy that begins *The Counterlife* (1986). Although Nathan Zuckerman cannot deliver his "morally inappropriate" reconstruction of the lost potency that drove his brother to his fatal surgery, he finds the story irresistible: "Henry wasn't dead twenty-four hours when the narrative began to burn a hole in Zuckerman's pocket" (*Counterlife* 13). This account initiates the dizzyingly self-contradictory chapters that burn a hole in the novel's coherence. Or consider the climactic scene in *The Anatomy Lesson* (1983), when a younger Zuckerman, crazed by bodily pain and tribal obligation, accompanies an elderly widower to his wife's grave. Screaming "'*We* are the dead! These bones in boxes are the Jewish living! These are the people running the show!'" (*Anatomy* 668; emphasis in original), he attempts a displaced oedipal patricide before blacking out, smashing his jaw on a gravestone, and metaphorically losing his capacity to tell a story that might change his life.[1] His timely date with the grave then heightens the bite of Roth's closing line, according to which Zuckerman acts "as though he still believed that he could unchain himself from a future as a man apart and escape the corpus that was his" (697)—where the *corpus* stands for both bodily mortality and the fatal commitment to write.

Consider, too, the briefest of passing references in Roth's late novellas, *Indignation* (2008) and *The Humbling* (2009), conflating sex and death under the sign of the burial ground. In *Indignation*, Roth's narrator, Marcus Messner, describes the sexual frustrations of 1950s America, when "there was almost no place where a student couple could be alone together. Some went out to the town cemetery and conducted their sex play against the tombstones or even down on the graves themselves" (*Indignation* 48–49). Roth drives the narrative in accord with Marcus's blindness to show how such "sex play" will, according to the social rules against which he strains, eventually send him to his death. With parallel effect, in *The Humbling*, the narrator describes the unrequited longings of a college dean for Simon Axler's sexual mate, noting that the dean "phoned from a local cemetery, where, she announced, she was 'stomping around in a fury' because of the way Pegeen had treated her" (*Humbling* 56). The reductive scare quotes around the dean's reported action convey the narrator's cynical detachment, aligned with Axler's own condescending feelings toward her. The scene thus lends a bitter foretaste of Pegeen's later abandonment of Axler, which motivates the suicide that closes his story.

Or look to the funeral of one of the first young polio victims in *Nemesis* (2010), when Bucky Cantor uncomprehendingly confronts the fact that the dead really no longer feel or think or grow: listening to the eulogy, Bucky "wound up instead imagining Alan roasting like a piece of meat in his box" (*Nemesis* 69), and he meditates on "That box from which you cannot force your way out. That box in which a twelve-year-old was twelve years old forever" (63). The box emphasizes, in Roth's imagination, the blank, mechanical geometry of death.[2] In attempting to control their own narratives, these figures are battered by the inescapable materiality of loss hinted at by the graveyard. Only *The Counterlife*'s Zuckerman finds solace, but that is because he embraces self-erasure, displacing his life into pure storytelling.

Consider, also, how some of Roth's most innocently deluded figures imagine that present deaths can be redeemed by a past whose story the cemetery signifies. For example, the alter-ego "Philip Roth" who narrates *Operation Shylock* (1993) fantasizes that "Jinx" Possesski, the necrophiliac consort of *his* doppelganger, buries the latter, "with traditional Jewish rites, in a local cemetery dating back to pre-Revolutionary Massachusetts. . . . To be surrounded in death by all these old Yankee families, with their prototypical Yankee names, had seemed to him exactly as it should be for the man whose gravestone was to bear beneath *his* name the just, if forlorn, epithet 'The Father of Diasporism'" (*Shylock* 366; emphasis in original). Roth identifies the naïve appeal to the imprimatur that American lineage might place on the lives and names of those who are, in pre-Revolutionary terms, far from "American"—just like Roth himself.[3] The delicious, reflexive irony that the name on Pipik's gravestone would, of course, be "Philip Roth" challenges death, since the narrating "Philip Roth" survives the "Philip Roth" who would be buried there. Finally, "Philip" imagines that Pipik had "chosen the *plot* there himself" (366, emphasis added). Roth thereby gestures figuratively at storytelling. The "plot" in which Pipik is buried is the (historical) plot of Jewish American life that he would consecrate in his wild (political) plot to return the Jews to Europe, all of which constitutes the (narrative) plot into which Roth—and "Roth"—has inserted him.

The intentionality of the "plot" becomes central to Roth's storytelling competition with death. *Patrimony* (1991) offers an example. At the end of the first chapter, Roth recounts driving by "accident" to the cemetery where his mother is buried instead of to his father's apartment, where he plans to tell Herman Roth of his fatal brain tumor: "Though I wasn't searching for that cemetery either consciously or unconsciously . . . I had flawlessly traveled the straightest possible route . . . to my mother's grave" (*Patrimony* 20). The scene signifies death's inevitability, preparing Roth for the memoir of his father's life, illness, and death, and its pairing of repression and confrontation with the fact of death encapsulates the central human problem of such knowledge. In the memoir's final pages, Roth circles back implicitly to that initial moment. Confessing how he incongruously chose to dress his father, a man "rooted all his life in everydayness" (234), in an ancestral shroud for burial, he recounts a dream in which his dead father "came in a hooded white shroud to reproach me," saying "I should have been dressed in a suit. You did the wrong thing." Roth realizes that "I had dressed him for eternity in the wrong clothes"—the dream blatantly displacing his anxiety that he has not told his father's story right (237). As at the narrative's beginning, the ending engages Roth in *error*, the psychological phenomenon according to which desire both belies and interpenetrates reality. Roth errs because he desires at once to evade and confront the knowledge of death's finality. This desire determines the arc of Roth's storytelling and means the most in its contradictions.

It seems as if all Roth's roads lead to the grave. Either "consciously or unconsciously," he "flawlessly travels" to the scene not of dying itself, which might elicit gestures of sentimentality or spirituality, but of burial: to the site of the body's vanishing, the hole in the earth that speaks of the final nothing-ness of material being. The obvious *memento mori* of the grave leads Roth to several motifs and formal strategies. First is that the voice of the mother, dead or alive, presides over the protagonist's traumatic confrontation with mortality. Second is that, according to the compulsion to remember and tell, Roth's linear plotting toward death may be embraced within circular narra-tive structures that feature traumatic repetition as well as closure that hovers ambiguously between oppositions—such as love and hate, transcendence and materiality, tragedy and irony. Third is the representation of the battle waged between eros and thanatos, perhaps most obvious in Mickey Sabbath of *Sabbath's Theater* (1995). Indeed, if every *third* thought is his grave, as Roth quotes Prospero in that novel's epigraph, the first thought, here and elsewhere, may be "mother," and the second, "sex."

Although many readers have remarked the death-haunted character of Roth's later work—Aimee Pozorski, for example, notes that gravesite scenes appear often in the major work since *Sabbath's Theater* (148)[4]—Roth has been preoccupied with mortality from the very beginning, as David Brauner observes (218). Indeed, the early short story "The Day It Snowed" (1954), published when Roth was just twenty-one, drives toward a climactic visit to the cemetery. In its relative simplicity, the story sketches the narratological pattern and some of the tropes I will explore briefly in a few of Roth's novels and in more detail in *Sabbath's Theater* and *Everyman* (2006).

"The Day It Snowed" focalizes the perspective of a child, Sydney, from whom the adults around him suppress the knowledge that some family mem-bers have died. Told that they have "disappeared," Sydney believes that if they have simply *chosen* to go elsewhere, then they might be found again. Roth narrates much of the story in free indirect style, capturing Sydney's childish inability to interpret the signs around him.[5] Beginning "Suddenly people began to disappear" ("Day" 34), the story explores Sydney's misun-derstanding of the word "disappear," which he takes as literal—the reverse of being *visible* and *present*—rather than as a euphemism veiling the knowledge of death. The word "disappear" supplies a structuring motif, repeating without clarification to invoke narrative principles that Peter Brooks identifies in *Reading for the Plot*. Drawing on Freud's account of eros and thanatos in *Beyond the Pleasure Principle* (1920) to describe the desires that propel narrative toward both continuation and the stasis of ending, Brooks notes how narrative "claim[s] overt authority for its origin, for a 'primal scene' from which . . . 'reality' assumes narratability." He calls the relation between "initiatory desire" and the "deathlike ending," when narratability ceases, "Freud's own masterplot" (*Reading* 96), where repetitions fill the space of the middle. Freud of course identifies in compulsive repetition a sign of repressed trauma. As Cathy Caruth explains, "the repetition at the heart of catastrophe—the experience that Freud will call 'traumatic neurosis'—emerges as the unwitting reenactment of an event that one cannot simply leave behind" (Caruth 2). The repetition of "disappear," then, from Roth's first sentence onward, suggests that the concealed meaning of death is the trauma that both initiates the narrative and drives it towards its close.

The story's turning point occurs with another incremental repetition, when Sydney asks directly of a nameless old man, "Why does everybody have to disappear on me?" Although the man explains that "'to disappear is to die'" ("Day" 42), the moment ironically fails to precipitate Sydney into knowledge. Rather, Sydney misplaces the emphasis and is overjoyed to learn that his family members "didn't do it [disappear] on purpose" (43). Sydney adapts the new fact into a new misconstruction and concludes that he can now stop his arduous search for the lost. By bringing Sydney in the closing paragraphs to the cemetery, where the funeral for his stepfather is occurring, Roth shows how the child fails to grasp what death is. Sydney asserts, "Momma, he is dead and that's good. Momma, you can stop looking, I can stop looking" (44), and, running heedlessly after the departing old man, he is crushed by the hearse, "shatter[ing] forever his thin glass voice" (44).

The new, displaced repetition—"can stop looking"—signifies Sydney's refusal of the *appearance* of absence, the gaze at the silent grave that might close the narrative with recognition. Repetition does not, according to the Freudian prescription, bring the repressed material into consciousness. Instead, Sydney does not so much *look* into the abyss as fall blindly into it, his trauma left unmastered. The death of the innocent child—senseless, mechanical, and unmotivated—suspends the story between tragedy and absurd irony. The only recognition achieved is that of the reader, for whom the repetition of "disappearance" *aesthetically* requires Sydney's death—the protagonist must fulfill the thematic pattern with which the story opens. In addition, the shattering of Sydney's "thin glass voice" in the final phrase emphasizes by synesthesia the conflation of *looking* and *speaking* embedded in the doubled perspectival effect of free indirect style, signaling the fundamental requirement of narrative—to

know and to tell.[6] The narrating voice indicates Sydney's stymied consciousness, stopping, unlike the reader, at the threshold of knowing and telling.

Sydney's mother is the source for him of concealed meanings and, therefore, despite herself, of his trauma and death. She informs him that his aunt
has "disappeared," and although he does not understand her meaning, he
neither asks for clarification, "because of her crying," nor asks his stepfather, "because his mother was the one he was supposed to ask questions of"
(35). Roth establishes the mother as the origin of both knowledge and the
comforts of its suppression; she thus figures both narratability and its limit.
Roth reinforces the mother's symbolic position at the end of the story when,
repudiating the knowledge that the old man gives Sydney, she screams the
lie that "'Poppa isn't dead!'" and demands that the old man be removed from
the cemetery (44). Roth's irony is obvious in the sense that the old man and
his news appear appropriately in the place where death discloses its indisputable material reality. Because Sydney desires not to be excluded from such
knowledge—seen when he desperately calls "'Mister Man'" (44) to come
back, rejecting his mother's assertion—he is killed.

In Roth's subsequent work, the voice of the mother remains a powerful
trope for the mediation or suppression of the traumatic knowledge of death
that the grave might otherwise convey. Although Zuckerman in *Zuckerman
Unbound* (1981) is forever bedeviled by the ambiguity of his father's last
word—whether he has called his "apostate son" (*Unbound* 373) "Bastard" or,
perhaps, is facing the void metaphysically, calling out "Faster," or "Vaster,"
or "Better" (379)—by the time, in *The Anatomy Lesson* (1983), Nathan's
mother's last word reaches him, its message is unmistakable. Asked to write
her name, "instead of 'Selma' [she] wrote the word 'Holocaust,' perfectly
spelled" (*Anatomy* 447). The knowledge that her death and word communi-
cate to Zuckerman stirs the stark summary that all is "Gone" (474), the word
that Roth also chooses to title the novel's second chapter (445).

Much later, when in *Exit Ghost* (2007) Roth renounces Zuckerman even as
his alter-ego starts to bid farewell to his life, the final chapter begins with a
wish-fulfilling dream of reversing time in a return to the womb. The pathetic
Zuckerman telephones his long-dead mother, a "corpse in a grave," to ask
her to commit incest with him; together with him, she obligingly "leave[s]
the cemetery for [his] bedroom" where, arousing his desire, she speaks the
"triumphant words . . . 'birth! birth! birth!'" (*Exit* 242). Needless to say, Roth
deflates such foolish fantasies, dashing Zuckerman's dream of escape from
the tomb, when he juxtaposes the scene to Zuckerman's reminiscence of his
friend George Plimpton, who "died as we all do: as a rank amateur" (264).

The forlorn fantasy of the maternal voice in *Exit Ghost*, mixing eros and
thanatos with infantile wishes, highlights the lengths to which, Roth finds,
the human imagination may go in cloaking the fundamental reality of death.

Roth makes such paradoxical gestures plain when, as the unmasked narrator of *Patrimony*, he notes, "If there's no one in the cemetery to observe you, you can do some pretty crazy things to make the dead seem something other than dead" (*Patrimony* 21). Starting from the weary insight that "while visiting a grave one has thoughts that are more or less anybody's thoughts" (20), Roth shrugs, "Oh, you can try talking to the dead if you feel that'll help . . . but it's hard not to know—if you even get beyond a first sentence—that you might as well be conversing with the column of vertebrae hanging in the osteopath's office" (21). As his paragraph tumbles toward its climax, however, his prose softens the arch tone: "you can even get down and place your hands directly above their remains—touching the ground, *their* ground, you can shut your eyes and remember what they were like when they were still with you" (21; emphasis in original). The tender specificity of the action and the familiar repetition—"their ground"—are only partly nullified by Roth's bitter insistence on the unvarnished facts: "But even if you succeed and get yourself worked up enough *to feel their presence*, you still walk away without them. What cemeteries prove . . . is not that the dead are present but that they are gone. They are gone and, as yet, we aren't" (21; emphasis in original). Roth's plain language, together with the tolling repetition of "gone," as in *The Anatomy Lesson*, demonstrates the incomprehensible distance that lies between the two states. The grave proves a black hole in more than one way.

Yet Roth's dismissal of talking to the dead in *Patrimony* reverses when, four years later in *Sabbath's Theater*, he takes it up as a desperately poignant endeavor. From the opening pages of the novel, Roth's narrator emphasizes how Sabbath, "ferociously a realist" who "had all but given up on making contact with the living, let alone discussing his problems with the dead," finds himself in constant communication with his dead mother: "His mother was there every day and he was talking to her . . . His dead mother was with him, watching him, everywhere encircling him" (*Sabbath* 16–17). James Mellard insightfully sees Mickey Sabbath's conversations with his mother's ghost in relation to the Lacanian narrative of the Real described by Slavoj Žižek. "In Lacanian terms," Mellard writes, "the ghost of the mother is an irruption of the Real into the structure . . . of ordinary existence" (Mellard 71).[7] Sabbath must, Mellard argues, resolve his mourning for the losses of his youth—for his brother, Morty, killed in the war, and for his mother's loving attention to Mickey, banished by her grief for her first son. His mother's ghost therefore "bring[s] Sabbath to the symbolization of the grief that has driven his outrageously transgressive life" (Mellard 71–72). Although Sabbath at first believes that "His mother had been loosed on him. She had returned to take him to his death" (*Sabbath* 17), he has it wrong, Mellard suggests, because she has instead appeared so as "to restore him to real, ordinary, meaningful life" (Mellard 71).[8]

It is thus that Roth locates the confluence of psychoanalytic and story-telling impulses at the cemetery. When Sabbath's mother brings him to the threshold of the grave, her figure, in all its resonant liminality, also brings the reader to the threshold of the narrative. Indeed, the metaphor of the threshold—the limit at which Sydney was stopped in "The Day It Snowed"—pinpoints how the graveyard scenes work thematically and narratively in both *Sabbath's Theater* and *Everyman*, which, despite their obvious differences, Roth organizes in much the same way. Several of the examples I've noted—"The Day It Snowed," *The Anatomy Lesson*, and *Exit Ghost*—lead *toward* a late cemetery or funeral scene as a pivotal or even climactic moment. The effect of this narrative structure is to make the apparently "unforeseen"[9] or repressed signification of death the goal of the discourse. Episodes in the graveyard, however, *frame* and incite the telling of *Sabbath's Theater* and *Everyman.* By appearing at both the narrative threshold and its close—and repeating at other points along the way—the gravesite scenes incite the protagonists to peer over the edge into their own mortality. Roth's form traces the psychoanalytic process that follows upon traumatic experience. The primal scene at the grave initiates each novel either in its *story* or in its *discourse*, in Seymour Chatman's terms (Chatman 9ff), and then the discourse returns to the gravesite through repetitions that organize the narrative middles around memory. In neither novel does this circularity produce the reconciliation or healing for its protagonist that Freud's masterplot prescribes—Roth is too fond of suspensive closure—but both give an inkling of what death *is.* Brooks writes of therapeutic narrative that "the analysis is an inquest, moving back from present symptoms . . . to the signs left by earlier events, and eventually back to the beginning in order to construct the chain of events" (*Body Work* 233). Roth's fictional form in *Sabbath's Theater* and *Everyman*, following the figure of storytelling as an "inquest," embraces a recursive structure, which is inscribed by the traumatic knowledge of death. At graveside, one can only look back.

The *discourse* of *Sabbath's Theater* does not begin at the grave as such, but its *story* does. Like *Everyman*, the narrative of *Sabbath's Theater* is analeptic, although its temporal zig-zaggings are far more complex than in the later novel, in keeping with its far greater density of rhetoric and incident. The opening chapter is a flashback telling of Sabbath's extravagant sexual relationship with Drenka, but the memories, recounted recursively in the "present" of the discourse and largely constituting the narration, logically begin around fifty pages into the novel, with Sabbath's visit to the cemetery where she is buried (*Sabbath* 50).

In the first chapter, Sabbath, in Roth's frequently deployed free indirect style, contemplates the central lesson of Roth's novel: "Take your pick. Get betrayed by the fantasy of endlessness or by the fact of finitude" (31). The story that follows is continually motivated by traumatic absences, which mock any innocent longing for the fantasy of endlessness that had duped Sabbath—that, indeed, he had first learned as a child from his mother: "He'd grown up on endlessness and his mother—in the beginning they were the same thing" (31). Sabbath's first guiding illusion was his oedipal fulfillment from his mother, which disguised her latent capacity to show how time rips the fabric of the Imaginary to expose the Real: "His mother, his mother, his mother . . . The ocean, the beach the first two streets in America, then the house, and in the house a mother who never stopped whistling until December 1944" (31). Morty is killed in December 1944—"Morty," whose very name signifies death and whose death marks the reversal of Sabbath's illusion, from endlessness toward the belief he cynically cherishes in his maturity, that life stops with loss.

Sabbath's Theater meditates on the dual betrayals of endlessness and finitude that Mickey marks by repeatedly visiting graves and burials once he understands that he "didn't have a life, except at the cemetery" (*Sabbath* 51). The gravesite scenes make literal the endless chain of loss that is the narrative of living, playing eros against thanatos. Sabbath's darkly comic first visit to Drenka's grave, there to invoke her ghost while he masturbates, repeats several times when he spies on Drenka's other lovers, who reenact his devotional desecration of her grave. Loss and absence gain materiality for Sabbath when he heads to the graveyard. Roth occupies much of the "present" of the narration with Sabbath's circuitous movement to pay respects to his old friend and theatrical producer, Lincoln Gelman, who has, as if whispering incitements to Sabbath, committed suicide. As Sabbath drives to New York for the funeral, his mind is filled with his other ghosts—his first wife, Nikki, and his mother: "All he could talk about with his mother, who was gliding about inside the car, drifting and plunging like debris in the tide, was what had led to Nikki's disappearance" (105). By vanishing without a trace, Nikki has created for Sabbath another kind of paradoxical endlessness. She leaves him no way to bring her story to a close so as to resolve her disappearance with the idea of finitude. If for Sabbath, to speak with the dead makes mourning meaningful, Nikki's disappearance leaves him in a condition of permanent trauma—without a grave, he finds no full stop. Her inexplicable, interminable absence stands for the enigma that is death. Nikki becomes the exception that proves the rule that Sabbath has a life only at the cemetery; no wonder he concludes, "'I could never again think about the future'" (144).

Roth takes the notion of disappearance to absurd lengths when even the *cemetery* seems to Sabbath to have disappeared. Driving to visit his family dead and "arrange . . . for his own burial" (351), he thinks that "the cemetery had disappeared! . . . A cemetery plowed under for a supermarket! *People were shopping at the cemetery,*" and it is only by driving "in circles" (352; emphasis in original) that he realizes his mistake and finds the place, untouched. Roth thereby inverts the error of *Patrimony*, when he flawlessly traveled to his mother's burying ground. Here, the meaning of Sabbath's error—to *lose* the cemetery—lies in his momentary repression of his abiding commitment to death, to which the narrative unerringly returns him.

Although, unlike Sabbath, the protagonist of *Everyman* seems to do everything in his power to avert consciousness of death, the novel's *form* represents the process of an inquest that reconstructs the chain of events leading back to the discursive beginning. *Everyman* opens at the protagonist's gravesite— "grave" and "cemetery" appear in the first sentence—which is at once the initiatory trauma and endpoint of the plot.[10] When Roth commits the novel to an analeptic structure, most events by definition appear in flashbacks. Although he includes many large and small digressions into memory, the circular narrative is also superimposed on a roughly V-shaped linear structure. *Everyman* first narrates the plot's *final* scene, looping at times into the past to provide back-stories for those attending the burial, insofar as they relate to Everyman. Then the scene shifts back in time to Everyman's penultimate night, explicitly announcing the narrative's structure of repetitions whereby Roth chronicles the protagonist's intertwined history of physical ailments and doomed entanglements with women—this novel's dry version of the oscillation between eros and thanatos: lying "in his bed the night before the surgery he worked at remembering as exactly as he could each of the women who had been there waiting for him to rise out of the anesthetic" (*Everyman* 15). An approximate chronology follows, finally returning, through narrated memories, to the "present" of his death. His earliest memories link two traumatic perceptions of death: hospitalized in 1942 for a hernia operation, he believes he "registered a death" (27), of the boy in the next bed; and he obsessively thinks about the "drowned body [of a seaman] that had washed up on the beach that past summer" (25). The description of the boy's perceptions, condensed into an overdetermined sign, could stand for the entirety of Roth's novel: "he couldn't get the word 'graveyard' to stop tormenting him" (26).

As Roth's novel traces the temporal progression of Everyman's life, consisting, as Ross Posnock identifies, of the twin betrayals of his flesh and of others (Posnock 55), it also cycles through his simultaneous repression and recognition of the traumatic knowledge of death. Victoria Aarons notes that Everyman is at once "preoccupied with his own death and in narcissistic denial of its inevitability" (Aarons 117), and Roth shows him oscillating between views in the cemetery scenes. The novel's second trip to the cemetery occurs when Everyman remembers his father's burial, which, as elsewhere, provokes a further embedded flashback.[11] The memory incited by this gravesite scene is of his father's devotion to his jewelry business, propelled by his wish to "have something to leave my two boys" and channeled into his faith in the transcendent properties of diamonds, which he believes offer "a piece of the earth that is imperishable" (*Everyman* 57). Roth exposes the vanity of the wish for imperishability by the logic of narrative juxtaposition; the novel immediately returns to the brutal realism of the framing memory, of "upright shovels with their blades in the large pile of earth to one side of the grave" (57). The cemetery scene recounts Everyman's existential panic by way of his epistemological confusion. He fantasizes that his father is being buried *alive*, the dirt "filling up his mouth, blinding his eyes, clogging his nostrils" (59–60), and concludes in his identification with the dead, as he "could taste the dirt coating the inside of *his* mouth" (62; emphasis added). Such confusion, bringing the dead object back to life within his own hysterical subjectivity, is one way of contesting reality, however futile.

Whereas this scene should by the logic of sequence lead toward Everyman's *recognition* of his own mortality, the climactic cemetery scene reverses the sense, leaving him, like Sydney, in a denial that readers may choose to understand either as opening up to tender, transcendent meaning or as piercing irony. This framing scene seems a more "objective" visit, as Everyman appears not to be on a purposeful errand. Instead, he diverts himself to the family burial place—once more echoing Roth in *Patrimony*—and never makes it to his intended destination. Such a physical detour again suggests the Freudian meaningfulness of error—an impression solidified when Roth almost immediately digresses into a flashback about two funerals Everyman has recently attended, at which he thinks: "death does not even seem natural. I had thought—*secretly I was certain*—that life goes on and on" (*Everyman* 169; emphasis in original). That is, his body travels to the site that should contradict his conscious convictions but fails to do so. The scene at first bears out his certainty as, weeping over the "bones in a box" that were his parents, he finds solace by claiming those bones as *his*: "This *was* what was true, this intensity of connection with those bones" (170–171; emphasis in original). Yet Everyman's poignant communing with his familial past, countered by his matter-of-fact conversation with the gravedigger about the technology of burial, tonally reflects the contradiction implicit in his truest and, at once, most self-deluded sentiment about the cemetery, expressed by yet another repetition: "He did not want to go" (173); "He never wanted to go" (177). He doesn't wish to *leave* the cemetery, which consoles him with his nearness to his parents, even though they are nothing more than "bones in a box." And if he does not leave—ultimately, of course, he *cannot*—he is proof that life does not go "on and on."

Yet this final perception is the reader's, not Everyman's. The irony of his failure to understand corresponds to his fantasy of speaking to the dead. Aarons is right to point out that this moment in the cemetery inserts Everyman into "the continuity of generations" (Aarons 123) and displaces him from his narcissism. His naked feeling of connection to his familial bones is indisputable. But his communion can only be one-sided; it is not his parents who speak to him, but only his desire. Unlike Sabbath, Everyman lacks imagination; he cannot conjure a mother's voice to offer him the fantasy of a return to the Imaginary. Unsurprisingly, then, as Aarons writes, "What he mourns over the graves of his parents is not only their deaths . . . but his own death" (Aarons 124), because that particular grief is arguably what any encounter with the grave evokes. Indeed, Roth prepares for this insight in the scene in which Everyman envisages that "life goes on and on." The husband of a woman who weeps uncontrollably at several funerals Everyman attends explains brusquely, "'That has been the story for fifty years . . . She's like that because she isn't eighteen anymore'" (*Everyman* 169). Grief is as much, or more, for the self as for the other.

Suffice it to say, then, that Roth lets no one—least of all Everyman—off the hook at the close of the novel, whose narrative juxtaposition of transcendence to materiality repeats the unresolved contradiction. As Everyman submits to his last surgery, the "words spoken by the bones [that] made him feel buoyant and indestructible" together with "the hard-won subjugation of his darkest thoughts" trigger his sensual memory of his child's "unscathed body" at the beach (181). Roth opens this most rapturous passage of the novel by uniting the man's delusion and act of repression. When the novel's final phrases bluntly announce Everyman's death—"He was no more, freed from being, entering into nowhere *without even knowing it*" (182, emphasis added)—Roth seals the irony that Everyman has repudiated this most obvious insight about his own mortality. The repetitions just produce more repetitions, the circularity of the narrative ultimately taking precedence over its linear promise of enlightenment. The ending returns us to the beginning, without concluding in insight; the inquest constructs the chain of events to find the body but finally no explanation. Death is nothing more than absence, the yawning grave, offered as a blank hole in the narrative if not as the character's reconciliation to fact.

And yet, and yet—in his professional competition with death, Roth seems to have it both ways. Roth's ambivalence is visible when, underscoring the analeptic form of both *Everyman* and *Sabbath's Theater*, he introduces a common trope, in scenes that perform climactically in each novel—the recitation of the names of the lost.[12] The appearance of the list is brief in *Everyman*, where Roth frames it with the beat of another powerful word: "leaving."

Dreaming that he is holding the corpse of Millicent Kramer, the suicide from his art class, Everyman names all those he has cared about and has lost or will lose: "'Momma, Poppa, Howie, Phoebe, Nancy, Randy, Lonny . . . Can't you hear me? I'm leaving! It's over and I'm leaving you all behind!'" The narrator is merciless in identifying Everyman's ontological anxiety and impotence: "*Leaving*—the very word that had conveyed him into breathless, panic-filled wakefulness, delivered alive from embracing a corpse" (165; emphasis in original). Only loss can wake him, however temporarily, from his own dream of endlessness.

A mordant, deflated irony closes *Everyman* and seems to trail off into nothingness. The extensive scene Roth narrates at the cemetery that Sabbath nearly missed, however, the scene in which the names of the lost appear, shows Sabbath not as fearful but as welcoming death. This is the longest cemetery scene in *Sabbath's Theater*, appearing more than three-quarters of the way through the novel, and is thematically and narratively transitional, driving home the ambivalence lurking within all these scenes. Here, the list of "beloveds" covers more than a page—beloved fathers, husbands, wives, mothers, sons, daughters, sisters, and brothers, each headstone read out with reverence and exactitude, though the buried are strangers to Sabbath, and though the epitaphs are wearyingly the same. Thus the narrator, in free indirect style, quips, "Nobody beloved gets out alive" (*Sabbath* 364). But the litany of names leads to Sabbath's own family and, again according to an analeptic narrative structure, toward a recounting of his richest, most comforting, most sensorily pleasurable memories of his family.

These root memories are as much the fount of Sabbath's being as his misplaced Oedipal complacencies, his vitriol, and his sexual transgressions, and they irrupt, as a rather different form of the Real, through the narrative's consistent tone of acerbic yet casual cynicism. Call it sentimental, perhaps, but the magnificent sweetness of this passage serves as a counterweight to the heavy reverberations of the compulsively repeated terms of loss in Roth's *oeuvre*: "gone," "disappear," "leaving," "graveyard."

It is both fitting and revealing, then, that Roth chose to read these very pages from *Sabbath's Theater* at the public celebration of his eightieth birthday, at the Newark Museum, on March 19, 2013. Roth began his talk that evening by referring to his recent announcement that he had finished writing novels.[13] The presentation was at once a beautiful farewell and a renewed avowal of the writer's mastery and grace with respect to both his subject matter and his prose. Like Prospero, to whom he alludes in the epigraph to *Sabbath's Theater*, and whose line about contemplating the grave he quoted on this occasion, Roth began by abjuring the rough magic of his art. He told the audience of all the familiar things that he would no longer write about—from the Gold Star Mothers of the Second World War and his childhood bicycle basket to stamp albums, glove factories, and fight night at Laurel Gardens. Roth's renunciation of storytelling took the form of an aesthetic of the real, of the "passion for specificity, for the hypnotic materiality of the world one is in" (*Philip Roth at 80* 53–54). Noting quietly that his turn to the excerpt from *Sabbath's Theater* "doesn't camouflage one's emotions quite so well" (58), Roth introduced the character who, he seemed to imply, might represent his own closely held feelings. Facing the "irksome law of cessation" (58), he said, Sabbath follows in the novel "a savage journey with the dead into his own raw wound" (59). Roth noted, however, that he does so with "great grief about the death of others and a great gaiety about his own" (59). In the writer's passion for the hypnotic materiality of the world, of course, nothing looks so real as the grave. But ultimately, Roth averred of Sabbath, "in his incompatibility he finds his truth" (61)—the truth of "Ungovernable laughter" (59).

This seesaw of feeling and knowledge, sadness and gaiety, acceptance and refusal, lies at the heart of Roth's professional competition with death and may explain why his fiction returns perpetually to the gravesite. Indeed, it seems no accident that the final words of the excerpt Roth read at his birthday celebration were the climactic words of Sabbath's visit to the ancestral graveyard. As the narrator observes when, preparing for suicide, Sabbath arrives at the cemetery to buy a plot near his familial dead, "He felt himself at last inside his life, like someone who, after a long illness, steps back into his shoes for the first time" (*Sabbath* 357). When he at last reaches his family's gravesites, Sabbath announces himself like Hamlet leaping into Ophelia's grave: "Here I am" (370). This statement of arrival and reconciliation, of an identity unmasked, of an embrace of the circle that links birth and death, served as Roth's birthday farewell. In the novel, however, Sabbath goes on to consolidate his identity by writing a satirical epitaph for his own monument, highlighting his most treasured and socially scurrilous behavior. The narrative then jumps, with a mid-sentence ellipsis, to trace Sabbath's encounter with the repressed memory at the chronological source of his trauma: the death of his brother and his mother's virtual death as a response to this loss. The abrupt transition, like the temporal delay of the scene's appearance in the novel's discourse, suggests the depth of psychic disruption that the memory holds for him. Only the grave can truly put Sabbath inside his life.

And so the closing scenes repeat his oscillation between accepting mortality ("He was dead, death was changeless, and there was no longer the illusion of ever escaping" [435]) and asserting his life force, as when he shrieks like a gorilla outside the window of his second wife, Roseanna (441), and, returning one last time to Drenka's grave, urinates there as an homage to their most intimate sexual transgressions. Unlike Everyman, Sabbath defiantly appears to embrace death in the face of a life dominated by loss, and the discourse closes with a fierce howl that epitomizes both the novel's and its protagonist's knowing perspective on death.

But like *Everyman* the novel, *Sabbath's Theater* hesitates on the brink of its own ambivalence. Sabbath's rejection of suicide in the final sentence invites endless repetition, a narrative that will not close—and its ambiguity with respect to the inevitability of death forecasts *Everyman* even as it repeats Roth's totemic words of loss: "How could he *leave*? How could he *go*? Everything he hated was here" (451; emphasis added). In Roth's marvelous closing ambiguities—is the "here" that he can't "leave" life? the cemetery? isn't his "hate" a testament to what he loves?—lies once again an intimation of endlessness. The equivocation resembles that in *Patrimony*. Roth's lines bear repetition: "What cemeteries prove, at least to people like me, is not that the dead are present but that they are gone. They are gone and, as yet, we aren't" (*Patrimony* 21). In his final contrast lies the conundrum of the burial ground. Where do we place the emphasis? On "*they* are gone"? Or on "as yet, *we* aren't"? In the encounter with the Real, it is, in the end, only every *third* thought that is the grave; in the others is, stubbornly, *something else.*

NOTES

Above text is a revised version of Shostak, Debra. "Roth's Graveyards, Narrative Desire, and 'Professional Competition with Death.'" *CLCWeb: Comparative Literature and Culture* 16.2 (2014): http://dx.doi.org/10.7771/1481-4374.2407. Copyright release to the author by Purdue University 2015.

1. Zuckerman is expressing a desire to which Roth repeatedly bears witness, which is probably most explicitly represented in the quotation, from Rilke's "Archaic Torso of Apollo," that concludes *The Breast* (1972): "for there is no place / that does not see you. You must / change your life" (89).

2. Roth repeats here, from *The Anatomy Lesson*, the figure of the "box" that also appears toward the end of *Everyman*, discussed in the following pages. There, the protagonist meditates at his parents' gravesite on the "bones in a box," both confronting their disappearance and taking comfort in the thought of their mortal remains (*Everyman* 170, 180–81).

3. Roth echoes himself a few years later, in *American Pastoral* (1997), when Swede Levov, who stakes his claim on America by moving from Newark to a pre-Revolutionary stone house in Old Rimrock out of a political innocence not unlike Pipik's, tours a Revolutionary-era cemetery with Bill Orcutt. Orcutt takes advantage of the Swede's sincerity to parade before him the gravestones of the many ancestors

who, dating back to 1774 (*Pastoral* 305), "prove" his own American birthright—an unsubtle snub that foreshadows his later claim on the Swede's wife.

4. See also Shipe on late style in *Exit Ghost*; Posnock 51; and Shostak.

5. The stylistic effect of cluelessness in the young voice recalls some of Faulkner's child narrators. Consider, for example, "That Will Be Fine" and "Uncle Willy" (Faulkner 265–288, 225–247), in both of which the naïve narrator participates actively in catastrophic events he fails to understand.

6. This basic condition of narrative—to know and to tell—is captured, as H. Porter Abbott reminds us, in the Latin etymology of the term "narrative." Abbott is in turn drawing on Hayden White's *The Content of the Form*, 215n (Abbott 10).

7. Mellard draws on Žižek's *The Metastases of Enjoyment*, 193–94.

8. Sabbath, as Mellard points out, Oedipally conflates his lover, Drenka Balich, with his mother, when, feverishly sucking Drenka's breast, he is "pierced by the sharpest of longings for his late little mother" (*Sabbath* 13; Mellard 70). Unsurprisingly, then, after Drenka's death, Sabbath likewise communes at her grave with her.

9. Especially in the later novels, Roth often uses the term "unforeseen" to highlight the disjunction between our knowledge, willed, refused, or occluded, and the contingencies of experience. See, for example, *Sabbath's Theater* 307; *American Pastoral* 36; *The Human Stain* 170; *The Plot Against America* 113–14; and *Everyman* 160.

10. Aarons describes the "voice" that "from the grave transcends [Everyman's] material being" (119). If the protagonist is, as he seems, resolutely secular, this notion of voice works only if the narrator's voice is taken for the protagonist's. Such conflation is another effect of Roth's use of free indirect style, which then emphasizes the temporal paradox of narration that could not be "told" otherwise "from the grave." If, however, the narrator is wholly an impersonal textual effect, it must be divorced from the transcendence effect to become external and, relatively speaking, "objective."

11. To be more precise, the narrator is describing Everyman's memories but Everyman is not "remembering" as such. This registers a narrative confusion that any argument about the Freudian plot fails quite to settle—that is, who or what is it that is repressing and remembering and eventually working through a trauma?

12. Such a list, in a much drier tone, appears in *The Professor of Desire* (1977), when David Kepesh visits the cemetery near Prague where Kafka is buried and sees many "familiar Jewish names. I might be thumbing through my own address book, or at the front desk looking over my mother's shoulder at the roster of registered guests at the Hungarian Royale: Levy, Goldschmidt, Schneider, Hirsch" (*Professor* 175).

13. Roth first announced his retirement in a French publication, *Les InRocks*, in October, 2012. See "Philip Roth: 'Némésis sera mon dernier livre.'"

WORKS CITED

Aarons, Victoria. "'There's no remaking reality': Philip Roth's *Everyman* and the Ironies of Body and Spirit." *Xavier Review* 27.1 (Spring 2007): 116–27. Print.

Abbott, H. Porter. *The Cambridge Introduction to Narrative.* 2nd ed. Cambridge: Cambridge UP, 2008. Print.

Brauner, David. *Philip Roth.* Manchester: Manchester UP, 2007. Print.

Brooks, Peter. *Body Work: Objects of Desire in Modern Narrative.* Cambridge: Harvard UP, 1993. Print.

———. *Reading for the Plot: Design and Intention in Narrative.* New York: Vintage, 1984. Print.

Caruth, Cathy. *Unclaimed Experience: Trauma, Narrative, and History.* Baltimore: Johns Hopkins UP, 1996. Print.

Chatman, Seymour. *Story and Discourse: Narrative Structure in Fiction and Film.* Ithaca: Cornell UP, 1978. Print.

Faulkner, William. *Collected Stories of William Faulkner.* New York: Vintage, 1977. Print.

Mellard, James M. "Death, Mourning, and Besse's Ghost: From Philip Roth's *The Facts* to *Sabbath's Theater.*" *Shofar* 19.1 (Fall 2000): 66–73. Print.

Posnock, Ross. "All's Well that Ends." Rev. of Philip Roth, *Everyman.* *Raritan: A Quarterly Review* 26.1 (Summer 2006): 51–63. Print.

Pozorski, Aimee. *Roth and Trauma: The Problem of History in the Later Works (1995–2010).* New York: Continuum, 2011. Print.

Roth, Philip. *American Pastoral.* Boston: Houghton, 1997. Print.

———. *The Anatomy Lesson.* New York: Farrar, 1983. Reprinted in Philip Roth, *Zuckerman Bound.* New York: Farrar, 1985. 407–697. Print.

———. *The Breast.* New York: Vintage, 1972. Print.

———. *The Counterlife.* New York: Farrar, 1986. Print.

———. "The Day It Snowed." *Chicago Review* 8.4 (Fall 1954): 34–44. Print.

———. *Everyman.* Boston: Houghton, 2006. Print.

———. *Exit Ghost.* Boston: Houghton, 2007. Print.

———. *The Human Stain.* Boston: Houghton, 2000. Print.

———. *The Humbling.* Boston: Houghton, 2009. Print.

———. *Indignation.* Boston: Houghton, 2008. Print.

———. *Nemesis.* Boston: Houghton, 2010. Print.

———. *Operation Shylock.* New York: Simon & Schuster, 1993. Print.

———. *The Plot Against America.* Boston: Houghton, 2004. Print.

———. *Patrimony.* New York: Simon & Schuster, 1991. Print.

———. *Philip Roth at 80: A Celebration.* New York: Library of America, 2014. Published version of "A Celebration of the Life and Work of Philip Roth." Public talk, 19 March 2013, Newark Museum, Newark, New Jersey. Print.

———. "Philip Roth: 'Némésis sera mon dernier livre.'" Interview with Philip Roth. *Les InRocks.* Les Editions Indépendantes, 7 October 2012. Web. 4 March 2016.

———. *The Professor of Desire.* 1977. New York: Penguin, 1985. Print.

———. *Sabbath's Theater.* Boston: Houghton, 1995. Print.

———. *Zuckerman Unbound.* New York: Farrar, 1981. Reprinted in Philip Roth, *Zuckerman Bound.* New York: Farrar, 1985. 183–405. Print.

Shipe, Matthew. "*Exit Ghost* and the Politics of 'Late Style.'" *Philip Roth Studies* 5.2 (2009): 189–204. Print.

Shostak, Debra. "Late Style in the Later Novels." *Critical Insights: Philip Roth.* Ed. Aimee Pozorski. Salem Press, 2013. 164–184. Print.

White, Hayden. *The Content of the Form: Narrative Discourse and Historical Representation.* Baltimore: Johns Hopkins UP, 1987. Print.

Žižek, Slavoj. *The Metastases of Enjoyment: Six Essays on Woman and Causality.* New York: Verso, 1994. Print.

Chapter Two

Roth @ 25

Publishing Goodbye, Columbus

Ira Nadel

The publication of Philip Roth's *Goodbye, Columbus* (1959) was neither simple nor swift—and its youthful author hardly a pushover. From the start of his career, Roth had a clear and absolute sense of the role of the author in the publishing process: to direct, guide and, if necessary, cajole the editor and his publisher to satisfy his goals. No one else would do it. The poet and editor George Starbuck initially wrote to Roth on Valentine's Day, 1958 because his father had read Roth's movie reviews in the *New Republic* and was using them in a course he taught. Starbuck had earlier admired Roth's stories in the *Chicago Review* and told him in early correspondence that publishers "are hard up for good young novelists." And if Roth was working on a novel or set of preferably interrelated short stories, he should let Starbuck know. Roth would be "assured of a favorably disposed reader as a well as a friendly eye on the production process if a book is accepted" (Starbuck, February 14, 1958). Three days later, a flattered Roth responded, pleased that someone else had the courage to leave graduate school for a writing life (Starbuck had been at Chicago and began the graduate program at Harvard but left because he needed money to support his young family). Roth tells him that he lasted only one quarter in the PhD program, taking an incomplete in Anglo-Saxon, but is now free to continue with his teaching and writing. He also mentions that in the previous year he was "dickering" with Harvard and wondered if he would have had the nerve to go if he was accepted. He wasn't and didn't have to make the choice, although he became bored with the doctoral program at Chicago. He also became "anxious as hell about writing, that is, about not writing" (Roth, February 17, 1958).

He then reports that he *is* working on a novel he calls *The Go Between*, suggesting that may send it on but is not sure how much he'll complete because of financial constraints. He says that he had been planning to apply for a Saxton award from Harper publishing, as well as a Houghton Mifflin Fellowship. This grant, founded in 1935, had previously been won by Robert Penn Warren, Elizabeth Bishop, and Anthony West and gave to the author, on the basis of newly submitted and publishable work, $2,500 plus an advance against royalties. He admits that he's impatient but if Starbuck could confirm fast results, Roth might try Houghton Mifflin (hereafter HM) first. He then says he's interested in a book of short stories, having recently sold material to *Esquire* and the *Paris Review*, as well as something to *Commentary*. His long story plus seven short ones might make a good volume. But he constantly revises and is not sure that he even has the seven best stories. He's now working on another, which he hopes "will crack the *New Yorker*" (Roth, February 17, 1958). But at 25, he wonders if he has enough credible material for a book.

Starbuck tells him he could ensure quick handling of the novel—that he took the job in publishing because the Harvard graduate program was a grind and he did well only in Archibald MacLeish's course. He went to Houghton Mifflin and the editorial job has actually given him time to complete five good-size poems and a book manuscript (Starbuck, February 20, 1958). Replying in mid-March 1958, Roth tells Starbuck from Chicago that he's completing a 42,000 word story—but is it long enough to enter into the HM Fellowship competition? He's excited about it, and although it is not the novel he earlier mentioned, he's had this in mind for quite a while and interrupted the longer work to get this one down on paper. It's called "Goodbye, Columbus"; Dick Stern, novelist and good friend of Roth, is the only one to have read it and he has been "euphoric" (Roth, March 14, 1958).

Roth goes on to outline combinations of stories but makes it clear that the fellowship interests him the most and "hard covers for Goodbye, Columbus, even more." He goes on to say: "I shall be twenty-five next week and stouter, and feel a tin knife in my side as I race to be a boy wonder" (Roth, March 14, 1958). He will also shortly apply for a Stanford fellowship for next year but now, unburdened from the graduate program, he writes "with a free mind and writes all the time." This summer, he adds, he's off to Europe on his *Esquire* money.

By early April, Roth sends Starbuck "Goodbye, Columbus" which he hopes can be published alone but if too short, he has some other stories in mind. Two of them are "The Conversion of the Jews"—which, he says: "you may remember reading last year in [Richard] Stern's course"—scheduled to appear in the next issue of the *Paris Review*; "Epstein" is the other story he's just finished. No publisher yet but he's entered it in the *Paris Review* short story contest. He would also like to submit "Expect the Vandals" for the proposed volume; it will soon be in Esquire. He then proposes a table of contents:

1. Goodbye, Columbus
2. The Conversion of the Jews

3. Epstein
4. Expect the Vandals
5. You Can't tell a Man by the Song He Sings
6. The Contest for Aaron Gold

The length of "Goodbye, Columbus" and "Expect the Vandals," however, makes the inclusion of other stories unlikely. And he's not excited about "The Contest for Aaron Gold" partly because it was written years ago in college and isn't currently representative of his work. (Roth, April 11, 1958).

Starbuck replied on May 8 with some reservations about "Goodbye, Columbus," especially the ending. Although the writing is rapid, satisfying, and well-paced, and the ruthlessness between the girl and her mother comes out indirectly, Starbuck wondered if Roth could sustain such a flat ending. That the narrator leaves the girl should be seen as a lucky thing. And the reader shouldn't be given any chance to go wrong. However, Starbuck added, the story creates tensions strong enough that Roth can give the story any ending he wants (Starbuck, May 8, 1958). Four days later, Roth replied in a long, single-spaced letter addressing the ending in particular, denying that it was "flat." He then analyzes Brenda and her decision to leave the diaphragm for her mother to find. Friends of Roth have given him a variety of psychoanalytic reasons for her action—a strong sign, he argues, that the fiction itself is right. But when Brenda fails to accept Neil's offer to go with him rather than her family, and fails to make a case for herself, "she submits to the circumstances" of her family; this is inevitable, Roth writes. For Neil, it is not a question of right or wrong. He has no choice but to leave, Roth explains, which is definitely not desertion.

He then adds: "I have no moral point. I think (or hope) that I let the story unwind itself and the characters do the deciding, not me" (Roth, May 12, 1958). This important statement expresses Roth's early aesthetic and view of his characters. The story and not the meaning interest him, he writes. He leaves for Europe on the 7 of June, he adds, and nervously awaits a decision about publication. Could HM let him know by June 1?

Starbuck writes almost immediately to report that Roth's stories have drawn, aside from himself, one "wildly enthusiastic," and one favorable but unimpassioned reaction. More troubling is that HM will not spend any more editorial time on them because they believe there is the strong likelihood that Roth has a full-scale novel under consideration at Harper. So, did Roth submit *The Go Between* for a Saxton award from Harper? Clarify, Starbuck asks—and also clarify the process of getting a diaphragm. In his experience, a gynecologist would give a prescription to be filled in a drugstore and not the diaphragm itself to the young woman (Starbuck, May 15, 1958).[1]

Roth replies two days later: no, I did not submit *The Go Between* to anyone: "so get off your editorial haunches and finish considering the stories." And if HM handles the stories, of course they'll have first crack at the novel: what is now 130 messy pages with 80 revised, plus an outline of the rest of the book. And on the diaphragm, it's up to the gynecologist and he's known doctors who have them stacked up on shelves. Starbuck, in response, says it would be easier to get the short stories out if we could get the novel out first. Send us the 80 pages and the outline (Roth, May 17, 1958; Starbuck, May 21, 1958). But Roth repeats his desire to have "Goodbye, Columbus" out first: his novel is a good ten or twelve months from completion. It would be too much time to wait. The stories are done; don't wait for the novel: Roth doesn't like to work at "too live [a] speed;" the novel is tough and tricky. Let me summarize, he writes: would you be interested in the stories with an option on the novel? (Roth, May 23, 1958). He admits that a novel-less writer offering a set of short stories first is not a good market strategy, but if pushed in certain ways "GC [Goodbye, Columbus] could have a very wide appeal perhaps to that same group who buy Salinger by the thousands. Am I mistaken?" (May 23, 1958).

Roth's surprising directness and self-confidence shows his early take-control attitude, which will later lead to debates and disagreements about advances, print runs, marketing budgets, and editorial judgment. But from the beginning, as even a young and inexperienced writer, Roth was sure of what he wanted. He realizes that a collection of short stories from a novice writer is something of a gamble but if publicized properly, with adequate advertising and marketing, the book could certainly sell. By June 28, from Paris, Roth has sent Starbuck pages from his drafted novel set in Germany and an application form for a Houghton Mifflin literary fellowship. Three weeks later, he writes again, asking Starbuck if there is news about either the collection or the fellowship: "since my next year's plans rest on your decisions, I would like to know as soon as possible" (Roth, July 25, 1958).

At last, on July 30, Starbuck wired Roth in Europe that HM would indeed publish "Goodbye, Columbus" with other stories. If he signs, he will receive a $1,000 advance and a 10 percent royalty on the first 5,000 copies sold. HM would also like an option for first refusal on his next completed book. Questions about the novel draft's atmospheric authenticity of post-war Germany, however, remained with one editor feeling that the novel was a little "out-of-the-blue" given the quality of the short stories, in which Roth knows the milieu "down to the last cuff-link" (Starbuck, July 30, 1958). Set in Frankfurt, the novel focuses on a neurotic American Jew who returns to Germany to look for traces of his family and possibly seek revenge on a German.

Roth received the congratulatory HM wire in Paris and he was delighted, although he was still anxious to discuss whether "Goodbye, Columbus" could stand alone or not. He then tells Starbuck he has another story, "Defender of the Faith," which he has recently finished. And he apologizes if he seemed anxious and pushy earlier but "now if I'm pushy it'll be about getting that book out: I'd love to see it printed tomorrow" (Roth, August 9, 1958).

By September, Roth was back in Chicago and preparing to visit Boston to review the contents of the collection. His preferred arrangement is now

Goodbye, Columbus
The Conversion of the Jews
Epstein
Defender of the Faith
You Can't tell a Man by the Song He Sings.

This would be almost the final sequence, which would see "Defender of the Faith" switch with "Epstein" and the addition of "Eli, the Fanatic" (finished in October 1958) as the final story, forming a book of 298 pages.

But the controversy surrounding "Defender of the Faith," originally in the *New Yorker*, began almost with its publication. Jewish religious groups and readers were upset and it had HM nervous. Roth tried to calm the publisher telling a member of the publicity department that he was not "Hitler reincarnate . . . but the fact that I have made Scarsdale mothers irate is not to be disregarded. As I said to Anne [Ford of HM], where there is a row there's an audience. I hope we can take advantage of it" (Roth, March 24, 1959). Starbuck tells Roth a few days later that if he wants to counter the label "anti-Semite," he should learn from others: "Harry Golden, but also Malamud, should teach you a disheartening lesson: to be safely a Semite, be less the comic artist than the sentimental buffoon" (Starbuck, March 26, 1959). Happily, Roth paid no attention to the idea. But every aspect of *Goodbye, Columbus* created concern. In a letter of November 4, 1959, Roth comically told Starbuck that he will keep the title "Eli the Fanatic" instead of "The Diaspora of Eli Peck" but that he felt "a little holier than thou about a volume including The Conversion of The Jews, and Defender of the Faith, and now the Diaspora. Perhaps the solution as to what to call the book is simply to call it The Revised Edition of the Old Testament. Or Goodbye, Columbus, a Gospel for Our Time."

The jacket was also a problem, resolved only by Roth convincing HM that his brother Sandy, a commercial artist in advertising, could draw it. Apparently, a draft image by the well-known Milton Glaser wasn't suitable; the new one by Sandy Roth is conventional but appropriate, says Starbuck: it also makes the book look like a novel, which may considerably boost sales. But the naked woman, now the focus of the cover, may be too sensational. No one at HM can recall a jacket for a novel with a nude on it other than Ross

Lockridge Jr.'s *Raintree County* (1948) featuring a woman's voluptuous shape worked into a landscape (Starbuck, February 2, 1959). Debate over the use of gray and orange on the cover then erupted: Roth felt it contradicted the mood of the cover, originally drawn to be gay, youthful, and sensuous. It is now too moody, melancholy, and unoriginal: "Instead of a girl standing in front of a window in day light, summery day light, it's a brooding girl looking oh so wanly out the window (anything but Brenda!) in back of a blob of orange fruit, ridiculous finally . . . truly a waste" (Roth, February 25, 1959).

Roth strongly objected to the changes and the failure of the production department to let his brother see them. He, himself, preferred a yellow cover, which has now been "blandized. Isn't there enough gray in the world?" Starbuck agreed that Sandy's image attempted to avoid the potential of wistfulness in "Goodbye" and apologizes that Sandy did not see the changes. But the final colors remained: The cover was gray with white lines outlining the figure of a naked woman from the back standing before a window in a contemplative pose and featured an oversized, floating orange bowl of fruit in the foreground.

But by July 1959, with the book receiving generally strong notice, Roth still expressed concerns: there didn't seem to be enough ads, and he was not receiving adequate sales reports. "Sometimes not knowing how the book is going," he tells Starbuck, "makes me feel like a Kafka Character, but this is my own problem" (Roth, July 23, 1959). Sales for a first-time author were, nonetheless, strong, as Starbuck told Roth in early September that sales crept over 10,000 and that 11,500 copies were in print (Starbuck, September 4, 1959). Roth at this time continued to work on another novel, now at 190 pages, and with varying titles: "The Craving or, the Confessions of a Distracted Young Man," or possibly "The Distracted Lover." This is likely a comic novel set in Chicago during the 1948 Wallace campaign (Roth, 1 December 1959). He was also beginning a work entitled "Debts and Sorrows" partly about teaching at the University of Chicago which would eventually become *Letting Go*.

However, other issues developed concerning the publication of *Goodbye, Columbus*, mostly having to do with Roth's unhappiness over its promotion and advertising campaign. He even prepared a draft ad to guide HM in its blitz; it reads in part.

Whoever knows New Jersey, Will Have Trouble
    Putting Down One of the Most
    Acclaimed Books of the Year–
     GOODBYE COLUMBUS
    By Newarker, Philip Roth.

He even suggests including a photo, perhaps the one used on the back jacket taken by his brother. Roth, now a "promoter" who combines advertising with marketing, does not want to overlook his special readership, but he also wants potential buyers to know that the book is being read all over the country. The volume will clearly sell but only as a product, he explains to the marketing department at HM. New Jersey women don't believe it [the book] exists until it's really merchandise he declares; it has to be something they can buy. Don't put the ad in the book section, he advises, but somewhere else in the paper (Roth, June 4, 1959).

One post-publication incident concerning *Goodbye, Columbus* was the Grossbart affair. While in Italy in April 1960 after the publication of the book, Roth received a letter from Houghton Mifflin saying a Mr. Sheldon Grossbart, through his lawyer, pointed out that he has the same name as a character in "Defender of the Faith" and was also in basic training with Roth. The use of the name in the story has caused him "anguish," as Grossbart claimed he was libeled and ridiculed. Dorothy de Santillana, an editor at HM, asked Roth if he knew this Grossbart. At this time de Santillana was dealing with Julia Child and a revised submission of *Mastering the Art of French Cooking*, which she praised but HM d rejected.

Replying on May 3, 1960, Roth denied any association or knowledge of Grossbart. He actually chose the name because he wanted the term gross to be hidden in the character's name, "the kind of playfulness even Henry James engaged in" (Roth, May 3, 1960). The name was entirely his invention, as his friend in Chicago had given him the germ of the story five years earlier. He notes that his brother reminded him that there was a Grossbart at Weequahic high who might have been a friend of his brother in Scouts, but he (Roth) never personally knew a Grossbart. Furthermore, the story had appeared two-and-a-half months earlier than the book—so why is Grossbart or his lawyer contacting the publisher only now? And he (Roth) had never been to either Germany or Missouri where the story was set and he never knew a Sheldon Grossbart in the army. The whole thing is suspicious and sounds like a "Grossbartian move—*my* Grossbart—and not a very crafty one," suggesting, or anticipating, the figure who actually impersonates Roth in Israel in *Operation Shylock*. It is also an early example of Roth's encounter with a playful counter-self and questions of identity. The matter was dropped.

The story of the publication and reception of *Goodbye, Columbus* anticipates Roth's response to the handling of his later books, from complaints about the layout of pages to the placement of the author's bio following the text and the use of font he thought too small in publishers' ads. A March 1969 letter to Jason Epstein, for example, his then editor at Random House, outlines in detail Roth's ideas for a further advertisement for *Portnoy's Com-*

plaint, indicating its layout, content, and where to place the Random House logo. His impatient reaction and at times demanding requests made to HM, atypical for a first-time author, are symptomatic of Roth's later control over publication matters. Indeed, final approval of jacket covers became a virtual requirement in future book contracts.

An activist concerning the production and promotion of his work, *Goodbye, Columbus* sets the tone for the release of all of Roth's later works, while difficulties with the production and (perceived) lackluster promotion of the volume contributed to Roth's decision to leave HM and move to Random House for his next book, *Letting Go*. William Styron and Donald Klopfer facilitated the change, but that is part of another story and one set in Italy.

NOTES

1. According to John McPhee, William Shawn supposedly rejected the short story "Goodbye Columbus" for the *New Yorker* because it contained the word diaphragm. The story would eventually appear in the *Paris Review* (McPhee 32).

WORKS CITED

Correspondence. Houghton Mifflin Archive. Houghton Library, Harvard University, Cambridge MA. bMS AM2105 (216), 1958–1960. Print. Material used with permission.

McPhee, John. "Editors & Publishers," *New Yorker* (July 2, 2012) 32. Print.

Roth, Philip. Letter to Connie [?]. June 4, 1959. MS. HM Archive. bMS AM2105 (216). Print.

———. Letter to Dorothy de Santillana. May 3, 1960. MS. HM Archive. bMS AM2105 (216). Print.

———. Letter to Anne Ford. March 24, 1959. MS. HM Archive. bMS AM2105 (216). Print.

———. Letter to George Starbuck. February 17, 1958. MS. HM Archive. bMS AM2105 (216). Print.

———. March 14, 1958. MS. HM Archive. bMS AM2105 (216). Print.

———. April 11, 1958. MS. HM Archive. bMS AM2105 (216). Print.

———. May 12, 1958 MS. HM Archive. bMS AM2105 (216). Print.

———. May 17, 1958. MS. HM Archive. bMS AM2105 (216). Print.

———. May 23, 1958. MS. HM Archive. bMS AM2105 (216). Print.

———. July 25, 1958. MS. HM Archive. bMS AM2105 (216). Print.

———. August 9, 1958. MS. HM Archive. bMS AM2105 (216). Print.

———. February 25, 1959. MS. HM Archive. bMS AM2105 (216). Print.

———. July 23, 1959. MS. HM Archive. bMS AM2105 (216). Print.

———. November 4, 1959. MS. HM Archive. bMS AM2105 (216). Print.

———. December 1, 1959. MS. HM Archive. bMS AM2105 (216). Print.

Starbuck, George. Letter to Philip Roth. 14 February 1958. MS. HM Archive. bMS AM2105 (216). Print.

———. February 20, 1958. MS. HM Archive. bMS AM2105 (216). Print.

———. May 8, 1958. MS. HM Archive. bMS AM2105 (216). Print.

———. May 15, 1958. MS. HM Archive. bMS AM2105 (216). Print.

———. May 21, 1958. MS. HM Archive. bMS AM2105 (216). Print.

———. July 30, 1958. MS. HM Archive. bMS AM2105 (216). Print.

———. February 2, 1959. MS. HM Archive. bMS AM2105 (216). Print.

———. March 26, 1959. MS. HM Archive. bMS AM2105 (216). Print.

———. September 4, 1959. MS. HM Archive. bMS AM2105 (216). Print.

Chapter Three

"A Human Being Lives Here"

Philip Roth on Scandals and the American Presidency

Claudia Franziska Brühwiler

In the Federalist Paper No. 51, James Madison observed that: "If men were angels, no government would be necessary. If angels were to govern men, neither external nor internal controls on government would be necessary" (67). In spite of our awareness that angels rarely tread on Earth, even less likely in the shape of politicians, the American presidency is often subject of unearthly expectations concerning the officeholder's character and personal conduct. As "the leader of the rituals of American democracy" (Rossiter 247), he reinforces the citizens' belief in the civil religious fabric of the country, demonstrating that there is more to statehood than political agreements and machinations.[1] In the eyes of the citizens, his representation of the country transcends the political connotations of the term:

> The embodiment of the presidency enables the President to present an image of the people to itself: singular, united, with a common material form and a single will. The legislature presents an image of the people in itself: divided, comprising a great diversity, debating, doubting, driving, sometimes finding expression in common judgments and a common will (Norton 121).

Those who effectively personify the nation gain the admiration not only of the generation of their voters, but far beyond, and in select cases they become part of the country's civil religious inventory. The nation's first president thus quickly became one of the saints or demigods of American politics, as a Russian diplomat came to observe in 1813: "It is noteworthy that every American considers it his sacred duty to have a likeness of Washington in his home, just as we have images of God's saints" (Mitnick 59).

However, only few presidents have such a claim on eternity, while the vast majority resemble more the earthly sinners James Madison had at the back of his mind. When humans err, the consequences can sometimes be grave; in the case of an erring president, they can be disastrous—and at times they cause scandals. "Scandal seems everywhere, inescapable," Michael Schudson felt when he contemplated America's political landscape (1231). While scandals are not a constant topos in presidential history, once they occur, they inevitably and lastingly taint a presidential legacy, possibly overshadowing any major achievements. "Scandal" broadly means an action or event "involving certain kinds of transgressions" which becomes "known to others" and is "sufficiently serious to elicit a public response" (Thompson 13).

The transgression as such is usually followed by attempts to conceal it which, once revealed, lead to public denunciation—the outcry of the public. The American public had to witness such presidential scandals time and again in the twentieth century, from Watergate to the Iran-Contra affair to Whitewater to a certain intern's affair with a president. As in Shakespearean tragedies, Robert Watson has remarked, scandals let us witness the great fall from grace, often due to all-too-human failures (411). These incidents thus become part of the nation's presidential gallery, yet seem to leave the desire for Madisonian angels unperturbed.

In his novels, Philip Roth observed, mocked, chastised, and recreated both sides of presidential scandals: on the one hand, he became a master of calling out the emperor for his new clothes, of unmasking those hiding behind status and tradition. On the other hand, he not only took political events as a starting point for his fiction to draw attention to those deeds and incidents that should have been considered scandalous for a long time, but also to unveil the bigotry of those shrieking "scandal!" in the first place. Consequently, he tackled two of the three types of political scandals identified by John B. Thompson (2000)—sex and power scandals, the unexplored third being financial scandals (90–115). However, as we will see in the following, Roth constantly changed mode and angle when contemplating presidential scandals: in a first instance, he used satire as his weapon against the Nixon Presidency, notably pre-Watergate; turning to the Clinton years, he directs the frustration at the presidential persecutors rather than the man in power; and, finally, he looks at the institution as such and asks the readers what might happen if all checks and balances fail.

TRICKY DICK'S COMEBACK: ROTH V. NIXON

Roth's protagonists often reference what seem to be "ideal" presidents in their story-worlds, presidents who, in the characters' eyes, came close to the angelic ideal Madison had declared unrealistic. As the son of a man who believed in "the sanctity of F. D. R. and the Democratic Party" (*Facts* 31), Roth gave his key protagonist, Nathan Zuckerman, a father who would be "famous for fanatical devotion. F. D. R. topped the list, followed by Mrs. Roosevelt, Harry Truman, David Ben-Gurion, and the authors of *Fiddler on the Roof*" (*Unbound* 190).

The same president would again be the ideal leader in *The Plot Against America* (2004), making his presence felt through the radio, giving each American the idea of being connected to him. Not only in the perception of Roth's characters would Franklin Delano Roosevelt (1882–1945) be considered more than a great communicator, but also he would generally be remembered as a president who seemed to embody his message and thus be perceived as "authentic" (Norton 105). Though less frequently, Roth likewise thematized the country's lasting admiration for Abraham Lincoln (1809–1865), and he had one of his characters underline that there was more to presidential greatness than superficial images and appearances. Criticizing an actor who played Lincoln, he asked: "Always impersonating and never the real thing. Because he was tall, that made him Lincoln?" (*Communist* 288).

Although his protagonists are susceptible to civil religious pathos and sentimentality, it is presidential failure and the public's ignorance thereof that is a more attractive subject to Roth. But while in later examples he would use a more pensive and thoughtful tone when tackling this topic, his "presidential beginnings" were rather aggressive, for he turned to a genre he only rarely played with: "Why have I turned to political satire? In a word: Nixon," Roth explained (*Reading* 41). Indeed, one could speak of satire as Roth's weapon of choice, as he set out to write *Our Gang (Starring Tricky and His Friends)* (1971) "to destroy the protective armor of 'dignity' that shields anyone in an office as high and powerful as the Presidency" (*Reading* 40).

The closet drama derides President Richard M. Nixon (1917–1993) by caricaturing his mannerisms and uneasy rapport with people. Thinly disguised under the fictitious character Trick E. Dixon, Roth's Nixon parades all the quirks of the president, from his obsessive hatred for "Jack Charisma" (59) and his related preoccupation with his perspiration, to his constant stressing of his lawyerly background by directly speaking of the "tradition in the courts of this land" (5) and of what "good lawyers" (6) should do, as well as minor rhetorical habits such as the constant usage of "now" to start sentences. We even get to relive one of the turning points in Nixon's pre-presidential career, namely his successful attempt at holding onto his nomination for Vice President in the midst of a financial scandal, i.e., the so-called Checkers Speech in 1952.

Having Tricky first reminisce about the sympathy he gained by instrumentalizing the family spaniel Checkers, Roth then has him reveal his financial circumstances, the one moment in the famed speech Pat Nixon found the hardest to bear in her husband's early career. Moreover, Roth surrounds Tricky with an entourage that is easily identifiable due to telling names, from the "Highbrow Coach" Henry Kissinger to "Vice-President What's-his-name" Spiro Agnew, and criticizes them as well for their involvement in the Nixon Administration. While one senses through the pages how much Nixon's persona irks Roth, the main stabs are directed at the president's sense of morality. The hypocrisy and lack of real convictions are shown as signs of a man who only wanted power for power's sake and failed to promote anything but his own career. Consequently, Roth has Tricky descend to hell at the end of the book. Comeback artist that he is, though, Tricky is not at the end of his wits and he runs for the last position of power open to him, the one of Satan. Thus he speaks to his "fellow Fallen" (185) and asks for their support, for "despite my brief tenure in the 'White' House, I firmly believe that I was able to maintain and perpetuate all that was evil in American life when I came to power" (191).

In a way, Roth sent Nixon to hell before the rest of the country wished him gone. As Roth explained proudly: "Richard Nixon was known as a crook in our kitchen some twenty-odd years before this dawned on the majority of Americans as a real possibility" (*Reading* 10). Roth seemed destined to become a satiric Cassandra and reveal the machinations of "the fine art of government lying" before they became apparent to others, not least the media (49). Published the same year in which the Pentagon Papers came to light, *Our Gang* suggests that there might be worse things to come, crying "scandal!" when everyone believed the wolves were at rest. The book's impact, though, was rather limited: Dwight MacDonald thoroughly enjoyed it, calling it "far-fetched, unfair, tasteless, disturbing, logical, coarse and very funny," but many felt that the obvious hatred and hyperbolic vitriol driving the narrative went too far to reach readers and provoke serious debate (Frick 140). Similarly, the man whom the accusing finger was pointed at seemed relatively unfazed by such artistic attacks, as we now know thanks to the taping system of the White House. When he learned from his aide H. R. Haldeman that a recently published satire vilified him, Nixon simply asked back whether the author was a Jew (Winkler).

With the Watergate conspiracy coming to light only two years after *Our Gang*, Roth had cause for triumph as incredulity took hold of a public that had only two years earlier re-elected Nixon with a landslide majority. Watergate meant for many citizens a loss of trust in the one political institution that was meant to represent the nation as such (Milkis 359–362). Roth's view of Nixon's character was suddenly shared by many more, who saw in the disgraced President a "hater" and "collector of lies" (Genovese 186). *Our Gang* had shown many facets of Nixon's public persona that were customarily referred to, starting with the anti-communist crusader and the trickster, to his image as a comeback artist, to his stiffness.[2] But only in the wake of Watergate would he—from a Rothian perspective, finally—be recognized as a villain. In a way, Nixon's public unraveling was the definite end of pastoral accounts of American politics and history, as it showed that even the most revered political position would only ever be in the hands of sinning mortals whose actions could tarnish the office as such. With *Our Gang*, Roth had effectively revealed just that, the vulnerability of the Presidency as an institution (McCann 191–196), by showing how it could be held captive by forces unworthy of public trust.

Looking at Roth's literary reaction at the Watergate scandal, though, one senses an echo of the public disbelief and anger that he would have to watch the administration come to this and fulfill his earlier prophecy. Instead of gloating about Nixon's fall from grace, Roth's writer-protagonist Nathan Zuckerman follows Watergate on TV, expressing mainly anger with "our President's chicanery—the dummy gestures, the satanic sweating, the screwy dazzling lies" (*Anatomy* 10). At the same time, however, in his personal misery, Zuckerman "almost felt for him, the only other American he saw daily who seemed to be in as much trouble as he was" (10). Rather than feeling vindicated in their creator's early disdain for Nixon, Roth's characters long for their pre-Nixonian belief in the Presidency and the political system as such:

> "Get Nixon. Get the bastard in some way. Get Nixon and all will be well. If we can just tar and feather Nixon, America will be America again, without everything loathsome and lawless that's crept in, without all the violence and malice and madness and hate. Put him in a cage, cage the crook, and we'll have our great country back the way it was!" (*Pastoral* 299–300)

The Watergate scandal could not inspire Roth to further descend into the abyss of the Nixon years, but it would show him that the catharsis hoped for during the investigation was unattainable. The pastoral could not be restored, whether the "crook" was on the loose or not. What Roth did not foresee, though, is that Watergate would unleash a persecuting spirit directed not at abuses of consequence, but at general impurities in the White House, as Martin Genovese would observe (186–195).

AGAINST THE TYRANNY OF PROPRIETY:
ROTH IN DEFENSE OF CLINTON

"Our republican robe is soiled, and trailed in the dust. Let us repurify it," Abraham Lincoln announced in Peoria, Illinois, in 1854 (54). The stains Lincoln made out on the republican robe stemmed from the persistent division

of antebellum America into a slaveholding South and a free North, a flaw in
the country's moral fabric. While Lincoln's America faced a fateful moral
decision that it needed to make, Roth's America (1990s) sought purification
in realms that it should have neglected. Instead of tackling the country's more
pressing issues, the public embarked on a crusade in the summer of 1998,

> the summer of an enormous piety binge, a purity binge, when terrorism—which
> had replaced communism as the prevailing threat to the country's security—was
> succeeded by cocksucking, and a virile, youthful middle-aged president and a
> brash, smitten twenty-one-year-old employee carrying on in the Oval Office like
> two teenage kids in a parking lot revived America's oldest communal passion,
> historically perhaps its most treacherous and subversive pleasure: the ecstasy of
> sanctimony. (*Stain* 2)

The man to suffer under said piety binge was President Bill Clinton, whose
affair with intern Monica Lewinsky would taint the memory of his tenure, rel-
egating other failures and actual achievements to the background. In Roth's *The
Human Stain* (2000), the presidential sex scandal is only of secondary interest,
yet it serves as a foil underlying the main plot and as an example of public outrage being misdirected. The latter is the case when Nathan Zuckerman learns of
his neighbor's alleged crime: professor of classics at a small liberal arts college,
Coleman Silk is fired for asking whether absent students were "spooks," thus
unwittingly insulting the African-American truants with a racist slur. As if that
humiliation were not enough, he later experiences scorn and contempt for pursuing an affair with a considerably younger woman and finds himself victim of
the same persecuting spirit taking possession of the Pharisees attacking Clinton.

In both cases, Zuckerman is disgusted by the public hypocrisy directed at
the wrong "crimes." For Silk hid a secret far graver than verbal abuse or an
affair with an unprivileged woman:

> His crime exceeded anything and everything they wanted to lay on him. He said
> "spooks," he has a girlfriend half his age—it's all kid stuff. Such pathetic, such
> petty, such ridiculous transgressions, so much high school yammering to a man
> who, on his trajectory outward, had among other things, done what he'd done
> to his mother, to go there and, in behalf of his heroic conception of his life, to
> tell her, "It's over. This love affair is over. You're no longer my mother and
> never were". (335)

Silk committed a "virtual matricide" by denying his roots and passing America's color-line (Kral 104). Thanks to his fair complexion, he could shed his
African-American identity and pass as a Jew, thus cutting the bonds with his
family and heritage. His robe is soiled not for the reasons the public sees as
his sins, but it is drenched in sentiments not completely dissimilar to those

cited by Lincoln in Peoria. If anything should scandalize anyone, Zuckerman seems to suggest, it is this betrayal of family and identity.

Similarly, it is not Clinton's marital infidelity that should stir the public. In that regard, Zuckerman would only want to remind his fellow citizens of the un-angelic nature of any of their leaders, making him wish for "a mammoth banner, draped Dadaistically like a Christo wrapping from one end of the White House to the other and bearing the legend A HUMAN BEING LIVES HERE" (3). We can therein read an exasperated echo of Alexander Portnoy who likewise felt tormented by the expectations of a label: "Jew Jew Jew Jew Jew Jew! . . . Do me a favor, my people, and stick your suffering heritage up your suffering ass—I happen also to be a human being!" (*Portnoy* 76). The stains on the White House are, again, not due to the all too human failures of its main resident, for he has himself committed worse errors. In *I Married A Communist* (1998), one of the protagonists relates the circumstances of Nixon's funeral in 1994 during which "the realists take command, the connoisseurs of deal making and deal breaking, masters of the most shameless ways of undoing an opponent, those for whom moral concerns must always come last, uttering all the well-known, unreal, sham-ridden cant about everything but the dead man's real passions" (278).

Instead of shunning the funeral or at least reminding the public of the moral shortcomings of the man to be put to his final rest, the honorable audience paid their respects and underlined how much the country owed the deceased leader. Even then-incumbent President Clinton commended Nixon for his "'remarkable journey' and, under the spell of his own sincerity, express[ed] hushed gratitude for all the 'wise counsel' Nixon had given him" (278). It seems that Clinton followed "Tricky Dick's" own wish, as the latter told his "fellow fallen" in *Our Gang* that it was "our whole lives that you should be judging here tonight" (200). The main irony of it all escaped Roth's observers, though. Without Watergate, some argue, Clinton would not have been punished as much for his adultery as he had been. In order to regain their faith in the White House, thus Genovese, voters changed their priorities: "The search for the pure, replaced the search for the capable. Personal virtue rose as the hunt for competence declined" (195). In other words, the search for the imaginary angels resumed.

PLOT AGAINST MYTHS:
ROTH'S VARIATION ON *IT CAN'T HAPPEN HERE*

Although *Our Gang* and *The Human Stain* depict presidents as being just human, as Zuckerman's dream of the Christo drape hanging from the White

House further accentuates, Roth does not attack the institution and the citizens' reverence of the presidency as such. Neither in the mode of satire nor with a presidential scandal as a backdrop does Roth suggest that the amount of power and trust granted to presidents is problematic *per se*, as rampant abuse can be counterbalanced by the political system and by alert citizens. Scandals thus assume one of the reassuring functions described by Thompson (2000), namely that their exposure ultimately confirms the citizens' trust in the State and in the institutions charged with its supervision (246). In other words, those who long for purity in government will feel vindicated and reassured in their ideals. However, in his novel *The Plot Against America* (2004), Roth does exactly the reverse—up to a point: he demonstrates that the presidency can, under certain circumstances, serve evil, unhindered. The novel is not in reaction to a presidential scandal; instead, it nearly provoked a scandal, as it cast in the role of the presiding evil none other than aviation hero Charles A. Lindbergh (1902–1974).

The Plot Against America is narrated from the perspective of seven-year-old "Philip Roth," modelled after his creator, who observes in 1940 how the changing political circumstances affect his small world and his family life in the Weequahic section of Newark. Philip's childhood idyll starts falling apart when Charles A. Lindbergh challenges the incumbent president, Franklin D. Roosevelt, the political idol of Philip's father. Lindbergh is not only revered for his bravado and pioneering spirit, but he is also known for his anti-Semitic views and sympathies for the German Nazi government. The prospect of a Lindbergh administration thus infuses Philip with fear—and with a feeling previously unknown to the child:

> Lindbergh was the first famous living American whom I learned to hate—just as President Roosevelt was the first famous living American whom I was taught to love—and so his nomination by the Republicans to run against Roosevelt in 1940 assaulted, as nothing ever had before, that huge endowment of personal security that I had taken for granted as an American child of American parents in an American school in an American city in an America at peace with the world. (7)

Lindbergh casts a spell over America, as his personality and the story of his achievements captures the public imagination and gives the citizens the kind of heroic figure they seek in a president. It is with ease that Lindbergh wins the presidency and starts transforming the country by setting up institutions that encourage companies to relegate their Jewish employees to regions of America where hardly any Jews have settled. Increasingly, citizens feel free to express openly their own anti-Semitic feelings, and Philip's family is not the only one that fears they may no longer have a future in the America they had believed to know so well. The Lindbergh Administration seduces distinguished members of the Jewish community, as well as Philip's older brother, and they start promoting programs that encourage assimilation and, as a consequence, tear families apart. At the novel's climax, pogroms erupt in the Midwest, and the country Philip and his family once believed to be a safe haven becomes just as dangerous as the world of their ancestors had been.

In the course of events, the Roth family does not idly watch their world fall apart, but they constantly try to reassure themselves of the strength of the American system and its safeguards against presidential abuse. Philip, for instance, tries to hold onto the order presented by his collection of stamps. Thinking of his fellow stamp collector, Roosevelt, he can reenact the pastoral beginnings of "his" America through the icons depicted by the stamps that perpetuate a consensus of who and what citizens should hold dear. With the eventual loss of his collection, though, Philip loses his grip on US reality.

In the same vein, a democratic pilgrimage of the entire family is bound to fail. A trip to the memory landscape of Washington, D.C., should lift their spirits, but even young Philip senses more than mere pleasure as their motive: "Inadvertently, we had driven right to the heart of American history, and whether we knew it in so many words, it was American history, delineated in its most inspirational form, that we were counting on to protect us against Lindbergh" (58). In particular, father Herman Roth is desperate to have his sons appreciate the legacy of the Founding Fathers and the great presidents following in their footsteps, and he does not tire in contrasting their achievements with the atmosphere reigning in Lindbergh's America. Still, accompanied by a guide who appears at the Roths' side as if summoned, the family struggles to focus on the grandiosity of the National Mall. They are only rarely in the thrall of its pathos, for instance at the foot of Lincoln's statue: "What ordinarily passed for great just paled away, and there was no defense, for either an adult or a child, against the solemn atmosphere of hyperbole" (63). Yet even standing in view of the Gettysburg Address does not protect the Roths from the charged spirit surrounding them, as Herman is insulted as a "loudmouth Jew" after an altercation (65). Lindbergh's plane passing over them becomes a final reminder that D.C. is no longer in the hands of those they so deeply admire and that the system they had relied on had effectively failed them completely (71–72).

Although the novel's dénouement re-establishes Lindbergh as a "good" American who had only turned to harsh methods under Nazi pressure, the fact remains that Roth had dared to cast an iconic figure as a source of evil. He put Lindbergh at the center of a plot that shows the alternative turns history could have taken. His story reveals the actual atmosphere of that time, namely the latent presence of anti-Semitism. As a so-called political scenario novel, or, as Roth put it in an essay for the *New York Times*, "an exercise in historical imagination," *The Plot* does not ask "what if?," but outlines the answer to the question and, at times, shows that it could have happened here, as did Sinclair Lewis in one of the most famous examples of the genre, the novel *It Can't Happen Here* (1935). Roth thereby implies, as in the other novels discussed, that the scandal is not what did or did not happen, it is rather scandalous that we close our eyes to such realities. Our ignorance of inconvenient truths becomes evident in a review in *The American Conservative* by Bill Kaufmann, who criticized the novel as "bigoted and libelous of the dead, dripping with hatred of rural America, of Catholics, of any Middle American who has never dared stand against the war machine."

While the latter reviewer felt scandalized by Roth's depiction of the United States in the 1930s and 1940s, other critics sensed a small scandal by reading *The Plot* as an allegory for the Administration of President George W. Bush. Allegories and *romans à clef* can often cloak or provoke a scandal as they show in an accusatory, yet secretive manner what is happening and where current events inevitably have to lead.[3] This prompted Roth to write "The Story Behind *The Plot Against America*" in the *New York Times*, in which he refuted such allegations, yet not unambiguously. He ended his note mocking President George W. Bush, as "unfit to run a hardware store let alone a nation like this one." In other words, Roth again left the readers speculating whether his scenario novel was in fact a masked critique of recent events deemed scandalous by many, or whether it was indeed just an exercise in "historical imagination." In any event, he succeeded in reminding his readers how both American present and history may be fraught with potential scandals that should, but rarely do make headlines.

CONCLUSION

> When power leads men towards arrogance, poetry reminds him of his limitations. When power narrows the areas of man's concern, poetry reminds him of the richness and diversity of his existence. When power corrupts, poetry cleanses. For art establishes the basic human truth which must serve as the touchstone of our judgment. (John F. Kennedy, 1963)

Dedicating Amherst College Library to the memory of Robert Frost, President John F. Kennedy (1917–1963) expressed greater hope in the powers of the arts and literature than Roth who would, in variations, stress that: "repeating . . . 'It can happen here,' does little to prevent 'it' from happening" (*Reading* 207). He may be right that it is hard to establish to what extent politicians are *ex ante* influenced by the arts and take cues from the realms of imagination. He also had to see how *Our Gang* and other negative accounts, factual and artistic, of Nixon's presidency did not prevent his re-election or his hero's treatment at the time of his death.

Still, writers and artists have the ability to shape the legacies of presidents and bring to light inconvenient truths. These may not only include Roth's "sickening disappointment of finding in the seat of power neither reason, nor common sense, nor horse sense—and certainly not charity or courage" (*Reading* 193), but also mirror the voters' failure to honor truly virtuous leaders. The many *gates* we nowadays read of usually only amount to "kid stuff," whereas the true scandals often remain at rest. Presidents may be performing, as Emmet John Hughes put it, for "two constituencies: the living citizens and future historians" (McDonald 439–440)—sometimes, however, we need writers like Philip Roth to remind both audience and officeholder of what they should stand up for.

NOTES

1. This chapter is based on a paper presented at Philip Roth Society's Roth@80 Conference on March 18, 2013, in Newark, New Jersey. I thank the organizers and editors David Gooblar and Aimee Pozorski for their comments and the opportunity to discuss my research with such a diverse round of Roth experts.

2. Since, to date, we have not seen a woman successfully claim the Presidency, I will use masculine pronouns throughout when I am speaking of US presidents in general.

3. Frick and Greenberg explore in their respective monographs the many public faces of Nixon, showing how his image constantly evolved, but some labels also stuck from the beginning.

4. The question whether *The Plot Against America* should be read in this manner was discussed by, among others, Brauner (192), Plax (77), and Safer (147).

WORKS CITED

Brauner, David. *Philip Roth*. Manchester and New York: Manchester UP, 2007. Print.

Dugan, Andrew and Frank Newport. "Americans Rate JFK as Top Modern President." *Gallup*. Nov. 13, 2013. Web. July 7, 2015.

Frick, Daniel. *Reinventing Richard Nixon: A Cultural History of an American Obsession*. Lawrence, KS: UP of Kansas, 2008. Print.

Genovese, Martin A. "The Long Legacy of Watergate." *Watergate Remembered: The Legacy for American Politics*. Eds. Michael A. Genovese and Iwan W. Morgan. Gordonsville, VA: Palgrave Macmillan, 2012. 183–196. Print.

Greenberg, David. *Nixon's Shadow: The History of an Image.* New York; London: Norton, 2003. Print.

Kaufmann, Bill. "Heil to the Chief." *The American Conservative.* Sept. 27, 2004. Web. May 20, 2012.

Kellman, Steven G. "It *Is* Happening Here: *The Plot Against America* and the Political Moment." *Philip Roth Studies.* 4.4 (2008): 113–123. Print.

Kennedy, John F. "Remarks at Amherst College, October 26, 1963." *John F. Kennedy Presidential Library and Museum.* Web. July 10, 2015.

Kral, Françoise. "F(r)ictions of Identity in The Human Stain." *Philip Roth Studies.* 2.1 (2006): 47–55. Print.

Lincoln, Abraham. *Lincoln Speeches.* Ed. Allen C. Guelzo. New York and London: Penguin, 2012. Print.

Madison, James. "Federalist No. 51." *Principles and Practice of American Politics: Classic and Contemporary Readings.* 3rd ed. Eds. Samuel Kernell and Steven Smith. Washington, D.C.: CQ Press, 2007. 66–68. Print.

McCann, Sean. *A Pinnacle of Feeling: American Literature and Presidential Government.* Princeton, NJ: Princeton UP, 2008. Print.

MacDonald, Dwight. "Our Gang." *New York Times.* Nov. 7, 1971. Web. May 20, 2012.

McDonald, Forrest. *The American Presidency: An Intellectual History.* Lawrence, Kansas: Kansas UP, 1994. Print.

Milkis, Sidney M. and Michael Nelson. *The American Presidency: Origins and Development, 1776–2011.* 6th ed. Washington, D.C.: CQ Press, 2012. Print.

Mitnick, Barbara J. "Parallel Visions: The Literary and Visual Image of George Washington." *George Washington: American Symbol.* Ed. Barbara J. Mitnick. New York: Hudson Hills, 1999. 55–70. Print.

Nixon, Richard M. "Checkers Speech." *NBC.* Sept. 23, 1952. Web. April 12, 2012.

Norton, Anne. *Republic of Signs: Liberal Theory and American Popular Culture.* Chicago and London: U of Chicago P, 1993. Print.

Plax, Martin J. "Thoughts on *The Plot Against America.*" *Society.* 42 (2005): 77–83. Print.

Rossiter, Clinton. "The Presidency—The Focus of Leadership." *New York Times Magazine.* Nov. 11, 1956: 247. Web. May 20, 2012.

Roth, Philip. *American Pastoral.* London: Vintage, 2005. Print.

———. *The Facts: A Novelist's Autobiography.* New York: Vintage, 1997. Print.

———. *I Married a Communist.* London: Vintage, 1999. Print.

———. *Our Gang (Starring Tricky and His Friends).* London: Vintage, 2006. Print.

———. *The Plot Against America.* New York: Vintage, 2004. Print.

———. *Portnoy's Complaint.* London: Vintage, 1999. Print.

———. *Reading Myself and Others.* New York: Vintage, 2001. Print.

———. "The Story Behind 'The Plot Against America.'" *the New York Times* Sept. 19, 2004. Web. May 20, 2012.

———. *Zuckerman Unbound.* New York: Vintage International, 1995. Print.

Safer, Elaine B. *Mocking the Age: The Later Novels of Philip Roth.* Albany: SUNY P, 2006. Print.

Schudson, Michael. "Notes on Scandal and the Watergate Legacy." *American Behavioral Scientist.* 47 (2004): 1231–1238. Print.

Thompson, John B. *Political Scandal: Power and Visibility in the Media Age.* Cambridge: Polity, 2000. Print.

Watson, Robert P. *Affairs of State: The Untold History of Presidential Love, Sex, and Scandal, 1789–1900.* Lanham, MD, USA: Rowman & Littlefield, 2012. Print.

Winkler, Willi. "Lebenslänglich." *Süddeutsche Zeitung.* April 23, 2011: 3. Print.

Chapter Four

"With an accomplice no less brilliant than Jean Genet"

A Comparative Approach to Roth's Autofiction

Patrick Hayes

The figure of Jean Genet does not loom especially large in Roth's *oeuvre*, and there are several other writers, such as Franz Kafka or Saul Bellow, with whom he had a more overt connection. Nonetheless, Roth taught Genet alongside other French writers, including Mauriac, Céline, and Colette, during his time as an instructor in comparative literature in the 1960s, and Genet appears on several occasions as an important point of reference—most notably in texts that explore the boundaries between fiction and autobiography.[1] He alludes to Genet in his first autofictional novel, *My Life as a Man* (1974), at a moment in which the narrative starts to undercut itself, exposing all the leading male protagonists as "useful fictions" that enable disclosure of difficult, even shameful experiences, many of which resonate with experiences later described in Roth's autobiography, *The Facts* (1988).[2] Genet reappears in *The Anatomy Lesson* (1983), the third in Roth's autofictional sequence of Zuckerman novels. "Leave the spurting hard-on to goyim like Genet," is the advice that Zuckerman thinks his critic Milton Appel (often identified with the critic Irving Howe) would give him: "Sublimate, my child, sublimate, like the physicists who gave us the atomic bomb" (161). And he returns at the outset of Roth's most spectacular autofictional text, *Operation Shylock* (1993), again when questions about the porous borders between fiction and autobiography are being raised. Having heard rumors that he is being impersonated by a man preaching a wacky political philosophy called "Diasporism," the Philip Roth character in this novel puts on a French accent and telephones his double. "My heart was pounding," he tells us, "as though I were out on my first big robbery with an accomplice no less brilliant than Jean Genet—this was not merely treacherous, this was *interesting*" (41).

Genet was indeed a thief, and in his teenage years he was sent to a prison for young offenders for the crime of stealing. Upon his release he entered into an itinerant life of petty crime, which culminated in a period of incarceration in Paris. While in prison he started to write a series of texts, culminating with *The Thief's Journal* (1949), each of which describe (with varying degrees of fictional transformation) different aspects of his life in crime. Edmund White, Genet's biographer, considered him—along with Marcel Proust—the origina- tor of the genre of autofiction, "that hybrid of genres," he put it, "character- istic of our century," and which found in Roth one of its greatest exponents (xl). Genet was himself very influenced by Proust, whom he read for the first time in prison, and White claims that Genet's five works of autofiction, which deal obsessively with criminal life, prostitution, and homosexual sex, can be understood as a "view from below" riposte to Proust's seven-volume account of the Parisian *beau monde*. But there is another, deeper, sense in which Genet's work was a riposte to Proust. "It is not a quest of time gone by," points out "Jean," the narrator of *The Thief's Journal*, "but a work of art whose pretext-subject is my former life. It will be a present fixed with the help of the past, and not vice versa. Let the reader therefore understand that the facts were what I say they were, but the interpretation that I give them is what I am—now" (63). As this suggests, Genet was impatient with Proust- ian ideas about the redemptive value of art, and more inclined to think of his writing as an act of revolt, and as an effort of self-transformation, whose aim was to generate new forms of life for the authorial self to inhabit.

By contrast, when Roth has chosen to discuss his own practice of autofic- tion, he has tended to make rather narrower claims about its nature and value. In a passage of his 1985 interview for the *Paris Review*, which focused on the handling of autobiographical material in the early Zuckerman novels, Roth disavowed any autobiographical aim, stressing instead that they should be read purely as works of art. Rather loftily pointing out that "you have to be awfully naïve not to understand that a writer is a performer who puts on the act he does best—not least when he dons the mask of the first-person singular," he went on to link this more narrow understanding of autofiction specifically with Genet. "I don't admire the Genet that Genet presents as himself any more than I admire the unsavory Molloy impersonated by Beck- ett," he explained. "I admire Genet because he writes books that won't let me forget who that Genet is" (*Reading* 125). Roth went on to amplify his view with reference to other writers of autofiction, including Witold Gombrowicz and Tadislav Konwicki. In Gombrowicz's novel *Pornographia* (1960), he pointed out, the author introduces himself as a character, using his own name, but in doing so his aim is purely aesthetic, "the better to implicate himself in certain highly dubious proceedings and bring the moral terror to life." Like- wise, in Konwicki's *The Polish Complex* (1977) and *A Minor Apocalypse* (1979), authorial self-staging is done exclusively to strengthen the "illusion that the novel is true—and not to be discounted as 'fiction'" (125).

While this rather formalist way of understanding autofiction simply as a device that can help to intensify the reality-illusion of a novel might conceivably work for some of Roth's fiction, such as *The Plot Against America* (2004), it hardly does justice to the fraught autobiographical contexts engaged by *My Life as a Man*; or to the early Zuckerman novels, with their teasing relationship to self-disclosure; or to *Operation Shylock*, where a Roth persona is brought into the text explicitly as a way of focalizing difficult questions about the responsibility of the public intellectual and the legacy of the Holocaust. And of course it is palpably untrue of Genet himself, who spoke of his writing as an action, an interpretation of his life that constitutes "what I am now." Without claiming that Genet had the same kind of significance for Roth as figures such as Bellow or Kafka, this essay will treat him instead as a "brilliant accomplice": a figure through whom Roth's practices of autofiction, which both compare with and diverge from Genet's, can be illuminated. Focusing first on the early Zuckerman novels (the series collected in *Zuckerman Bound* [1985]), and then on *Operation Shylock*, this essay will use a comparison with Genet to build up a more complex picture of the aims and effects at stake in Roth's autofictional writing than his public statements about the nature and value of this literary idiom tend to suggest.

***

In order to address Roth's first series of Zuckerman novels I am first going to consider what was, at the time Roth was teaching Genet in the 1960s, the single most influential way of understanding the nature and value of Genet's autofiction. This was Sartre's model of existential psychoanalysis, which he developed in no small part through his interest in Genet himself.

In *Saint Genet* (1962), Sartre described Genet as someone who had heroically extricated himself from the condition of "bad faith."[3] Labelled a thief and a homosexual early in life, Genet was forced to accept these pejorative terms, living under the hostile judgement of others. But, Sartre argued, Genet's writing changes this condition of bad faith: while never escaping the scorn of other people, his books are free and creative actions, not expressions of some putatively static socially-imposed identity. In becoming a writer, Sartre's argument goes, Genet chose a project of freedom, of free self-creation, through which he was able to transvalue the pejorative definitions of his life. Through his self-legendizing, Genet is in fact choosing a path to authenticity—not of being thrown into an unchosen identity, but of doing, of actively creating himself. "Since he cannot escape fatality," Sartre claimed, "he will be his own fatality; since they have made life unlivable for him, he will live the impossibility of living as if he had created it for himself, a particular ordeal reserved for him alone. He wills his destiny, he will try to love it" (49–50).

This effort to emerge from bad faith takes place through a form of self-mythologizing defined by Genet as "the rehabilitation of the ignoble" (*Thief's Journal* 20), or more aggressively, "my break with your world" (61). For an example of Genet's "rehabilitation of the ignoble," consider the following passage, where Genet finds himself in a Spanish prison, having been arrested in a police raid on the homosexual ghetto where he was turning tricks. The police search him, and find a tube of Vaseline, which he has clearly been using as a lubricant. Strapped for cash, though, Genet has only been able to procure mentholated Vaseline, which leads the police to make a series of humiliating jokes about how he must be taking it "in the nose." Then he starts to reflect:

> When I was locked up in a cell, and as soon as I had sufficiently regained my spirits to rise above the misfortune of my arrest, the image of the tube of Vaseline never left me. The policemen had shown it to me victoriously, since they could thereby flourish their revenge, their hatred, their contempt. But lo and behold! that dirty, wretched object whose purpose seemed to the world—to that concentrated delegation of the world which is the police and, above all, that particular gathering of Spanish police, smelling of garlic, sweat and oil, but substantial-looking, stout of muscle and strong in their moral assurance—utterly vile, became extremely precious to me. (17)

As his imagination starts to honor the tube of Vaseline, he associates it—in a way that resonates with the leaps of metaphor Genet admired in Proust—with an "oil lamp," perhaps because of its unctuous character, and "a night-light beside a coffin." Then the train of associations starts to take flight: the night-light leads to a lamp-post, and the "pallid face of a little old woman" beneath it. Who is the little old woman? Perhaps she is a thief, or perhaps—Genet goes on—she is the mother who abandoned him at his birth. "The tube of Vaseline," Genet triumphantly concludes:

> . . . which was intended to grease my prick and those of my lovers, summoned up the face of her who, during a reverie that moved through the dark alleys of the city, was the most cherished of mothers. It had served me in the preparation of so many secret joys, in places worthy of its discreet banality, that it had become the condition of my happiness, as my sperm-spotted handkerchief testified. Lying on the table, it was a banner telling the invisible legions of my triumph over the police. (18)

The Vaseline tube becomes a Proustian *madeleine* of Genet's underworld life, but one that is involved in a powerful act of self-transformation. It brings him back to his lost mother—not through an involuntary memory, but through an audacious act of imagination that pushes his prick, and (he is keen to point out) those of his lovers, right up into his mother's face, triumphing over the "invisible legions" of disapprovers.

While Genet disavowed any interest in a more general cultural politics that would transform the perception of homosexuality, those who followed on from him often had a broader sense for how the enterprise of self-mythologizing could be socially useful. Genet became at times a model for queer writers, particularly within the Violet Quill Club, a group of seven gay male writers including Andrew Holleran, Robert Ferro, Felice Picano, George Whitmore, Michael Grumley, and Christopher Cox, who met in New York City between 1980 and 1981, and who became some of the most influential gay autofictionalists. It is not easy to picture Roth in this company, and at first glance the Sartrean idiom seems quite alien to him. However there is one quite particular sense in which the Zuckerman novels might be understood as a variation upon Sartre's way of understanding the nature and value of an autofictional literary project.

Unlike Genet, who loathed the idea of a literary career, preferring to see himself as roving opportunistically between several very different kinds of life, Roth had from an early age seen himself precisely in those terms: as a professional novelist with a career to build and an *oeuvre* to create. As he reveals in *The Facts: A Novelist's Autobiography* (1988), going along with this sense of a writer's vocation was a very clear idea—and this at times made Roth seem a somewhat precious young man—of the serious standing of literary art, and the high calling of a literary vocation. But where Roth does compare to Genet is in the way a particular negative identity, which he did not choose, was imposed upon him in his professional life as a writer. Roth's first collection of short stories, *Goodbye, Columbus* (1959), which deals with the increasing affluence, and consequent deracination, of East Coast American Jews in the postwar economic boom, was hailed by leading critics as a striking success, but some of the stories were derided by certain sections of the Jewish community who found Roth's portraits of Jewish people not only unflattering, but dangerously conducive to anti-Semitic stereotyping. Roth claims he was shocked by these attacks, in which he was labelled a "self-hating Jew"—but his deeper reaction was one of embarrassment and confusion at being wrenched into an authorial identity he had in no sense chosen. How could such palpably high-minded artifacts, and a vocation so manifestly devoted to intellectual seriousness, be dragged down into the mire of identity politics in this crude way?[4] If it was a shock to find his early fiction labelled anti-Semitic, the reception given to *Portnoy's Complaint* (1969) massively intensified the bad faith into which his professional identity was thrown. The same critics who lauded his early work seemed deaf to the comic energies of this novel, and now intellectuals who Roth actually respected started to label him as anti-Semitic, even in one case having the temerity to cite one particular line spoken in anger by the adolescent Portnoy (his invitation to "stick your suffering heritage up your suffering ass") as somehow exemplary of Roth's own attitude (72).

But even more damagingly, in the wider culture Roth became recast as the literary celebrity who made a million dollars out of writing a pornographic book. The sexual explicitness of *Portnoy* (not only masturbation, but some casual sex and a rather fraught threesome) led to his being seen both as a hero of the sexual revolution, and as a masturbator whose hand you would not wish to shake.[5] Now internationally famous, Roth once again found his own conception of his professional identity dragged into something much cruder and shallower.[6]

In the years after *Portnoy*, Roth's career went into something of a creative lull: so defined was he by the popular reception of that book that his work of the 1970s tended to replay its themes, at times—as in *The Breast* (1971), and *The Professor of Desire* (1977)—to the point of self-caricature. Roth's way out of this impasse as a writer was to follow Genet's example, and create a series of autofictional novels that would transvalue the fate he had been handed—yet in a special way that diverges from Genet. Through the figure of Zuckerman (the name derives from "suckerborn," alluding to the cruel fate Roth felt he was handed as an American writer with pretentions to high seriousness) Roth created a figure through whom he could write about his particular fate as a professional writer—heightening it, and transforming it in a self-legendizing way.[7] But his interest in doing so was not, as with Genet, in transvaluing the moral concepts (anti-Semite, pornographer, sell-out to the consumer society, and so forth) that had been used to denigrate him. Instead, in a different take on Sartre's existentialist model of self-transformation, Roth transforms the muck of his reputation into the gold of serious art, making his professional catastrophe into a new basis for artistic success.

In *Zuckerman Unbound* (1981), the second novel in the series, Roth used the period of his life immediately after the success of *Portnoy*. Whereas Roth himself left New York City immediately upon publishing the book for a trip to London, followed by several months at the Yaddo Artist's Colony (where he began to invent Zuckerman), after the release of *Carnovsky* Zuckerman stays in New York, where he has overnight become so famous he gets mobbed in the street by turned-on women and crazy celebrity-addicts. Throwing Zuckerman into the shallow unrealities of celebrity in this extreme way enabled Roth to build up an evocative, and often very troubling, exploration of what has become known, since Baudrillard, as the culture of simulacra. In an increasingly dark series of scenes, Roth explores the difference between the cultural products of the mass media, and the seemingly more "real" objects and people we assume they obscure, using Zuckerman to test more conventional and reassuring assumptions about the difference between the simulated and the real, often to the point of destruction. The book culminates in a disturbing comparison between the banality of a celebrity funeral, into which Zuckerman aimlessly wanders, and the funeral of his own father, hinting darkly at the ways in which the same potential for human disconnection and emotional emptiness lurks in both experiences.

In *The Anatomy Lesson* (1983), Roth deepened this exploration of the culture of simulacra by transforming himself into a Zuckerman who is bewildered by the vacuity of the response to his work, and who is (moreover) debilitated by an undiagnosable pain that stubbornly has no meaning, either psychological or medical. Again, an unpromising authorial situation became Roth's way into a novel that powerfully focalizes what it means to inhabit a society in which—as Roth put it in an interview—"everything goes and nothing matters." Zuckerman inhabits a vast modern democracy in which the old criteria for seriousness no longer apply: where the sex he has is a meaningless commodity, where the suffering he undergoes is medicalized, and where the great books and artworks he had learned to value are also palpably just commodities. The subtlety and resonance of this novel lies in the way it carefully avoids portraying postmodern America's affluent consumerist democracy as in some sense tragic, without ever understating the restriction of human experience it entails.

However it is the first novel in the series, *The Ghost Writer* (1979), which uses the idiom of autobiographical disclosure most provocatively. Here Roth returns to the reaction to his early fiction by parts of the Jewish community in the late 1950s, but considerably heightens the forcefulness of the accusations levelled at him. Whereas the worst Roth had to combat was a grilling by some students at a writers' conference at Yeshiva University in New York City, the young Zuckerman confronts a Newark judge, who asks him if there was anything in his story (called "Higher Education," about the efforts of a Jewish man to enrich himself at someone else's expense) that would not have given pleasure to Goebbels and Goering, and who instructs him to take Anne Frank as his example of how to write more sympathetically about Jews.[8] In contrast to Roth's own fiercely loyal and supportive father, Zuckerman's father joins in the chorus of disapproval as one of its loudest voices.[9]

The Ghost Writer uses the seemingly unpromising material of his early humiliation to focalize a series of questions about (on one level) the relationship between intention and meaning in literature, and (on another level) about what is at stake in memorializing the Holocaust in postwar America. In the middle of the novel there is a chapter entitled "Femme Fatale," which turns out to be a story Zuckerman wrote as a riposte to his Jewish critics. The story is his fantasy of what might have happened if Anne Frank survived Belsen and emigrated to America, only to find her diary on sale, and her life being staged as a kitsch Broadway play (later a Hollywood film). In one sense, Roth is using Zuckerman, and Zuckerman's story, to explore the manifold ways in which texts can slip their intended frame of reference: just as Zuckerman's story was read into a series of questions about anti-Semitism that he didn't choose, so is Anne's diary, inside Zuckerman's story, being used as a way to memorialize the Holocaust in a way she may well not have chosen. Zuckerman's story is a great retort to his Jewish critics, because the Anne Frank he creates, one who has survived Belsen, is a world away from the somewhat asinine young girl who appears on stage, mouthing optimistic, crowd-pleasing lines like "I still believe that people are really good at heart."[10] Zuckerman's Anne decides to keep her survival a secret, and thus ensure the success of the Broadway show: partly out of revenge, a pleasure in seeing so many Christian tears spilt for her; but also out of sheer self-delight, as she realizes she could never write another hit this big.

However the text becomes particularly interesting through the way it plays with authorial intentions. While we know that within the plot of *The Ghost Writer*, Zuckerman wrote "Femme Fatale" in the late 1950s to upstage his Jewish critics, what we don't know is why Philip Roth in the late 1970s wants us to read about Anne Frank, and about his fictional alter-ego Zuckerman's tribulations with the Jews. The contrast to Genet is especially salient here. Whereas Genet projected a version of himself as Genet, Roth here projects himself as Zuckerman, but also at the same time projects his own identity, and his own intentions, as a tantalizing secret that the reader of the novel must try to discover: what is it that Roth, who is acting as Zuckerman's ghost writer, wants us to realize? We can only speculate as to Roth's intentions, but any speculation would have to take into account the very changed context for Holocaust memorialisation in 1979, when *The Ghost Writer* was published, *vis-à-vis* 1956, when the novel is actually set.

As Peter Novick has argued, whereas in the late 1950s the prevalent ethos around Jewish American identity was assimilationist, by the late 1970s there was an increasing tendency to connect ethic identities with victim status, and a widespread use of the Holocaust as a form of "symbolic capital," both to generate military and financial support for Israel, and (particularly from religious leaders) to shore up a distinctive Jewish identity (209). In these changed times, the naïve and optimistic figure of Anne Frank was no longer seen as a suitable way to memorialize the horrors of the Holocaust. But does Zuckerman's Anne Frank give us a new icon to conjure with? She is certainly more sassy and wised-up than the 14 year old girl in the Broadway show. Naturally, she is marked by pain and anger at what happened to her. But above all, Zuckerman's Anne loves her freedom from group identities, and is impatient with any attempt to say the Holocaust defines who she is. "Responsibility to the dead?" asks Zuckerman's Anne at one point: "Rhetoric for the pious! There was nothing to give the dead—they were dead" (107).

Do we hear Roth's voice coming through Zuckerman's story, and speaking to us, about our own lives? Should we read Zuckerman's story about a fantasized Anne Frank as Roth's invitation to shake off the victim culture as so much rhetoric for the pious? Layering this idea through a speculation about possible intentions ensures that this finely-judged provocation doesn't collapse into didacticism. Instead, Roth's autofictional devices, most especially the ghostliness he creates around his own identity, generate a text that bristles with imaginative possibilities.

***

Roth's first series of Zuckerman novels do not in any simple sense exemplify Sartre's understanding of autofictional writing as a free act that transvalues the bad faith into which a subject is thrown. However they might nonetheless be understood as a "public act," as Roth called them in his *Paris Review* interview (126), that do indeed recuperate and transform the terms on which Roth's career as a writer was defined. As such they were successful not only as works of art, but as acts of self-transformation. These novels decisively changed the terms upon which Roth was considered important as a writer, and established for him a new kind of literary seriousness: an art that would derive its energies and its powers precisely from treating seriousness as a problem.[11] It is thus by no means irrelevant to note that coming out of the Zuckerman novels, Roth entered into an extraordinary period of creativity that transformed his literary reputation: first through a series of interlinked autofictional texts, from *The Counterlife* (1986) to *Operation Shylock* (1993); then in a series of major novels, from *Sabbath's Theater* (1995) to *The Human Stain* (2000).

However the early Zuckerman novels are not, of course, the whole story of Roth's autofiction, any more than the Sartrean reading of Genet is the whole story of Genet. I am going to turn now to another way of thinking about Genet's self-staging, one that is best articulated by the critic Leo Bersani. I do not wish to suggest that Roth was familiar with Bersani's reading (there is no evidence to suggest he was), only that the way of thinking about authorial self-staging that Bersani develops through Genet offers a useful inroad into *Operation Shylock*, Roth's most ambitious autofictional text.

Rejecting the emphasis of *Saint Genet*, Bersani claimed that all that Sartre had succeeded in doing in his study of the writer was describing "the best-known Genet"—the Genet of the popular imagination, "frozen in fussily obscene, self-theatricalising postures, the Genet wondering as he writes if he has found the perfect 'gesture'" (9). Only to focus on this aspect, Bersani argued, is to "blunt the originality of his work," and he brought to the fore another, more dissonant aspect of Genet's self-staging. "Genet's use of his culture's dominant terms (especially its ethical and sexual categories)," he claimed, "are designed not to rework or to subvert those terms but rather to exploit their potential for erasing cultural relationality itself (that is, the very preconditions for subversive repositionings and defiant repetitions)" (6). Genet is at his most original and unsettling when he attempts instead to push himself into a state that is unconfined by any terms of moral definition: "a form of revolt with no citational relation whatsoever to the laws, categories, and values it would contest and, ideally, destroy" (5).

Genet's pursuit of this experience of excess is closely tied to his interest in betrayal. In *Prisoner of Love* (1986) Genet figured betrayal as an experience that has a strange kind of value in and of itself, through the way it engages what he calls an "erotic exaltation" (59). And in *Funeral Rites* (1948) he hymns the treachery of his partners in crime: "Saying of them, 'They're treacherous' softened my heart. Still softens me at times. They are the only ones I believe capable of all kinds of boldness. Their sinuousness and the multiplicity of their moral lines form an interlacing which I call adventure. They depart from your rules. They are not faithful" (75). But as Bersani argues, betrayal is not just a theme in Genet's fiction. His novel *Funeral Rites* is inspired by death of one of his lovers—Jean Decarnin, the twenty-year-old Communist resistance fighter shot down in 1944 on the barricades in Paris "by the bullet of a charming young collaborator"—and Genet claims that the book will "tell the glory" of his lover (75). However he also confides at the outset that the work "perhaps has more unforeseeable secondary aims," and a very curious aim does indeed take over (13). Genet starts singing the praise of the very collaborator (Genet names him Riton) who killed Jean, openly admiring the Nazis who were Jean's (and France's) enemy, and even celebrating Adolf Hitler himself. In other words, Genet mourns Jean through an act of betrayal, but this self-betraying structure doesn't just valorize betrayal insofar as it might be understood most conventionally, namely as a transgression of loyalty. "In his most original move," Bersani argues, "Genet imagines a kind of *nonrelational betrayal*," in which the act of betrayal is so multiple it challenges comprehensibility itself (9). Describing his admiration for the traitor Riton, murderer of his lover, Genet celebrates betrayal as a process that might "exhaust . . . the social being or gangue from which the most glittering diamond will emerge; solitude, or saintliness, which is also to say the unverifiable, sparkling, unbearable play of his freedom" (160). Immersion in the movement of betrayal achieves not a transvaluation of moral norms, but an existential solitude that exceeds any form of moral definition: "a kind of metatransgressive *dépassement*," as Bersani puts it, "of the field of transgressive possibility itself."

What is important to recognize here is that betrayal for Genet becomes a matter of literary style: he develops it into a series of instabilities, organized around the figure of the authorial self. The main sign of this betrayal is an extensive play with the identity of the Genet figure, involving frequent shifts of tone, and disruptions of subject position. In the course of mourning his lover, the Genet character at times moves into drag, masquerading as Riton and even (in one notably extreme episode) assuming the identity of Hitler, while he engages in anal sex with his dead lover's brother. This is the passage in which Genet becomes a camp version of Hitler:

> Puny, ridiculous little fellow that I was, I emitted upon the world a power extracted from the pure, sheer beauty of athletes and hoodlums. In the secrecy of my night I took upon myself . . . the beauty of Gérard in particular and then that of all the lads in the Reich: the sailors with a girl's ribbon, the tank crews, the artillerymen, the aces of the Luftwaffe, and the beauty that my love had appropriated was retransmitted by my hands, by my poor puffy ridiculous face, by my hoarse, spunk-filled mouth to the loveliest armies in the world. Carrying such a charge, which had come from them and returned to them, drunk with themselves and with me, what else could those youngsters do but go out and die? (133)

Genet runs his homosexuality into Hitler's will to power, destabilizing both through a comic energy that is full of a perverted inventiveness. The Genet-Hitler figure delights in his Nazi armies, yet doing so in a fey rhetoric of male beauty, that takes in "the sailors with a girl's ribbon" alongside the "aces of the Luftwaffe," into "the loveliest armies in the world"; his excitement at destructiveness—the murderous violence of Nazism—is run through a camp voice that emerges from "my hoarse, spunk-filled mouth." Notice in particular the turn at the end, which brings back a note of grief, touching upon the subject of the book, Genet's grief for Jean; but it is a pathos played through Hitler's death-drive, which is itself layered onto the orgiastic scene of a homoerotic frenzy: it is a grief betrayed into a murderous lust, a grief both estranged and realized through that relation. It is passages like this, Bersani argues, that Genet "betrays the ethic of seriousness that governs our relation to art," and liberates his writing from "the co-optive operations of institutionalized culture" (18). His poetics of betrayal allows Genet to take his self-projection into a more enigmatic space that exceeds the normal kinds of moral accounting.

While Roth frequently turns to the theme of betrayal in an explicit way, particularly in *I Married a Communist* (1997), his most sustained literary practice of betrayal comes in *Operation Shylock*.[12] Recall the passage quoted at the outset: "My heart was pounding," the Roth persona tells us, "as though

I were out on my first big robbery with an accomplice no less brilliant than Jean Genet—this was not merely treacherous, this was *interesting*. To think that he was pretending at his end of the line to be me while I was pretending at my end not to be me gave me a terrific, unforeseen, Mardi Gras kind of kick" (40). What the reference to Genet draws attention to is the way in which the writing is an adventure in betrayal, charged-up with the betrayal's erotic charge. Exactly what is to be betrayed is specified at the start of the text, where a contract of serious intentions is drawn up with the reader: the book, we are told, will be a "confession," the most deeply reflective of the auto-biographical genres. Moreover, by alluding to the trial of John Demjanjuk in a prefatory note, Roth suggests that *Operation Shylock* will be a confession dealing in a serious way with his understanding of the Holocaust, and its impact on postwar Jewish life—signalling that this notoriously irresponsible Jew is now getting serious about his public responsibilities. But when Roth starts to deal with the serious matter of the Holocaust by introducing a second Roth, putting on a fake French accent, and calling himself (in a moment of madness) Pierre Roget, after the Thesaurus, all the time talking about the fun he is having while doing so, the "ethic of seriousness," as Bersani called it, starts to slip. And as the phone conversation with his double gathers pace, it creates a disconcerting effect: the serious exploration of big questions about the lessons of the Holocaust, the status of Israel, and violence in the Middle East, are betrayed by the comic situation in which they are articulated, and the overt laughter of the Roth persona.

However while there clearly seems much to connect *Operation Shylock* with the mode of autofiction that Bersani identifies with Genet, the differ-ences between the two writers are every bit as salient. As in the first series of Zuckerman novels, Roth's interest again has less to do with the performative possibilities of revolt for his real-life identity, than for what he might do with his identity as a professional author.

Whereas in Genet "cultural relationality" was perceived as a force that makes the self conform to certain moral shapes, in *Operation Shylock* it emerges most powerfully as a force that threatens to crudely reduce Roth's literary vocation to a public identity that is made to yield up easily-digestible answers to oversimple political questions. Roth had first explored what it means for the writer to get drawn onto the field of international politics in *The Counterlife* (1986), where, visiting Jerusalem, Zuckerman is surprised to find his books being read by some individuals as a manifesto for a liberal, cosmopolitan, and diasporic Jewish identity, over and against a rooted, more Zionist notion of Jewishness. By his own account, Zuckerman had never en-tertained such an aim in his writing, and he claimed to be startled at this new reduction of his literary seriousness.

In the later novel, Roth enlarges the political misreading of his work into a character masquerading as "Philip Roth," who he dismissively names "Moishe Pipik," and whose vision of diasporism slyly glances at R. B. Kitaj's *The First Diasporist Manifesto* (1989), in which Roth's longstanding friend Kitaj had claimed (in a tongue-in-cheek way) Roth's allegiance to his own artistic ideals.[13] As the Roth persona becomes ever more entangled with events taking place around the Demjanjuk trial, he starts to draw very specific attention to the ways in which different political powers are trying to use him. In the courtroom in Jerusalem, watching the trial, he wonders whether he is beholding the true evil of the Holocaust, or whether it is better understood as an Israeli publicity stunt that is victimizing a harmless old man, in order to garner support for its own oppression of the Palestinians. Later, outside a courtroom in Ramallah, where the Palestinian activist George Ziad has taken him to witness Israeli oppression at first hand, the Roth persona reflects explicitly on how easily a writer's identity can be manipulated. "They're thinking," he reflects, of his Palestinian friends, "of the infantile idealism and immeasurable egoism of all those writers who step momentarily onto the vast stage of history by shaking the hand of the revolutionary leader in charge of the local egalitarian dictatorship; they're thinking of how, aside from flattering a writer's vanity, it lends his life a sense of significance that he just can't seem to get finding the *mot juste*" (164).

As with Genet—or at least the aspect of Genet's autofiction that Bersani foregrounds—Roth's response to the dominant powers that try to enclose his identity is not one that aims to subvert and reclaim, for himself, a set of values and convictions that are superior to those on offer in Israel. Instead Roth pushes his authorial persona into a process of betrayal, through which—to recall Bersani—there might emerge a "potential for erasing cultural relationality itself." One of the ways this happens, which bears close resemblance to Genet's practice in *Funeral Rites* of going in drag, is through the Roth persona's play with the misrecognition of his identity. Returning to the scene set outside the Ramallah courtroom, his friend Ziad starts to regale him with a seemingly-unending lecture on the manifold nefarious ways in which the Holocaust is being put to use by the Israeli state. After the Six Day War, the "public-relations campaign cunningly devised by the terrorist [Menachem] Begin" took off, and a "mythology of victimization that they use to justify their addiction to power and the victimizing of *us*" was propagated, he claims (132–134). But just as Ziad's potent rhetoric starts to take flight, we are reminded that he has mistaken Roth's identity: he thinks he is talking not to the skeptical Roth persona that we know through the novel, but to a Roth who is masquerading as "Moishe Pipik," the cranky Messiah of Diasporism. When Ziad starts describing Roth as a "Jewish *seer*" (137), a new Moses who will redeem the Palestinians, a disturbing thought enters the text: are we supposed to be respectfully listening to a lecture given by one of the world's oppressed, or can we laugh at his mistake, and his clownish participation in what has already been exposed as a silly fantasy?

Here, outside the Ramallah courtroom, we start to taste the illicit pleasure that Genet identified in betrayal, as the text tempts us to take pleasure in Ziad's humiliation. And when we enter Ziad's home the betrayal—and the pleasure of the betrayal—cuts deeper, in an even more transgressive way. Having been introduced to Ziad's resentful son and his silent, embittered wife Anna, the Roth persona lets rip with his Pipik impersonation, "obeying an impulse I did nothing to quash . . . without a trace of conscience to rein in my raving" (156). Out pours a tirade in which Roth takes all of Ziad's most cherished fantasies about the departure of the Jews from his homeland and ruthlessly parodies them. The sadistic pleasure of the betrayal is all the more potent for the fact that it transgresses against the taboo on mocking human suffering. Ziad becomes a figure of fun, blissfully unaware he is being made a fool of: Roth even draws specific attention to the "thoughtfulness with which George sat there" taking in his "Diasporist blah-blah" (158). Our pleasure in the humiliation of this tormented man is so reckless that, as in the passage from Genet's *Funeral Rites*, a sense of moral chaos is created: what kind of political novel makes author and reader the moral equivalent of "two children playing in a sandpit" (163)?

One of the things that Roth is particularly skilled at orchestrating—and here he goes beyond his accomplice Genet—is how to deepen the experience of transgression through the handling of a dramatic situation. Having taken us into the betrayal of Ziad's moral seriousness, the betrayal now cuts in a different and unexpected direction, which has exactly this deepening effect. We are now confronted by the mysterious spectacle of Ziad's wife Anna metamorphosing into a more primal human form: "Either to warm herself or to contain herself," we are told, "she'd enwrapped herself in her own arms and, like a woman on the brink of keening, she began almost imperceptibly rocking and swaying to and fro" (158). Then, from this "tiny, almost weightless woman," comes a torrent of invective that articulates the rage and bitterness that Ziad's rambling lecture only succeeded in covering over. Rearing up against "the sentimentality of these childish, stupid ethnic mythologies" she reminds Ziad of his cosmopolitan university days, when he "plunged into a big, new free world with all your intellect and all your energy." Ziad tries to make a retort, but he only provokes this quiet woman into a more powerful counterstatement:

> "You just prefer," [Ziad tells her] "the high-minded idiocy of universities to the low-minded idiocy of political struggle. No one says it isn't idiotic and stupid

and perhaps even futile. But that is what it's like, you see, for a human being to live on this earth."

"No amount of money," she said, ignoring the condescension to address me again about my check, "will change a single thing. Stay here, *you'll* see. There is nothing in the future for these Jews and these Arabs but more tragedy, suffering, and blood. The hatred on both sides is too enormous, it envelops everything. There is no trust and there will not be for another thousand years. 'To live on this earth.' Living in Boston was living on this earth—" she angrily reminded George. "Or isn't it 'life' any longer when people have a big, bright apartment and quiet, intelligent neighbours and the simple civilized pleasure of a good job and raising children? Isn't it 'life' when you read books and listen to music and choose your friends because of their qualities and not because they share your roots? Roots! A concept for *cavemen* to live by! Is the survival of Palestinian culture, Palestinian people, Palestinian heritage, is that really a 'must' in the evolution of humanity? Is all that mythology a greater must than the survival of my son?" (161)

Anna so powerfully turns the tables that she silences the Roth character's derisive laughter: the simple dignity of her outburst takes hold of all the anger and frustration bubbling somewhere beneath Ziad's rambling lecture; her brief intervention, which brings this section of the chapter to a sudden end, discloses a sense of the desperation that underlies the situation as a whole. The pathos she commands is only strengthened by the fact that, after all we have heard about the complexity of the situation in Israel, there seems something oddly naïve about her cosmopolitanism—her fantasy of winding back the clock to 1950s Boston, before the messiness of history overtook their lives.

But the betrayal now stacks up in multiple ways. If Anna's outburst betrays Roth's betrayal of Ziad, the power of her voice is rapidly betrayed by the unruly movement of the text. As the Roth persona takes his leave from the Ziad household, we find ourselves in another very different literary idiom: a bizarre taxi ride with a driver who keeps stopping the car to relieve himself, and which ends with him being rescued by the Israeli army—with whom he starts impersonating Pipik again. Through this multiple layering of betrayal Roth's text generates a way of experiencing the situation of Israel that is unconfined by the different moral discourses that seek to regulate and define that experience, and which also try to define his authorial identity. As such, Roth shares Genet's interest in betraying "the ethic of seriousness that governs our relation to art," as Bersani put it, and liberating his writing from "the co-optive operations of institutionalized culture," as those operations play out in Israel. But he also diverges from Genet, reconceiving what is at stake in transgressiveness and revolt at the level of literary vocation, more concerned than Genet to defend the serious status of the literary text as a value-creating artefact in its own right, most in revolt against the power-play of those forces that attempt to co-opt it.

There are of course other aspects of Roth's autofiction that pull away from Genet into other directions entirely: think of the almost Wildean interests on display in *Deception* (1990), with its aesthete's fascination with the movement of voice; or the highly-wrought metafictional involutions of *My Life as a Man*; or the countervoice structure of *The Facts*, which uses Zuckerman as a way into the truth of Roth. But nonetheless, for some of Roth's most compelling autofictional writing, Genet does deserve his accolade: never quite Roth's guide or master, but certainly his brilliant accomplice.

NOTES

1. Roth describes aspects of his role as an instructor in comparative literature in an interview filmed for *Web of Stories*.

2. Here the narrator describes himself as longing for "a full-scale unbuttoning, a la Henry Miller or Jean Genet" (231).

3. For a discussion of "bad faith," see Jean-Paul Sartre, *Essays in Existentialism*, ed. Wade Baskin (New York, 1965) 160–180.

4. See "Writing About Jews" (1963), in *Reading Myself and Others* 195–211.

5. "He's a fine writer," quipped Jacqueline Susann, "but I wouldn't want to shake hands with him." See Barbara Seaman, *Lovely Me: The Life of Jacqueline Susann* (New York, 1987) 382.

6. For Roth's reaction, see his (unsent) "Letter to Diana Trilling" in *Reading Myself and Others* 22–27, and the discussion of his early career in his essay "On *The Great American Novel*," 66–78.

7. See the Philip Roth Papers, Library of Congress, Box 144, Folder 4.

8. This picks up Marie Syrkin's review of *Portnoy's Complaint*, which famously said parts of that novel were "straight out of the Goebbels-Streicher script."

9. See Roth's account of his parents' reaction in ch. 5 of *The Facts*, "All in the Family."

10. Frances Goodrich and Albert Hackett, *The Diary of Anne Frank* (New York, 1954) 92.

11. David Gooblar offers a penetrating account of Roth's quarrel with ideas of literary seriousness: see *The Major Phases of Philip Roth* (New York, 2011) 33–57.

12. *I Married a Communist* features an extended discussion of the sexual dynamics of betrayal in the McCarthy era that resonates very profoundly with Genet: "You retain your purity at the same time as you are patriotically betraying—at the same time as you are realizing a satisfaction that verges on the sexual with its ambiguous components of pleasure and weakness, of aggression and shame: the satisfaction of undermining . . . Betrayal is in the same zone of perverse and illicit and fragmented pleasure" (264).

13. Kitaj's book begins with a playful quotation from *The Counterlife* ("The poor bastard had Jew on the brain"), and a full-page sketch of Roth himself; later Kitaj

positions Roth with Primo Levi—again with a certain playfulness—as "two great Diasporists" (79).

WORKS CITED

Bersani, Leo. "The Gay Outlaw." *Diacritics* 24 (1994): 5–18. Print.

Genet, Jean. *Funeral Rites*. 1947. Trans. Bernard Frechtman. London: Faber, 1971. Print.

———. *The Thief's Journal*. 1949. Trans. Bernard Frechtman. London: Faber, 1965. Print.

———. *Prisoner of Love*. 1986. Trans. Barbara Bray. New York: New York Review of Books, 2003. Print.

Gooblar, David. *The Major Phases of Philip Roth*. London: Continuum, 2011. Print.

Kitaj, R. B. *First Diasporist Manifesto*. London: Thames and Hudson, 1989. Print.

Novick, Peter. *The Holocaust and Collective Memory: The American Experience*. [1999] London: Bloomsbury, 2000. Print.

Roth, Philip. *The Anatomy Lesson*. 1983. London: Vintage, 1995. Print.

———. *The Counterlife*. 1986. London: Vintage, 2005. Print.

———. *Deception*. 1990. London: Vintage, 2006. Print.

———. *The Facts: a Novelist's Autobiography*. 1988. London: Penguin, 1989. Print.

———. *I Married a Communist*. 1998. London: Vintage, 2005. Print.

———. *My Life as a Man*. 1974. London: Vintage, 2005. Print.

———. *Operation Shylock*. 1993. London: Vintage, 2000. Print.

———. *Portnoy's Complaint*. 1969. Harmondsworth: Penguin, 1986. Print.

———. "Reading." *Web of Stories*. Web of Stories, n.d. Web. March 4, 2016.

———. *Reading Myself and Others*. 1985. New York: Vintage, 2001. Print.

———. *Zuckerman Bound: a Trilogy and Epilogue*. 1989. London: Vintage, 1998. Print.

Sartre, Jean-Paul. *Saint Genet, actor & martyr*. 1962. Trans. Bernard Frechtman. London: Heinemann, 1988. Print.

———. *Essays in Existentialism*. Ed. Wade Baskin. New York: Kensington, 1965. Print.

Syrkin, Marie. "The Fun of Self-Abuse." *Midstream*, April 1969: 64–68. Print.

White, Edmund. *Genet*. London: Chatto & Windus, 1993. Print.

Chapter Five

Performance Anxiety

*Impotence, Queerness, and the
"Drama of Self-Disgust" in Philip Roth's*
The Professor of Desire *and* The Humbling

David Brauner

In David Baddiel's *The Death of Eli Gold* (2011), whose eponymous character is a fictional (half-)Jewish American novelist frequently referred to as "the greatest living writer," Philip Roth is described by Gold's estranged son, Harvey, as "the dark bard of American sex" (Baddiel 13), explicitly evoking what Debra Shostak has referred to as "a pseudo-autobiographical 'Roth persona'" (Shostak unpublished) and implicitly invoking the greatest of all dead writers, William Shakespeare (whose own public persona as "the bard" has made his name a synecdoche for the Western literary tradition and an idea of the poet/playwright as the repository of a timeless wisdom). Long before he himself began to be called the greatest living writer, Philip Roth was renowned and reviled for his candid and sometimes explicit representation of sex.[1] Even before the publication of *Portnoy's Complaint* (1969), Roth was harangued in certain quarters for depicting "depraved and lecherous creatures" (qtd. in Isaac 84)[2] and as late as 1982 John Gross complained of what he calls "an intolerable knowingness about . . . menstruation and masturbation" in his work (Gross 41). More recently, critics have tended to discuss Roth's interest in sexuality in less censorious terms, but there is still a widespread impression that, as Robert McCrum puts it, Roth's "lifelong subject" has been "the adventures of the ordinary sexual (American) man" (McCrum).

Less attention has been paid to the dramatic qualities of Roth's work, qualities that, this essay will argue, shed new light on the supposedly settled case of Roth's representation of sex and sexuality. The theater has always played a prominent role in Philip Roth's life, from his own thespian activities as an undergraduate at Bucknell University to the active interest he took in the career of his long-term partner, the celebrated actress Claire Bloom, whom he notoriously charged, during the course of divorce proceedings, for the time he claimed to have spent advising her on her theatrical and screen performances.[3]

Further, some of the earliest non-fiction he published took the form of reviews of contemporary drama and, as Mike Witcombe has demonstrated, after authoring a number of plays early in his career and some stage adaptations in the late 1970s, Roth developed "a renewed interest in playwriting during the mid-to-late 1980s," during which period he adapted a Chekhov play (*The Pregnant Wife*) and two of his own works—*The Ghost Writer* (1979) and *The Prague Orgy* (1985)—for television (Witcombe 110). James Duban has also written compellingly on Roth's investment in and debt to drama, particularly *Macbeth*, with reference to *The Humbling*.

In Roth's fiction, his keen interest in the theater manifests itself both thematically—in literary allusions to the great canonical playwrights (particularly Ibsen, Chekhov, and Shakespeare) and to post-war American dramatists such as Arthur Miller, Eugene O'Neill, and Clifford Odets—and formally, in the frequent use of theatrical metaphors and tropes in his prose and in the appropriation of dramatic conventions.[4] Dialogue plays a conspicuous role in most of his fiction and sometimes takes over all together, as in *Deception* (1991) and the "He and She" sections of *Exit Ghost* (2008). Several of Roth's protagonists over the years have also worked in the theater: the protagonist of an early uncollected story, "An Actor's Life for Me," is a playwright; Mickey Sabbath, the eponymous hero of *Sabbath's Theater* (1995), is both a puppeteer and a theater director, whose first wife is an actress; Ira Ringold, the tragic hero of *I Married A Communist* (1998), gains fame as a radio actor and marries the screen and stage star Eve Frame, whose marriage to her second husband, Carlton Pennington, was arranged by her studio to disguise his homosexuality; and Simon Axler, the protagonist of *The Humbling* (2009), is "the last of the best of the classical American stage actors" (2). In *The Professor of Desire* (1977), David Kepesh initially aspires to become an actor, before becoming abruptly disillusioned with the stage and disgusted with himself for having been formerly infatuated with it. In these last two novels, performance in the thespian context is repeatedly linked, implicitly and explicitly, with performance in the sexual sense, and with a queerness attended by self-disgust that disrupts, distorts, and ultimately disables the masculinity of Kepesh and Axler, resulting in psychological collapse and physical impotence. In the remainder of this essay, I will explore the relationship between impotence, queerness, and what Kepesh calls "the drama of self-disgust" (*Professor* 34–35) as it plays out in *The Professor of Desire* and *The Humbling*.

Although Roth has been celebrated for "his focus on the male libido and the testosterone-driven lust of red-blooded American men,"[5] in recent years there has been an increasing recognition that Roth's men, while they may aspire to the healthy sexual appetites and powerful virility of this archetype, more often than not fail to conform to this image.[6] Neil Davison and Warren

Hoffman go further in their readings of *Portnoy's Complaint.* For Davison, the "homosocial environment" of Alex Portnoy's father's generation of Jews represents an idealised space that Portnoy, as a cripplingly self-conscious second-generation American Jew, cannot inhabit (187), while Hoffman claims that "Portnoy's attempts to pass as a butch American man . . . ultimately read as hysterical," and that "one of the most heterosexual characters of all Jewish American literature is actually inherently queer" (17). Hoffman's argument overlaps with my own, in a companion piece to this essay, that "there is a strong thread of homosocial discourse running through Roth's *oeuvre*, that the series of intimate relationships with other men that many of Roth's protagonists form are conspicuously couched in this discourse; and that a recognition of this ought to reconfigure our sense of the sexual politics of Roth's career" (Brauner unpublished). The terms in which Hoffman couches his discussion of what he calls Portnoy's "heterosexual performance" are also pertinent to the discussion that follows here. Hoffman repeatedly invokes theatrical metaphors to describe Portnoy's attempts to "pass" as a "butch American man," foregrounding the "vast linguistic energies Portnoy has mustered to maintain his heteronormative act" (112).

For a writer conventionally associated with "testosterone-driven lust," impotence is curiously conspicuous in Roth: from Portnoy in Israel and David Kepesh in *The Professor of Desire* to Norman Cowan in *Sabbath's Theater* and Nathan Zuckerman in the American Trilogy and *Exit Ghost*, Roth's novels are populated by men who cannot perform, sexually. Perhaps even more striking are the instances of emasculating disabilities and disorders suffered by Roth's male characters: Novotny's mysterious malady in "Novotony's Pain" (1962), Herbie Bratasky's "damaged eardrum" in *The Professor of Desire,* Zuckerman's chronic back troubles in *The Anatomy Lesson* (1983), Alvin Roth's amputated leg in *The Plot Against America* (2004), Simon Axler's "perennial spinal pain" (13) and "dead leg" (54) in *The Humbling* and Bucky Cantor's congenitally weak eyes and polio-damaged legs in *Nemesis* (2010).[7] If, as Freud contends, "[t]he genitals may . . . be represented in dreams by other parts of the body" then these congenital weaknesses, injuries, illnesses, and signs of decrepitude are all also symbolic castrations (48). Moreover, if we read Steinberg's and McCrum's references to "red-blooded" and "ordinary" men as underpinning an assumption of heteronormative sexuality, then a close reading of *The Professor of Desire* and *The Humbling* would suggest that a mythology has grown up around Roth's men that needs to be challenged; that in fact Roth's representation of male sexuality is much queerer than has been generally acknowledged.[8]

The Professor of Desire is a relatively neglected text in Roth's *oeuvre.* When it is discussed, it tends to be in terms of its place in the Kepesh tril-

ogy—chronologically it is the middle of the three, published five years after
the first version of *The Breast* (1972) and 24 years prior to *The Dying Animal* (2001), but in narrative terms it is the first, since the events it describes
precede Kepesh's transformation into a breast—or as part of Roth's mid-
career engagement with Kafka, spanning *Portnoy's Complaint*, *The Breast*,
"'I always wanted you to admire my fasting'; or, Looking at Kafka," "Our
Castle," the Penguin "Writers from the Other Europe" series, and *The Prague
Orgy*. As well as Kafka's work, the novel's intertextuality has been explored
in relation to the other European fiction that Kepesh teaches in his professional capacity. As far as I am aware, however, there has been no detailed
consideration of Kepesh's early infatuation with the theater or of what I will
argue is the novel's emphasis on the performance of the sexual act and sexual
performance as an act.

The novel begins with Kepesh's description of himself, as a young boy,
enthralled by the theatrical antics of Herbie Bratasky, an all-round entertainer
and master of ceremonies at his father's Hungarian Royale hotel whose
"shameless exhibitionism" constitutes what Kepesh calls, in the opening
line of the novel, his first "temptation" (3). As such, the opening pages of
the novel are devoted to a semi-satirical eulogy of the talents of Bratasky: a
figure of fascination as much to the aged clientele of the hotel as to Kepesh.
An impressive physical specimen, in his "elasticized muscleman's swim
trunks" and immaculate tan, Bratasky is a disreputable version of *American
Pastoral*'s Seymour Levov: like "the Swede," he is feted by the Jewish community (or at least its male members) as "the wonder of our tribe," a "Jewish
Cugat" or "Krupa"(4, 3).[9] Whereas the Swede excels at sports and enlists to
do his bit for Uncle Sam's war effort, Bratasky specializes in musical performances and mimicry and is unfit to fight because of an injury to his ear,
which some guests speculate might have been self-inflicted. As his name
suggests, Bratasky is brash and brattish but he is also charming, and Kepesh
falls "under the demon drummer's spell," becoming his "awestruck acolyte"
(7). "Who else," he asks rhetorically, "is so richly endowed as to be able to
mimic Cugie's accent, the shofar blowing, and, at my request, a fighter plane
nose-diving over Berchtesgaden—*and* the Fuehrer going crazy underneath?"
(6). Bratasky saves his lewdest performances for the young Kepesh, simulating the sounds of defecation ("the full Wagnerian strains of fecal *Sturm und
Drang*") and micturition ("a most enviable stream belting an enamel bowl"),
while his disciple almost literally genuflects in adoration ("I could fall down
and worship at his feet") (7).

After the end of the summer season, the nine-year-old Kepesh carries on
a covert correspondence with Bratasky, concealing a letter in which his hero
details his struggle to "perfect the last of his lavatory impressions" "hidden

away in the button-down back pocket of my knickers" and eagerly rereading it "every chance I get" (8) while at the same time asking himself: "why do I persist in carrying the incriminating document around with me all day long?" (9). The terms of Kepesh's self-inquiry implicitly raise another question: why does Kepesh think of the letter as "incriminating"? Can Bratasky's vulgar humor really account for Kepesh's shame and fear, and for his anguished incredulity at Bratasky's alacrity in enlisting him as an "accomplice" to some unnamed crime—or, in Kepesh's words: "Does Bratasky really fail to understand how decent people feel about such things?" (9).

Like the young Nathan Zuckerman's view of the Swede, Kepesh's idolization of Bratasky is partly the hero worship of an impressionable young boy in awe of an older male role-model but there is also, in each case, a homoerotic dimension to the adoration. What Kepesh describes, retrospectively, as his "susceptibility to the . . . flamboyant, the bizarre" can easily be read as a coded confession of sexual deviance, both because of the associations of these words ("bizarre" can be a synonym for "queer," while there is a long history of "flamboyant" being used as a euphemism for "homosexual") and because of the larger discourse of which it forms a part (8). Almost everything Kepesh says about his feelings for Bratasky—from the opening line of the novel ("Temptation comes to me first in the conspicuous personage of Herbie Bratasky") to the terms in which he praises the talents with which he is "richly endowed," to his fetishization of his letter (keeping it in his knickers at all times and furtively re-reading it) would, if the object of his adoration were female, be understood as evidence of an erotic attachment. But Kepesh does not—or cannot bring himself to—recognize the nature of his attraction to Bratasky because of the self-disgust that such feelings arouse in him, self-disgust that he has internalized from his awareness of "how decent people feel about such things" (9). Indeed, the phrase "such things" here makes much more sense as a euphemism for homosexuality (still a very strong taboo in the 1940s, when sodomy was illegal in all forty-eight states and gay marriage unthinkable) than as an allusion to genteel distaste for toilet humor.

The extent of the stigma attached to homosexuality in the post-war period is made clear in two later episodes in the novel. The first of these is Kepesh's reaction when he is told by a fellow student at college that his best friend, "a nervous, awkward, and homely philosophy major named Louis Jelinek" (17) is a "'practicing homosexual'": "*My* friend? It cannot be. 'Sissies,' of course, I am familiar with . . . But as for a practicing homosexual? Never, never, in all my nineteen years" (18–19). From this initial incredulity, Kepesh swiftly moves to accept that perhaps "while my shameful secret with Louis is that under it all I am altogether ordinary and respectable, a closet Joe College, his with me is that he's queer?" and then imagine scenarios in which Louis attempts to initiate physical intimacy: "Will he tell me he loves me and stick his tongue in my mouth?" (20). In spite of these fears (which are also of course fantasies), Kepesh "continue[s] to visit him in his odoriferous room and sit across the litter [of discarded kleenexes] from him there talking loudly for hours . . . and praying that he will not make a pass" (20).

If Kepesh's veneration of Bratasky anticipates Zuckerman's of the Swede, then his relationship with Jelinek anticipates that of Zuckerman with his gay college mentor, Leo Glucksman, in *I Married A Communist*. Just as Zuckerman, on his weekly Friday-night visits to Glucksman's room, where they talk intensely about literature and philosophy, feels "like a girl . . . when she wound up with an intimidating boy who too obviously liked her breasts" (220), so Kepesh places himself in the female subject position, imagining himself rebuffing Jelinek's advances in the same way as the "innocent, tempting girls" at college do his: "No, no, please don't! Oh, Louis, you're too smart for this!" (20).

The uneasy mixture of homophobia and homoeroticism that characterises Kepesh's representation of his friendship with Jelinek recurs later in the novel, when Kepesh sublets an apartment from Mark, a gay actor. After moving in, he finds a box of wigs in the closet and decides to "indulge my curiosity and try a couple on" (104). Before long, he begins receiving calls on his intercom from Wally, who seems to believe that Kepesh has become Mark's lover and attempts to flirt with Kepesh, addressing him as "sweetpants" and responding to his attempt to explain that Mark has moved to California with inane innuendo ("'Then who are you?' 'His tenant.' 'Is that what they call it in the thee-ayter?'" [105]). Although ostensibly infuriated by the attentions of the man whom he dubs his "homosexual suitor," Kepesh admits that during his "loneliest . . . nights" he has "to suppress a powerful urge to call for help into the intercom" (105). When his parents find out about Wally, Kepesh tries to pacify his father, who threatens first to "crack open the head" of, and then to pour boiling water on, the "lousy stinking fairy" (115). Kepesh plays down the significance of Wally's visits ("you mustn't make too much of it" [216]), lying about the frequency of his visits and later claiming, dishonestly, that they have stopped altogether, just as earlier in the novel he lies to the FBI when they question him about Jelinek following his expulsion from college and subsequent flight from the army after being drafted to fight in the Korean War:

Agent McCormack asks, "What about his homosexual record, Dave?" Flushing, I reply, "I don't know about that." . . . "Listen, they tell me you're quite the Casanova. . . . That you really go after the girls. Is that so?" "I suppose," turning from his gaze, and from the implication I sense in his remark that the girls are only a front (21).

Kepesh's unease here might be attributed to the anxiety any young man would have felt under interrogation by the FBI during the McCarthy era in the early 1950s, particularly on suspicion of associating with a draft-dodging homosexual. Yet his prevailing emotion seems to be not fear but embarrassment—and the fact that he blushes when asked about Jelinek's "homosexual record" suggests that he feels himself to be implicated in that "record." Similarly, his inability to meet McCormack's eyes when he asks himself about his own sexual appetites might be explained as natural diffidence were it not for the particular gloss that Kepesh puts on the question—his suspicion that the question is evidence of McCormack's suspicion that his aggressive heterosexuality is a performance, that he is trying to "pass" as "a butch American man," to quote Hoffman on Portnoy again (112).

This reading is reinforced by the emphasis throughout *The Professor of Desire* on the sexual act as precisely that: an act, a self-conscious performance. Refining the "penchant for mimickry" (9) that had originally been inspired by Bratasky, at college Kepesh takes on "leading roles in university productions of plays by Giraudoux, Sophocles, and Congreve" and responds to his father's queries about his intended career by declaring "I want to act" (11). But then Kepesh has an abrupt change of heart, "[s]avagely turn[ing] upon [him] self," recalling the thespian exploits in which he had previously reveled with "the utmost self-disgust" and feeling "so humiliated by the nakedness of what I have been up to that I consider transferring to another school" (11). Why Kepesh feels such visceral shame at what he has been "up to" is never made clear, but Wally's allusion to the stereotypical associations between acting and homosexuality ("'Is that what they call it in the thee-ayter?'") might provide a clue. Like the interview with McCormack, Kepesh's experiences on the stage provoke feelings of shame, embarrassment, and self-disgust. In both cases, there is a powerful sense of exposure, which is compounded by the image that Kepesh deploys to describe his reinvention as a "young man devoted to European literature" with "the power . . . to dramatize myself . . . and . . . to shed a skin . . . by inserting the scalpel and lacerating myself from end to end" (12). The apposition here between self-dramatization and self-laceration manifests itself strikingly elsewhere in the novel in the sexual arena.

The Professor of Desire is a double-edged title: it refers both to Kepesh's profession as an academic and his interest, academic and otherwise, in the nature of desire; but also it implies that desire is something that Kepesh *professes*: an attribute he claims dubiously. The ironic disparity between these two meanings—between an image of Kepesh as an authority on sex, a connoisseur of eros, and an image of him as a pathetic charlatan, relying on rhetoric to disguise his own inadequacies—is reflected in the novel by the juxtaposition of his two bouts of therapy with Dr. Klinger for impotence with

accounts of his prodigious sexual adventures. After a brief dalliance at college with Marcella "Silky" Walsh, whose "strong tomboyish legs" tantalize
him (25), these adventures begin in earnest when he travels to London on a
Fulbright Scholarship and embarks on a *menage a trois* with two Swedish
students: Elisabeth and Birgitta. This is not the first or the last threesome to
be described in Roth's *oeuvre*. Portnoy's relationship with Mary Jane Reed
founders after they pick up a prostitute named Lina in Rome one night, a
night that begins with Portnoy imagining their activities being filmed (127)
and finishes with Portnoy vomiting, Mary Jane weeping and mutual recrimi-
nations in which Portnoy complains that Mary Jane had monopolized Lina
and Mary Jane responds with indignation and self-contradiction: "I am not a
lesbian! . . . Because if I am, *you made me one!*" (128). Kepesh's threesome
follows a similar trajectory, albeit over a longer period of time. At the start of
the relationship he is consumed by "an egotistical frenzy over this improbable
thing that is happening to me, not just with one but with two Swedish girls"
(31) but when Elisabeth attempts suicide it precipitates a "drama of self-
disgust" (34–35), self-recrimination and, finally, impotence (when Kepesh
visits a prostitute the "fifteen minutes of hard labor she . . . puts in over the
recumbent lump is without significant result" [38]).

Recalling his time with the two Swedes later in life, Kepesh marvels at his
sexual athleticism, but in this context it appears a self-serving distortion, a
convenient fiction that disguises the insecurity underpinning his enthusiasm
for the *menage*. Kepesh's staging of the three-way sex sessions is both an
attempt to achieve validation for his performance of heterosexual desire and
an implicit admission of anxiety about this performance, a recognition of its
inadequacy, of the necessity to enlist another lover to satisfy the needs of his
lover. And it is very much a staged event: Kepesh describes "proceed[ing]
as . . . I was being directed to," just as later he characterizes his sex life with
his wife, Helen Baird, in terms of "theatrical display" and "passionate performances" (61) and with his final lover, Claire Ovington, as an "underground
theater of four furtive selves—the two who pant in performance, the two who
pantingly watch" (200). In this respect, as in many others, Kepesh anticipates
Simon Axler, the protagonist of Roth's penultimate novel, *The Humbling*.

The most infamous scene in that novel—arguably the closest Roth gets
to pornography in his fiction, with the exception of the transcript between
Mickey Sabbath and Kathy Goolsbee in *Sabbath's Theater*—occurs after its
protagonist, Simon Axler and his lover, Pegeen Stapleford, pick up a woman
they meet in a restaurant bar.[10] The description of the three-way sex session
that ensues is framed by dramatic metaphors, from Axler's decision to "let
Pegeen appoint herself ringmaster" (112) to his self-conscious entrance into
the action: "'Three children got together,' he said, 'and decided to put on a

play,' whereupon his performance began" (114). In spite of Axler's apparent insouciance here, and his representation of Pegeen's mastery as one that he magnanimously permits, in fact Pegeen has been in charge from the outset, and it comes as no surprise to the reader when, soon after this episode, she ends the relationship as abruptly as she had started it, inviting herself into Axler's house and life just at the point when he "was sure he was finished: finished with acting, with women . . . with happiness" (45). Although it is Axler who makes the first move physically, Pegeen stage-manages the scene, directing Axler even if he is unaware that he is being directed. When they have sex, Pegeen is always on top since "[t]he pain from the spinal condition made it impossible for him to fuck her from above or even from the side and so he lay on his back and she mounted him" (90). And it is Pegeen who dictates the terms of their sexual play, pleasuring herself with a green dildo with which she offers to sodomize Axler. Axler's response is revealing: "'I would prefer you to suck me off,' he said. 'While I wear my cock,' she said. 'Yes' . . . 'And after I suck you off,' she said, 'you'll suck me off. You'll go down on my big green cock.' 'I could do that,' he said" (93). Axler's resistance to Pegeen's attempt to assert her dominance over him further by penetrating him is equivocal, since he acquiesces to her suggestion that he performs fellatio, thereby implicitly adopting the female role that she has assigned him, or rather that of a gay man, since what is proposed is reciprocal fellatio.

Similarly, although Axler ostensibly gives Pegeen a thorough make-over, buying her an entirely new wardrobe and restyling her hair in order to cast her as the lover in his production of an idealized May-December relationship, his motivation for doing this might be to convince himself that what he desires is a feminine woman rather than the androgynous "girl-boy" whom he was first attracted to (87). Rather than, as most readers of the novel have assumed, trying to persuade Pegeen to embrace a more conventionally feminine identity, perhaps the aim of Axler's reinvention of Pegeen is to construct a conventional female subject opposite whom he can put on a convincing heterosexual performance.

Such a reading gains traction if we accept that the crisis with which *The Humbling* begins: the sudden loss of Axler's "magic" as an actor functions as a metaphor for the loss of sexual potency (1). It is pertinent in this context that Axler's power as an actor is implicitly linked with his masculinity. Roth's nameless narrator describes him as "a man conscientiously on the grand scale who looked as if he could stand up to anything and easily fulfill all of a man's roles" (6). The phrase "stand up" connotes sexual potency and takes on greater resonance by virtue of the emphasis on his stature both on and off the stage suggested by "*all* of a man's roles." When Pegeen recounts to Axler the awkward conversation she has had with her mother about the

nature of their relationship, she reports that in response to her mother's queries about Axler's stint in a psychiatric hospital she "told her that you were
there for twenty-six days a full twelve months ago and that it had to do with
performance problems on the stage" (72). Although she is ostensibly trying to
reassure Axler about having reassured her mother about his mental health, Pegeen's diction reveals a fundamental tension between certainty (the duration
and timing of Axler's stay are specified with precision) and vagueness (the
grounds for his admission are articulated only in the most generalized terms).
Moreover, given Axler's famed acting abilities (which Pegeen's mother witnessed first-hand when she played the role of Pegeen Mike opposite Axler's
Christy Mahon in a production of Synge's *The Playboy of the Western World*)
the refinement that Pegeen offers to her explanation of Axler's predicament
("it had to do with performance problems *on the stage*") ought to have been
redundant.[11] That Pegeen feels obliged to clarify that Axler's performance
problems occurred only in the context of the theater paradoxically suggests
that they might not have been restricted to the stage, as does the narrator's
observation that Axler's experiences in the theater during his calamitous run
as Macbeth "became a night-after-night exercise in trying to get away with
something" (3). The word "something"—that most generalized, abstract of
terms—reinforces the sense that there is a reluctance on the part of the narrator to provide any detail as to the nature of Axler's "performance problems."

The fact that Axler's collapse is precipitated by, or at least coincides with,
his taking on the roles of Prospero and Macbeth concurrently in a double-
bill is pertinent here. Prospero's relinquishing of his staff at the close of *The
Tempest* might be seen in symbolic terms not simply as a renunciation of
his magic but also of his phallic power, while Macbeth is repeatedly taunted
by his wife for displaying insufficient manliness ("When you durst do it,
then you were a man" [I vii 49]; "Are you a man?" [III iv 57]; "What! quite
unmann'd in folly?" [III iv 72]). This is the greatest fear of Axler, and of
Kepesh: that they will not measure up as men, that their "heterosexual performances" will seem as hollow, inauthentic and as "ludicrous" as the critics
found Axler's rendition of Macbeth (4), that their very lives will be exposed
as "a bad act" (5). As James Duban points out, Pegeen "assumes characteristics of Shakespeare's witches and Lady Macbeth," goading him to perform
increasingly extreme acts (11). Similarly, at one point Helen Baird reproaches
Kepesh after the manner of Lady Macbeth, asking "Why didn't you take me
into your world like a man?" (91).

The more pertinent question, however, might be why he marries her in the
first place, at the end of "an interminable drama of vacillation" that leads him
to "the ineluctable conclusion that [he] ought never to see the woman again"
(66) and with the conviction that "another man still holds the claim upon her

deepest feelings" (67). Or indeed why she singles him out as her likely savior, after years of being nursed through her unhappy affair with a married man by, as Kepesh puts it, a "wealthy Hong Kong circle of English homosexuals who had 'adored' her" (76). Or why, later, she taunts him for his "prissiness" and for being a mother's boy, the former being etymologically a conflation of "prim" and "sissy"[12] and the latter a common euphemism for male homosexual in the post-war period.[13]

The suggestion that Kepesh's heterosexuality may be more honored in the profession than the performance is reinforced by the recurrence of his impotence at the end of his relationship with Helen. During the subsequent sessions with his psychoanalyst, Dr. Klinger, Kepesh tells him that he feels his problems originate from the fact that as a young man there was "something in me that I turned against . . . before I even understood it," something that he "throttled to death" (102). As with the "something" that Axler tries to "get away with," the referent of this "something" is not clear. Kepesh identifies it with his fleeting ambition to become Birgitta's pimp, but does not confide to Klinger that this fantasy was motivated by "the thrill it had given me imagining her with men other than myself" (52). He does, however, proceed to "speak at length now not just of Helen but of Birgitta as well. I go back to Louis Jelinek, even to Herbie Bratasky, speak of all that each meant to me, what each excited and alarmed, and how each was dealt with, in my way" (102). Placing Bratasky and Jelinek in apposition with his former lovers, Helen and Birgitta, Kepesh implicitly categorizes them as objects of erotic attraction.

Even if Kepesh himself seems to be unaware of the queer implications of his own narrative, others are less oblivious. The quasi-homicidal rage that Kepesh's father, Abe, exhibits towards Wally is matched by the near-hysterical euphoria with which he greets Claire Ovington, the woman who helps Kepesh rediscover his desire, thereby apparently redeeming him. The extremity of both reactions can be explained by an unspoken fear, a fear that can be inferred from the terms Kepesh uses to describe his father's relief that "it looks from the girl as though his renegade son has decided to go straight" (241). The primary meaning of this of course is that Abe sees in Claire's appearance and demeanor evidence that Kepesh has decided to settle down with someone who can make him happy, but the phrase "go straight" in the context of the queer reading that I have been pursuing also signifies a resolution to leave his queer desires behind and adopt the conventional role of the heterosexual husband. Similarly, if the emphasis in the phrase "it looks from the girl" is placed on "girl," it suggests a fear on Abe's part that his son might have chosen a boy for a companion. This fear is palpable throughout the scene in which Abe overhears Wally on the intercom in Kepesh's apartment, not only in his agitation at the presence of the man himself, but also at what he fears it portends:

it is clear from the anguished question he poses to David—"Why do you hang *around* with such people?"—that he doesn't believe his son's earlier assurance that he does not know Wally personally (116).

However, *The Professor of Desire* does not end with this reassuring vision of domestic harmony. Instead, Kepesh acknowledges that his desire for Claire "has mysteriously vanished" (262) and tries desperately to suppress a growing "fear of transformations yet to come" (263), a phrase that seems to anticipate the emasculating fate that awaits Kepesh in *The Breast* and that anticipates the title of the second section of *The Humbling*: "The Transformation." Kepesh also envisages himself "back in Klinger's waiting room . . . like Gogol's berserk and mortified amputee, who rushes to the newspaper office to place a maniacal classified ad seeking the return of the nose that has decided to leave his face" (261). This allusion to Gogol's satirical short story "The Nose," whose protagonist, Kovalyov, wakes up one morning to find that his nose has absconded, reinforces the sense of dread that permeates the closing pages of the novel. More specifically, it suggests that Kepesh's impotence is about to return; that his latest "heterosexual performance" is about to falter. Kepesh's identification with Kovalyov and his description of him as a "mortified amputee" makes clear that he sees the waning of his passion as a symbolic castration.

Although Kepesh expresses bewilderment and indignation at being "robbed" of the prospect of a life of marital bliss with Claire, he also concedes that he is sabotaging the relationship: "And robbed by whom? It always comes down to myself" (261). Even at the start of the relationship, when Kepesh bids farewell to Klinger, having convinced himself that Claire has restored his physical and mental health, he betrays profound doubts about the longevity of this miraculous cure: "*Can* it be that I've come through? Just like that? Just because of Claire? What if I awaken tomorrow morning once again without a man's capacity and appetite and strength and judgment, without the least bit of mastery over my flesh" (158). The italicized opening word here, followed by the repeated question marks, suggest that Kepesh does not really believe that he has left his problems behind. Again, the precise nature of these problems is left somewhat obscure but the reference to "a man's capacity and appetite" implies that at the very moment that Kepesh is supposedly celebrating the disappearance of his impotence and the resuscitation of his desire he is already anticipating the recurrence of the former and the failure of the latter. Finally, the fear of losing "mastery" over his "flesh" seems to be both another proleptic allusion to the events of *The Breast* and a reference to his inability to control his own bodily urges, a moment of quasi-confession that is echoed later in the novel when Kepesh, on his visit with Claire to Prague, tells Professor Soska about the "sexual despair" that resulted when he "turned against my flesh, or it turned against me—I still don't know quite how to put it" (171). Once again, Kepesh retreats into abstraction when faced with the task of describing his performance anxiety. By acknowledging the inadequacy of his own formulations—"I still don't know quite how to put it"—Kepesh draws attention to the fact that he is repressing something that remains, as ever, unnamed.

A similar reticence characterizes the narration of *The Humbling*. Like Kepesh with Claire, Axler has barely embarked on his affair with Pegeen before he finds himself speculating about its demise:

> What is the draw of a woman like this to a man who is losing so much? Wasn't he making her pretend to be someone other than who she was? Wasn't he dressing her up in costume as though a costly skirt could dispose of nearly two decades of lived experience? Wasn't he distorting her while telling himself a lie—and a lie that in the end might be anything but harmless? What if he proved to be no more than a brief male intrusion into a lesbian life? (65–66)

This proliferation of questions seems to demand cogent answers but instead they simply fade away: as soon as Pegeen's hair is cut to Axler's specifications "she seemed so transformed that all these unanswered questions ceased to trouble him" (66). As Ross Posnock has observed, *The Humbling* is a novel that poses "a series of unanswerable questions." It is also a novel that represents transformations as intrinsically suspect. Pegeen leaves her long-term lover, Priscilla, when she resolves to undergo sex reassignment surgery, becoming "a man with a mustache named Jack" (62) and Axler himself is abandoned by his wife when he metamorphoses virtually overnight from an actor whose work is "strong and successful" into someone who "couldn't act," whose "impulse was spent" and to whose performances "nobody came" (1). Bereft of the ability to act himself, Axler finds consolation in creating a role for Pegeen, casting her in a production demanding a heterosexual performance that he tries in vain to sustain. His relationship with Pegeen is an exercise in vicarious fulfillment, in which he takes on the roles of dresser, director, and producer; the "draw of a woman like this"—which is to say a lesbian woman going straight—is precisely that she offers him the opportunity to reimagine himself through her. The "lie" that he tells himself is not that Pegeen has, to adapt Kepesh's phrase, turned against her own flesh to become a heterosexual woman, but that she is attracted to him because of his own performance of heteronormative virility. On the contrary, it is Axler's abject impotence—his complete emasculation—that attracts Pegeen, since, as her former partner Louise informs Axler, she is a "cunning naif" (87–88), a conniving opportunist who uses her sexual power and her own disingenuous performance of ingenuousness to exploit her partners.

When Pegeen first visits Axler he "tripped and fell hard on the wide stone step as he led Pegeen into the house, gashing the meaty side of the hand with which he broke the fall" (52), and subsequently allowing her to tend to it, Axler immediately cedes the power in their incipient relationship. The fact that his fall is the result of the "dead leg" that afflicts him periodically—"One of his legs would intermittently go dead *so that he couldn't raise it properly*" (45, emphasis added)—reinforces the sense that Axler's impotence has been metaphorically exposed to Pegeen from the outset. Later, when her jilted lover, Louise Renner, visits Axler and asks him where Pegeen's "power" comes from, he answers that "Something about her is sexually very potent" and then watches Renner "cringe at the words" (87). But Axler himself is also arguably cringing here: there is, in his attribution of *sexual potency* to his female lover, an implicit admission of his own impotence and a resigned acceptance of his own passivity. In this resignation lie the seeds of his eventual suicide.

After Axler's wife leaves him—unable to cope with, or to understand, the extent of his collapse, given that in the past his "performance [had] never faltered" (8) even during personal traumas such as the sudden death of his parents in an automobile accident—he checks into Hammerton, a psychiatric hospital, in order to prevent himself committing suicide. Although he discharges himself after only twenty-six days, his psychiatrist, Dr. Farr, is never able to get to the bottom of his depression, as Axler only goes through the motions during his sessions: "[H]e talked to the doctor, each time he showed up. Why not? At a certain stage of misery, you'll try anything to explain what's going on with you, even if you know it doesn't explain a thing and it's one failed explanation after another" (13). Unilaterally deciding that there is no identifiable cause for his collapse but maintaining the pretense of cooperating with his doctor (a performance that belies his conviction that he can no longer act) Axler conveniently provides himself with an alibi for his condition: if it is inexplicable, then he is off the hook. Yet the precipitate nature of both his initial breakdown and his subsequent liaison with Pegeen suggests that there is "something" going on that Axler cannot or will not acknowledge. Pegeen comes closest to identifying Axler's problem when she observes that "you're . . . a very twisted man to be turned on by a girl like me," "twisted" being etymologically linked with the term "queer" (93).[14]

So shameful is queerness for Axler and Kepesh that it fills them with self-disgust, a self-disgust that results in a psychosomatic condition: in other words, they react to their queer desires by denying themselves of potency altogether, "turn[ing] against their own flesh" in a modern, secular version of the mortification of the flesh practiced by Catholic penitents. Initially, thespian and sexual performances offer a solution: through constant self-reinvention on the stage, they can elude those parts of themselves that are authentically queer; and through the performance of hyper-heterosexuality, they can convince themselves of their own heteronormativity. However, the strain of such performances takes a toll, resulting in physical and psychological collapse. Because impotence is so fundamentally inimical to their view of themselves as virile, heterosexual men, ultimately the only response left is the complete annihilation of the self. For Axler, this means the literal acting-out of the role of a failed writer who kills himself at the end of the play he appears in (Konstantin Treplev in Chekhov's *The Seagull*). For Kepesh, who shares Axler's reverence for Chekhov (he discusses a number of his stories in some detail in the course of the novel and works for many years, on and off, on a monograph devoted to his work entitled *Man in a Shell*), it entails a Kafkaesque metamorphosis into a literal embodiment of the symbolic antithesis of phallic power: the breast.

In his memoir *Worlds Apart* (2015) the gay American novelist David Plante tells an anecdote about how, while accompanying Roth on a trip to Jerusalem, on the first morning of their stay, when he emerged from his bedroom in their shared guest house, Roth told him: "I heard you last night . . . shoving furniture against the door so I wouldn't be able to come in." Plante comments, "Never before have I felt so accepted for my homosexuality by a heterosexual" (89). Roth's teasing representation of himself as a queer sexual predator might indeed be seen as a well-judged defusion of any potential tension between the men regarding Plante's sexual orientation and the fact that he has been invited to be Roth's companion in Israel in the stead of Roth's partner of the time, Claire Bloom. Equally, it might be adduced as evidence not of how sensitive he is to Plante's sensibilities (of how comfortable he is with his friend's sexuality), but rather as a sign of sensitivity in the sense of exacerbated awareness (an uncomfortable self-consciousness). Both kinds of sensitivity are visible in his fiction, but the protagonists of *The Professor of Desire* and *The Humbling* are clearly ill at ease with the idea of queer sexuality. What Duban says about Axler—"his unrelenting bisociation cripples his ability to act spontaneously, because he is ever actor and audience" (Duban 10)—applies equally to Kepesh and this crippling self-consciousness accounts to a large extent for the uncharacteristic awkwardness of the prose in both novels, and consequently for their reputation as minor or even failed works.[15] A recognition that the roots of this stylistic agitation lie in the relationship between notions of impotence, queer sexuality, and performance in the novels, and that this imbues them with a compelling energy born of unresolved tensions, might not necessarily rehabilitate their reputations, but should lead to a reevaluation of their place in the Roth canon.

NOTES

1. By 2011, Ben Jeffrey was able to assert unequivocally that "He is America's Greatest Living Writer: a national monument and the country's outstanding candidate for the Nobel Prize. In other words, Philip Roth, now, is about as celebrated and successful as it is possible for a novelist to be."

2. This quotation is from *To our Colleagues,* a "little journal circulated among Reform rabbis in the U.S." (Isaac 84).

3. Sean O'Hagan reports: "he billed her at $150 an hour for the 600 hours he had supposedly helped her work on scripts." He also refers to the "two-handed comic routines" for which Roth and Bloom were "renowned" on "literary London's dinner-party circuit" (O'Hagan 2004).

4. See Shostak 2004 for a discussion of "Theater [a]s the principal metaphor of *Sabbath's Theater*" (49) and Brauner 2007 for an analysis of how the "various realities" depicted in *The Counterlife*, and "the very processes of that depiction, are dramatised in theatrical and metatheatrical tropes" (65).

5. By Paul Steinberg, a psychiatrist who credits Roth's novels with "saving [his] life," since his reading of them persuaded him not to accept medical advice to undergo castration in order to treat his prostate cancer.

6. See, for example, Astruc; Fulk; Kalisch; McKinley; Shostak 1999.

7. In the cases of Bratasky and Cantor, their physical defects make them ineligible to serve in the Second World War; in the case of Novotny, his condition leads to a discharge from the army before he can be sent to fight in the Korean War. These circumstances reinforce the sense that these ailments signify a deficiency in manhood.

8. I am using the term "queer" here and throughout the essay in the sense that Warren Hoffman, taking his cue from Daniel Boyarin's formulation in *Unheroic Conduct: The Rise of Heterosexuality and the Invention of the Jewish Man* (1997), defines it: "not as an indication of a necessarily homosexual or gay subject position but as a marker of any sexual practice that 'puts into question any praxis, theoretical or practical, of 'the natural' in sexuality'" (Hoffman 5).

9. Xavier Cugat and Gene Krupa were American bandleaders who were known for their flamboyance as much as their musical prowess.

10. Although Ross Posnock makes a spirited defense of it, arguing that it "may be the richest passage in the novel" and celebrating the way in which Roth "conjures a primal scene of dramatic art, magically fluid transformations, originating in the totemic rituals of the shaman's shape shifting, that bring animal and human together while dividing spectator from performer" (Posnock).

11. Pegeen's mother is two months pregnant when she plays the part of Pegeen Mike and decides to name her child Pegeen if a girl and Christy if a boy.

12. The *Oxford English Dictionary* defines the word as "Precise and over-particular; (affectedly) prim or prudish, esp. in a manner considered feminine or effeminate" and cites its origin as "perhaps a blend of prim and sissy."

13. In Darden Asbury Pyron's biography of Liberace, for example, he refers to critics of the entertainer habitually identifying him "as a 'Mama's Boy,' a euphemism for queer and sissy" (22).

14. In an essay on Eve Kosofsky Sedgwick, Jane Gallop quotes from Sedgwick's foreword to *Tendencies* (1993) in which she points out that "the word queer . . . comes from the Indo-European root *twerkw*, which also yields the Latin *torquere* (to twist)" (77).

15. Kepesh suffers from a debilitating self-consciousness as a narrator that manifests itself in frequent (often parenthetical) refinements, qualifications, and clarifications—in sentences that seem to correct themselves as they proceed. Although the narrator of *The Humbling* is not Axler, his narration is very much focalized through the protagonist and is often inflected by his self-doubts and self-delusions. The initial critical reception of *The Professor of Desire* was mixed and the terms in which Robert Towers reported his ambivalence are suggestive in the context of my reading of the novel: "If the book is finally disappointing, it is so because Roth fails to mount and sustain an action that is commensurate with its stylistic achievement; about two-thirds of the way along, the momentum falters, and the rest is a tour de force that is more eloquent than convincing" (Towers). *The Humbling* received probably the least enthusiastic reviews of any of Roth's fiction since the 1970s, William Skidelsky's judgment of it as "dismayingly poor" being broadly representative. Skidelsky also revived the perennial complaints of negative reviewers of Roth, observing that "the novel's sexual politics could be construed as highly offensive" and, in less measured tones, that it is "an old man's sexual fantasy dressed up in the garb of literature" (Skidelsky).

WORKS CITED

Astruc, Remi. "The Circus of Being a Man," *Shofar* 19 (2000): 109–116. Print.

Baddiel, David. *The Death of Eli Gold*. London: Fourth Estate, 2012 [2011]. Print.

Brauner, David. *Philip Roth*. Manchester: Manchester UP, 2007. Print.

———. "Queering Philip Roth: Homosocial Discourse in 'An Actor's Life For Me,' *Sabbath's Theater* and the American Trilogy." Unpublished.

Davison, Neil. *Jewishness and Masculinity from the Modern to the Postmodern*. New York: Routledge, 2010. Print.

Duban, James. "To Dazzle as Macbeth: Bisociated Drama in Philip Roth's *The Humbling.*" *Comparative Drama* 46.1 (2012): 1–16. Print.

Freud, Sigmund. "Chapter 6E," *The Interpretation of Dreams*. EServer.org. Iowa State University, n.d. Web. July 6, 2015.

Fulk, Mark. "Tracing the Phallic Imagination: Male Desire and Female Aggression in Philip Roth's Academic Novels." *Academic Novels as Satire: Critical Studies of an Emerging Genre*. Ed. Mark Bosco and Kimberley Rae Connor. Lewiston, New York: Edwin Mellen, 2007. 72–84. Print.

Gallop, Jane. "Sedgwick's Twisted Temporalities, 'or even just reading or writing.'" *Queer Times, Queer Becomings*. Ed. E. L. McCallum and Tikko Tuhkanen. Albany: SUNY P, 47–74. Print.

Gross, John. "Marjorie Morningstar Ph.D." Rev. of *Letting Go*, by Philip Roth. *Critical Essays on Philip Roth*. Ed. Sanford Pinsker. Boston: G.K. Hall, 1982. 41–43. Print.

Hoffman, Warren. *The Passing Game: Queering Jewish American Culture*. New York: Syracuse UP, 2009. Print.

Jeffery, Ben. "What's next Isn't the Point: Philip Roth in Age." *The Quarterly Conversation*. Quarterly Conversation, September 6, 2011. Web. June 7, 2015.

Isaac, Dan. "In Defense of Philip Roth." *Chicago Review* 17 (1964): 84–96. Print.

Kalisch, Michael. "A Late Adventure of the Feelings: Eulogising Male Intimacy in *I Married a Communist* and *The Human Stain*." Unpublished.

McCallum, E. L. and Tikko Tuhkanen, eds. *Queer Times, Queer Becomings*. Albany: SUNY P, 2011.

McCrum, Robert. "Philip Roth more than deserves his Booker." *The Observer*. Guardian News and Media Ltd, May 18, 2011. Web. June 7, 2015.

McKinley, Maggie. "'I wanted to be humanish: manly, a man': Morality, Shame and Masculinity in Philip Roth's *My Life as a Man*." *Philip Roth Studies* 9.1 (2013): 89–101. Print.

O'Hagan, Sean. "One Angry Man." *The Observer*. Guardian News and Media Ltd, 26 September 2004. Web. June 7, 2015.

Oxford English Dictionary. Oxford UP, 2015. Web. June 7, 2015.

Plante, David. *Worlds Apart*. New York: Bloomsbury, 2015. Print.

Posnock, Ross. "Art's Humbling." Rev. of *The Humbling*, by Philip Roth. *Michigan Quarterly* 48:4. Web. June 7, 2015.

Pyron, Darden Asbury. *Liberace: An American Boy*. Chicago: U of Chicago P, 2000. Print.

Roth, Philip. *I Married a Communist*. London: Jonathan Cape, 1998. Print.

———. *The Humbling*. London: Jonathan Cape, 2009. Print.

———. *The Professor of Desire*. Harmondsworth: Penguin, 1985 [1977]. Print.

Shostak, Debra. *Philip Roth—Countertexts, Counterlives*. Columbia, SC: U of South Carolina P, 2004. Print.

———. "Return to the Breast: The Body, the Masculine Subject, and Philip Roth." *Twentieth-Century Literature* 45 (1999): 317–335. Print.

———. "Roth at the Movies: Portrait of the Artist as a Narcissist." Unpublished.

Skidelsky, William. Rev. of *The Humbling*, by Philip Roth. *The Guardian*. Guardian News and Media Ltd, Oct. 25, 2009. Web. June 7, 2015.

Steinberg, Paul. "Philip Roth Saved My Life." *Publisher's Weekly*. Publishers Weekly, 8 May 2015. Web. June 7, 2015.

Towers, Robert. "One-Man Band" Rev. of *The Professor of Desire*, by Philip Roth. *New York Review of Books*. New York Review of Books, Oct. 27, 1977. Web. 7 June 2015.

Witcombe, Mike. "Goodbye, *Goodbye, Columbus*: Experimental Identities in Philip Roth's Early Dramatic Works." *The Review of Contemporary Fiction* 33.3 (2015): 108–124. Print.

Chapter Six

Stalkers, Furies, and Comforters

Roth's Grave Comedy of Persecution

Aurélie Guillain

A curious fascination for unexpected, excessive *insistence* is obvious in most novels by Philip Roth. Many characters outstay their welcome in a bewildering way: In *I Married a Communist* (1998), the daughter who will not leave her mother shows the same ghoulish persistence as the wife who clings to her husband in succubus-like fashion in *My Life as a Man* (1974). This domestic persecutor is the uncanny counterpart of the stalker, the complete stranger who should belong to the public sphere of impersonal interaction and yet shows an intense, lasting *personal* interest in the protagonist: for instance, Alvin Pepler who stalks Nathan in *Zuckerman Unbound* (1981) or even the character of Philip Roth when he decides to hound his *doppelgänger* in *Operation Shylock* (1993).

In *The Human Stain* (2000), Les Farley shadows Coleman Silk until his victim is killed in a car accident, and in the novel the stalker's mute insistence is echoed by the unrelenting way in which poison-pen letters are sent to Coleman, or even by the stubborn insistence of his lawyer's comforting words: any kind of insistence, including the loyalty of faithful relatives and friends, seems likely to appear as a form of persecution. Roth's dialogues will bring out the combative quality of any conversation, staging them as verbal matches in which neither interlocutor is ever willing to "let go." The recurring motif of undiagnosed, chronic pain can also be viewed as a form of malicious insistence, possibly on the part of some dæmonic persecutor, for instance in *Novotny's Pain* (1962), *My Life as a Man* (1974), or *The Anatomy Lesson* (1983). As the ailment becomes *chronic,* it becomes the hyperæsthetic manifestation of *chronos*, of passing time that has to be endured as a shapeless continuum: in the experience of endless persecution at the hands of some human being or in that of permanent pain inflicted by some invisible persecutor, time is without perceptible "*telos*," devoid of the prospect of "*kairos*," crisis or turning point: in Roth's novels the experience of chronic pain thus radically contrasts with what Kermode defined as the experience of time when it is shaped by a teleological and "apocalyptic" narrative pattern (Kermode 17).

In this vision of time as shapeless *chronos*, of the other man as potential persecutor, of human existence as exposure to invisible threat, Steven Milowitz has read a metaphorical displacement of the "concentrationary experience" to an American setting (14). I would like to argue, on the contrary, that Roth's singular emphasis on the theme of *mutual* persecution suggests an attempt at transforming the silenced victim of European persecution into a vocal "counterpuncher" (*Stain* 90) who is provoked into speech and who becomes, in a way, fully Americanized in the process. This will lead me to explore an aspect of the transformative quality of Roth's poetics as I will focus on its capacity to transform the theme of crushing persecution into the burlesque motif of mutual persecution, notably in the *Zuckerman Bound* tetralogy. I will argue that in Roth's texts, persecution is paradoxically associated with a renewal of the subject's energy and self-authoring power, in a consistently agonistic vision of human existence. I will finally focus on the American trilogy, to show that the endless arguments between the protagonist and his friends, relatives and enemies, are modern echoes of the persecution of the tragic hero by the Furies, but also echoes of the verbal persecution of Job by his comforters: in the protagonist's answers to his persecutors, one can still hear the strains of Orestes' lament and the sound of Job's outrage, as well as the sheer energy of their protest.

Instances of persecution abound in Roth's representations of the American scene: the political correctness of the 1990s is viewed as a renewal of the Puritans' "persecuting spirit" in *The Human Stain* (2) and political persecution in the 1950s is made the subject of *I Married a Communist*. Yet the American experience of persecution is always scrupulously distinguished from any European experience of persecution, be it that of the pogroms, the Nazi holocaust, or political persecution suffered by unorthodox writers in East Europe.

In "Roth and the Holocaust," Michael Rothberg examines Roth's fiction in the context of changing representations of the Holocaust in popular American culture and convincingly contends that Roth always insists on an "unbridgeable distance" between the American Jew's and the European Jew's experience of persecution at the hands of Nazi persecutors. Rothberg argue[s] that "it is less the Holocaust and its impact on American life that obsesses Roth than the unbridgeable distance between the Holocaust and American life— and the inauthenticity of most attempts to lessen that distance" (53).

Indeed, in *The Ghost Writer* (1979) Nathan Zuckerman dreams of giving Anne Frank a second chance as his American bride and the daydream is mocked as a self-exonerating fantasy on the part of a young Jewish writer who is being accused of being disloyal to the Jewish community. The experience of the American Jew is often described as the antithesis of the Jewish experience of persecution at the hands of the Nazi: for instance Aharon Appelfeld is described as the inverted mirror-image of Philip in *Operation Shylock* (1993): "Aharon and I each embody the reverse of the other's experience; because each recognizes in the other the Jewish man that he is not" (200–201). In *The Plot Against America* (2004), a more complicated move is made by Roth to suggest the unbridgeable distance between the European and the American experience. The alternate history begins, as it would, with a consistent attempt at showing that anti-Semitic persecution *might very well* have taken place in the United States; the novel thus begins by giving credibility and an aura of verisimilitude to a story of anti-Semitic persecution taking place on American ground. The epilogue even portrays the American boy as a permanently terrified child, one who will symbolically share his bedroom with Seldon Wishnow whose mother was killed by her anti-Semitic persecutors. The shared bedroom becomes a metaphor for the shared space of a common traumatic memory. In the remarkable final sentence, the bond existing between Philip, the subject of the autobiography, and Seldon, his orphaned companion, is designated as the relationship between a prosthesis and a stump: "the boy himself was the stump . . . I was the prosthesis" (362). The metaphor does not evoke mere bonding but rather a pseudo-organic unity achieved between Philip and Seldon: the autobiographical subject and the victim of anti-Semitic persecution are imagined as two components making up one single body. Nevertheless, this powerful symbiotic image is not the novel's last word: it is immediately followed by a sobering paratext, which reminds the reader that the novel is a piece of fiction and the symbiotic image, a fantasy. The appendix then goes on to distinguish the counterfactual elements from historically established facts, once more in a scrupulous way. This harrowing finale does acknowledge the strong pull of the compassionate fantasy but it also recognizes the fantastical nature of the prosthetic brotherhood between 11-year old Philip and the figure of the victim of anti-Semitic persecution. Returning to the historical fact of Philip Roth's protected American childhood, the novel eventually discriminates between fantasy and ineluctable fact: the novelist, as novelist, will indulge the dream of appropriating a suffering which is, ultimately, not his own; but being a fundamentally ironic novelist he will also, scrupulously and somehow ruthlessly, expose the fictitious quality of that fantasy.

When Roth's other novels deal with persecution in the United States, and they often do, they remain scrupulously focused on a specifically American "persecuting spirit." In the opening of *The Human Stain*, Nathan Zuckerman rails against the self-righteous frenzy that presided over Bill Clinton's impeachment in 1998 and the writer traces it back to the moral and religious intolerance of the Puritan Fathers:

> In the Congress, in the press, and on the networks, the righteous grandstanding creeps, crazy to blame, deplore, and punish, were everywhere out moralizing to beat the band: all of them in a calculated frenzy with what Hawthorne (who, in the 1860s, lived not many miles from my door) identified in the incipient country of long ago as "the persecuting spirit." (2)

The singularity of this American atmosphere seems to lie in the interplay between the persecuting drive and the individualistic spirit, which is conjured up by the explicit reference to Hawthorne and the more implicit one to *The Scarlet Letter*. Even if it is the butt of satire, the American persecuting spirit nevertheless acts as the moral environment in which a free individual will assert himself, uncrushed and unvanquished. In *The Human Stain*, the ostracized and harassed Coleman Silk is marked out as a free individual by the very fact of his isolation, like the minister who was ostracized for remaining true to himself in Hawthorne's "The Minister's Black Veil" or like Hester Prynne whose stigma gradually became a symbol of growing self-awareness and moral dignity in *The Scarlet Letter*. In *The Facts* (1988), as Roth reflects upon his having been stigmatized as a self-hating Jew, he underlines the dialectical process linking external persecution and the self-authoring process. Being "branded" by a segment of the Jewish community as a self-hating Jew turned out to be "the luckiest break" and a kind of fortunate fall:

> Fanatical security, fanatical insecurity—nothing in my entire background could exemplify better than that night did how deeply rooted the Jewish drama was in this duality. After an experience like mine at Yeshiva, a writer would have had to be no writer at all to go looking elsewhere for something to write about. My humiliation before the Yeshiva belligerents—indeed, the angry Jewish resistance that I aroused virtually from the start—was the luckiest break I could have had. I was branded. (130)

In this version of the "facts," being branded as a self-hating Jew appears to consolidate the writer's identity as a *literary* author and as a *self-authoring* subject. Like Hester Prynne, the "branded" subject who has been exposed to public shame is also on his way to becoming a free individual defined, in Emersonian manner, as a self-progenitive subject.

Indeed, in *Zuckerman Bound*, Roth used as literary material his American experience of being harassed and taken to task by his readers. And this was indeed a self-defining act: in the portrait of Zuckerman, the fictional alter ego, Roth authored an image of himself as comic "counter-persecutor" and developed the original comic treatment of "guilt and persecution," a path he had begun to explore in *Portnoy's Complaint*:

> I realized the course [I was giving at the University of Pennsylvania] might have been called "Studies in Guilt and Persecution" . . . fascinated, obviously, as I still was by these dark books, I was actually looking for a way to get in touch with another side of my talent . . . I was aching to be writing something freewheeling and funny. (*Reading* 19)

In 1976, Roth praised Kafka's ability to make "strange grave comedy" out of the "tedious enervating rituals of accusation and defence" ("In Search of Kafka" 6). In the *Zuckerman Bound* tetralogy (1979–1985), the repetitive rituals of accusation and defence are made the stuff of Roth's own "grave comedy of persecution."

In *Zuckerman Unbound,* the farcical opening derives most of its comic power from the quick succession of unwanted followers, fans, and stalkers popping up on the protagonist's path like so many Jack-in-the-boxes. This bewildering proliferation of *followers* is perceived by the writer as a sudden swarm of *persecutors*, an over-consistent interpretation which often proves to be the comic misreading of deceptive appearances, as in the opening section when a harmless Christian lady with a bible is immediately suspected by Zuckerman of carrying a lethal weapon. More often than not, the persecutors are not visible: they are disembodied voices over the phone, disembodied scripts sent through the mail, accusing the writer of being a bad son and a traitor to the Jewish community. Eventually, when Nathan's father utters the word "Bastard" at the moment of his death, the accusing word immediately takes on a ghostly, haunting quality with the demise of the one who uttered it. With the father's curse, it seems that the accusing voice is being heard in its original and purest version, as if the insults and accusations coming from the reading public had been nothing but weak anticipations of the father's powerful Word, a curse in which the prosecutor's accusation coincides with the judge's sentence. Yet even at this point when the spirit of farce seems to be fading away from the narrative, the tone of "grave comedy" survives. This is mostly due to the element of Hawthornian skepticism which prevails in the epilogue: in the concluding pages, the narrative foregrounds the multiplicity of interpretations that are given to the father's rather indistinct dying words, depending on the limited perspectives and personal grudges of the surviving interpreters, in this particular case, the Zuckerman brothers: and then the *pathos* and the paralysis involved in the persecution of the son by a ghostly paternal curse are replaced, at the last minute as it were, by the comic dynamics of mutual persecution between two estranged brothers.

In "*Zuckerman Bound*: the Cerebrant of Silence," Donald Kartiganer argues that the tetralogy is haunted by the submerged but omnipresent figure of the silenced victim of the Holocaust (43). Yet I would rather argue that the exuberant comedy of the Zuckerman tetralogy is not a veil that half-conceals and half-reveals the latent motifs of death and silence, but rather a triumphant illustration of the book and the protagonist who "will not shut up." If the victim crushed by the concentrationary universe is present in Roth's fiction, one must recognize that this figure has been transformed into a burlesque, aggressive counter-persecutor. This literary transformation obeys a poetic imperative, which consists in finding a way out of seriousness and into grave comedy, and this poetic imperative is clearly mingled with an ethical and political imperative, the one which Roth thought was at work in one of Primo Levi's narratives: "staging the bravery of Jews who fought back" ("Primo Levi by Philip Roth" xvii).

In his representation of persecution, Roth seems to break free from the allegorical logic that was still found in Saul Bellow's *The Victim* (1947) in which the victimization of Asa Leventhal by Allbee could easily be regarded as an allegorical reenactment of European situations. Even if Roth's persecutors are endowed with the same uncanny, daemonic viciousness as Bellow's Allbee, Roth's persecuted victims are endowed with a far greater talent for sheer verbal aggression than Bellow's Leventhal: in Roth's dialogues, the victim's exchange with the persecutor soon becomes an instance of comic, *mutual* persecution. If one does postulate that the harassed American victim is the projected shadow of some archetypal European victim, one must also concede that the archetypal figure has been novelized, Americanized, and thus given a "second chance" on American ground.

In the context of Roth's "grave comedy," persecution is not the agent of paralysis and obstruction but rather a dynamic element that will set the plot or the character into motion. In *Zuckerman Unbound*, the most dangerous of Nathan's persecutors is Alvin Pepler, the stalker who threatens to abduct Nathan's mother. Significantly, he is also the most effective source of comedy in the narrative: a highly entertaining character, even in the eyes of his victim. In one critical conversation with his obviously deranged fan, Nathan drops his guard and begins to enjoy himself, even feeling that he is being picked up in the amorous sense of the phrase. As soon as Nathan Zuckerman begins to exchange jokes with Pepler, a passage in free indirect speech grudgingly admits in so many litotes that this stalker is "not unentertaining": "Once you relaxed with this guy, he wasn't unentertaining. You could pick up worse on the way home from the delicatessen" (29). Pepler has just characterized himself as a literal and metaphorical glutton, "Pepler the human garbage can," a man who can absorb anything from food to information; when Pepler is referred to as something Nathan has "pick[ed] up on one's way home from the delicatessen," the cannibalistic yearning to engulf the other man's existence is recognized as an impulse that is present in both the stalker and his victim (28). To Zuckerman, engaging in playful banter with a potentially dangerous stranger is a way of indulging his own gargantuan appetite for new material.

When Nathan thus admits to taking an interest in Alvin Pepler, an element of added self-awareness and assertiveness is curiously entangled with the more obvious element of self-destructiveness. Pepler acts as a grotesque but efficient muse: he praises but also stimulates Zuckerman's talent for the "one-liner": "No, you don't run away from phenomena like Alvin Pepler, not if you're a novelist with any brains you don't. Think how far Hemingway went to look for a lion" (139). Unexpected analogies expressed with virtuosic concision keep cropping up in Nathan's mind, as if losing control of the situation mysteriously increased the comic writer's control over language.

Pepler is not a silent shadow but on the contrary, an extremely talkative stalker, a human version of the book that "will not shut up": when Pepler offers Zuckerman a sample of his talents at remembering American love songs beginning with a given word, Zuckerman recognizes in this form of verbal persecution the good work of a fellow comic artist:

> He had Zuckerman laughing away now. "Alvin, you're amazing."
> To which Pepler rapidly replied, "You're sensational." "You're devastating." "You're My Everything." "You're Nothing Till Somebody Loves You." "You're Breaking My Heart." "You're Getting to Be a Habit with Me." "You're –" "This, this is quite a show. Oh, this is heaven, really." He couldn't stop laughing. . . . Priceless. The *vrai*. You can't beat it. Even richer in pointless detail than the great James Joyce. (*Unbound* 138–139)

The expressive power of anaphoric repetition, the quick, trochaic beat of the sentence, the metonymic power of the list that is able to conjure up, with precision and concision, a great variety of cultural and historical contexts: Pepler's enumeration is hailed by Zuckerman as a form of *art brut*, a rough, prototypical form of the great realist novel, unwittingly emulating Flaubert or Joyce's use of "pointless detail" to create a reality effect. Although the freewheeling Alvin is obviously declaring his flame to his victim (as in "You're getting to be a habit with me," which ironically applies to Pepler's aggravated fixation on Zuckerman), the persecutor is above all perceived by Nathan as a comic artist in the rough—both an "oppressive" threat and a "wonderful" source of inspiration for someone in the literary business: "instead of phoning [his agent], [Nathan] began to record what he could still recall of the previous day's business: not buying and selling, but seeing and believing. Oppressive perhaps from a personal point of view, but from the point of view of business? My God, from the point of view of business, yesterday was wonderful!" (119). Through his encounters with the *doppelgänger*, Zuckerman is going through a rejuvenation process which parallels the revival of Roth's own *vis comica* in the *Zuckerman Bound* series.

Later, in *Operation Shylock* (1993), confronting one's *doppelgänger* will also appear to be a perplexing experience, but not one of loss, deprivation, or even fear. After the psychic disintegration caused by the sleeping pill Halcion, the experience of mutual persecution between the protagonist and his *doppelgänger* is rather described as an awakening, a phase of hyperæsthesia following the anæsthesia of depression. The confrontation triggers the recovery of the old "obstinate, energetic, independent self":

> I felt absolutely rapturous over the decision to take on this impostor by myself, for on my own and by myself was how I'd always preferred to encounter just about everything. My God, I thought, this is me again, finally the much pined-for natural upsurge of my obstinate, energetic, independent self, zeroed back in on life and brimming with my old resolve, vying once again with an adversary a little less chimerical than sickly, crippling unreality. (37)

Finding a funny demeaning name for his antagonist ("Pipik") will be associated with "a return of [his] force": inventing an insulting nickname is the seminal element, the starting point of the verbal match that structures the loose, episodic plot of the whole novel (117). The mutual persecution taking place in verbal jousting gives unity to the narrative just as it restores the embattled protagonist's sense of personal integrity. Far from being associated with a circular pattern of stagnation, the mutual persecution of protagonist and *doppelgänger* rests on a spiraling movement and it sets into motion a loose, episodic plot which does not derive its structure from a picaro's potentially endless discoveries about unfamiliar social spheres, but from the amateur sleuth's potentially endless discoveries about his *doppelgänger,* about the version of himself that is already roaming about the world. Persecution is again used as a dynamic principle, a *primum mobile* setting the plot into motion as well as reviving the protagonist's powers. Roth's use of the *doppelgänger* is thus in sharp contrast with Dostoyevsky's use of a similar figure. In *The Double* by Dostoyevsky, the encounter with an articulate, self-assertive, masculine *doppelgänger* marks the beginning of a disintegration process for Goliadkine, the focal character whose internal contradictions can only be expressed by stuttering, self-correction, verbal inconsistency. Quite to the contrary, Roth uses the encounter of the *doppelgänger* as the starting point of an empowering process for the focal character whose eloquence will thrive in the context of antagonistic dialogue.

More generally, the Rothian persecutor is a pro-*vocative* figure in the etymological sense: he goads his interlocutor into raising his *voice.* Even when the persecutor is not his victim's *doppelgänger*, he provokes the victim into verbal retaliation and by doing so, ironically rescues him from speechlessness, which is implicitly the worse possible kind of paralysis.

In *Patrimony* (1991), a verbal match between the son and the anti-Semitic nighttime caller results in the defeat of the stalker: the son triumphs as his father's champion and emerges as a powerful counterpersecutor who symbolically murdered his opponent with words: "at the other end, the phone was dead" (102). Similarly in *Exit Ghost* (2007), a much older Zuckerman recovers his youthful energy at the same time as his ability to act as the champion of a worshipped father figure. Kliman, the ambitious editor who dogs Nathan Zuckerman's steps succees in inflicting increasingly serious narcissistic wounds on the older man, yet the repeated challenge of these conversations allows Zuckerman to unleash his own hostility with all the "rashness" of a young man: so once again verbal persecution causes a rejuvenation process. Just as the young seaman in Conrad's *The Shadow Line* made a rash decision in accepting his captainship, similarly Zuckerman shows youthful rashness and determination when accepting the mission entrusted to him by the dying Amy Bellette on behalf of the ghostly E. I. Lonoff: the mission precisely consists in preserving the ghostly writer's authorial control over his work and therefore, to oppose Kliman's publication project. Paradoxically, while the aging man is thus acting as the champion of a dead writer and his dying spouse, the sheer power of antagonism restores to Zuckerman his youthful energy, a rash, irrational impulse exposing him to trouble and therefore to existence itself.

Indeed, the writer's persistent interest in scenes of persecution reflects a view of human existence as a fundamentally agonistic situation, in which opposition and conflict are the defining circumstances of both action and self-knowledge. Even in *The Counterlife* (1986), which is often cited for its definition of the self as theatrical performance, one should keep in mind that the freedom of this performer is not conceived as absolute freedom; it is exercised within the specific bounds of classical *agôn*: a codified dispute between two contestants who put forward their arguments in turns. Self-definition then arises from disagreement. This is why a theatrical definition of the self as performance and the definition of the self as circumcised Jew are not mutually exclusive in *The Counterlife*: because Roth's theatre is a theatre of *agôn*, both the circumcised body and the performer's act bear witness to the endless "strife" that the world is: "Circumcision is everything that the pastoral is not and, to my mind, reinforces what the world is about, which isn't strifeless unity" (*Counterlife* 327).

In the later phases of Roth's fiction, the dream of living in a state of "strifeless unity" with one's environment is consistently referred to as "the pastoral" or "the pastoral mode." In *Operation Shylock*, the pastoral will be called the dream of an *unhaunted* existence: no accuser and no persecutor are to be found in the pastoral garden, which is the most conspicuous mark of its unreality. The epilogue of *The Human Stain* deconstructs the vision of a world without persecutors as it stages the encounter between Nathan Zuckerman and Les Farley, the man who stalked and probably caused the death of Nathan's friend, Coleman Silk. The persecutor has survived his victim and Nathan meets him on the blank, frozen surface of a mountain lake, where the man is ice fishing. The indelible presence of the evil persecutor at the heart of an "arcadian mountain in America" symbolizes the irreducible presence of strife and conflict at the heart of human existence: "the icy white of the lake encircling a tiny spot that was a man, the only human marker in all of nature, like the X of an illiterate's signature on a sheet of paper" (361). "[The] tiny spot that was a man" is a metaphorical script reminding Nathan that he is not looking at a wilderness but at a world composed of human signs, human markers, human words that are bound up in the universal *agôn*. Albeit an "illiterate's signature," the trace left by Farley belongs to the logic of Roth's agonistic grammatology, in which natural space is always already inscribed with a script signalling conflict. The final contemplation of the wilderness is overshadowed by the consideration by Zuckerman of the risks involved in the publication of his coming book, the whodunit that will indict Farley: very likely, the text that will give away Farley's "secret spot" will get the author of the *roman à clef* into trouble (360). The final ironic image of pastoral peace on the mountain lake is a description that conspicuously leaves out the metaphor of the illiterate's signature. And indeed what is being suppressed in the pastoral dream is precisely the consciousness of having to live in a world of human markers that is also a world of mutual persecution carried out *in and through* language. The persecution of Silk by Farley will lead to the literary persecution of Farley by Zuckerman, and this textual persecution will probably, in turn, cause the man with the pen to be tracked down by the man with the auger. The endless spiral of potential retaliation is not presented as an eccentric vendetta but rather as the open structure of *human existence* itself: it is the spiraling structure of existence unfolding within *human* time, a spiraling structure existing apart from the cycles of nature, not in tune with them.

As Debra Shostak argues in *Philip Roth—Countertexts, Counterlives*, the existential principle of agonistic dispute also applies to the very process of writing in the Rothian text, which can be regarded as a process of self-incrimination: the literary pursuit consists in not letting go of the argument, notably by inventing new voices that will argue against the case made in the latest book. Saul Bellow suggested similar views on the literary pursuit when he wrote: "The degree to which you challenge your own beliefs and expose them to destruction is a test of your worth as a novelist" (46). In Roth's *oeu-*

vre, similarly, the existential dynamics of *agôn* is inextricable from the poetic dynamics leading from texts to countertexts.

In *American Pastoral* (1997), *I Married a Communist*, and *The Human Stain*, Roth returns to the paradoxical vision of persecution as empowering provocation and he gives the voices of his outraged protagonists a distinctly tragic tone. Explicit references are made in the texts to the tragic genre and the persecutor figures appear to be novelistic avatars of the tragic Furies, or *Erinyes*, the allegorical figures materializing both the tragic hero's remorse and the hostility of Nemesis, the Greek goddess of retribution. When Fate appears in the guise of the Furies, it punishes the tragic hero for some past error (*hamartia*) even if the *hamartia* results from the possession of the hero's soul by daemonic forces (such as *hubris*) and more generally from the intrusion of divine forces lying outside man's control into the sphere of human action. The paradox of tragic responsibility and tragic self-awareness is fully revived and exploited in Roth's novelistic trilogy: the protagonist is accounted responsible for some error although he committed this error because of forces lying utterly beyond his control. As the protagonist is being hounded and assaulted by modern avatars of the tragic Furies, the verbal persecution is used to problematize the very notion of *meaningful* human suffering.

In *I Married a Communist*, Eve Frame and her daughter are not fully realistic characters: they are daemonized, Gorgon-like figures. Like Aeschylus's Furies, who appear only as a swarm, Eve and Phoebe are not individualized and the significance of their symbiotic love is ultimately symbolic, not psychological. They are two separate manifestations of the same vengeful force and their unity is symbolically conveyed in the climactic, grotesque scene when Phoebe straddles her mother and forms only one hybrid, chimerical body with her. At first, the two women appear as the daemonized agents of a radically unjust fate plaguing a virtuous Ira Ringold, but when Ringold's murderous and shameful deed is eventually revealed to the reader, the two women appear, in retrospect, as the agents of tragic retribution. Even if Ira Ringold's persecution and downfall is anchored into the historical context of McCarthyism, the fundamental significance of the two female daemons is not historical but mythical.

In contrast to *I Married a Communist*, *The Human Stain* may seem to question the adequacy of the tragic interpretation of the protagonist's predicament. In *The Human Stain*, the *hubris* of the protagonist resides in his crossing racial boundaries and in denying his family bonds to pass for white, an action in which the narrator sees a reenactment of the "savagery of *The Iliad*, Coleman's favorite book about the ravening spirit of man," Nathan even uses the metaphor of murder when referring to the unthinkable cruelty involved in Coleman's denial of his mother (335). In using the image of matricide, Zuck-

erman does not only elevate Coleman's betrayal of racial and family bonds
to a transgression of epic proportion: he also invests his friend's deed with
tragic meaning. Indeed, if the explicit intertextual reference is to Homer's
Iliad, the reference to Orestes' murder of his mother Clytemnestra is implied
in Zuckerman's interpretation of his friend's action as a matricide. One can
regard Zuckerman's version of Coleman's life as a rewriting of Aeschylus's
Oresteia; more specifically one could view it as a rewriting of the last two
plays in Aeschylus' trilogy, *The Libation Bearers* and *The Eumenides,* in
which Orestes is plagued and hounded by a group of Gorgon-like Furies
until a trial organized by Athena results in his acquittal. Indeed, Aeschylus's
Eumenides begins with the suffering and persecution of the matricidal son by
the Furies, but ends with a trial in which Athena and Apollo (the god who
ordered Orestes to punish his mother for the murder of Iphigenia) stand as
Orestes' defenders while the Furies act as his prosecutors. But in *The Human
Stain*, the tragic hero never faces trial; his swarm of persecutors never turns
into a party of *prosecutors*. Whereas Aeschylus' Furies eventually became
the prosecuting party opposing the party of defence, Roth's own persecuting
Furies swarm the whole fictional stage and beset the tragic protagonist from
all sides of the social and political spectrum, from the left-wing, privileged
academic Delphine Roux to the working class bigot and Vietnam veteran Les
Farley. In the novel, the *prosecution* of the tragic Orestes degenerates into a
blind, universal, and potentially endless *persecution* of Coleman: when the
novel turns Delphine Roux into a burlesque oracle and into a persecutor, the
modern text playfully inverts the role of the oracle of Delphi in Aeschylus'
play, which is that of a helper to Orestes. When the novel shows the college of
Athena turning against the ostracized Coleman, the modern text reverses the
function of Athena in Aeschylus's play, which was to protect rationality and
the rule of law and to preside over Orestes's acquittal. Through these playful
inversions, Roth's modern novel defines itself as a degenerate tragedy, one
in which the leading Fury, Les Farley, proves utterly unable to make a case
against his victim: as Farley mechanically repeats that it's "*all* payback" he
appears as an unthinking character ("What were you thinking?", a psychologist asks him, a year after the deaths of Coleman and Faunia. "No thinking,"
Farley replies.)—the living embodiment of a mindless principle of mechanical retribution (67, 257).

In *American Pastoral*, the daemonized figures of Rita Cohen and Merry
Levov can also be characterized as modern avatars of the tragic Furies
tormenting the tragic hero through unrelenting accusation. Rita Cohen and
Merry Levov never appear together in the same room, and the fanatical Rita
Cohen is implicitly a stand-in for fanatical Merry Levov once Merry has per-
formed her vanishing act: like the Furies, Merry and Rita are the interchange-

able accusers whose function consists in questioning the very notion of the tragic hero's innocence. Moreover, in *American Pastoral*, the protagonist's trajectory is a close fit to the tragic plot as defined in Aristotle's *Poetics*: in the initial situation represented in the prologue, the virtuous Seymour Levov enjoys a conspicuously good fortune and a good name. When the Old Rimrock post office is bombed by Seymour's daughter, the reversal of the initial situation (*peripeteia*) inaugurates what Aristotle defines as a complex tragic plot, in which the tragic hero's downfall suddenly causes him to realize the causes of his predicament. The tragic hero thus reaches *anagnorisis,* namely a state of tragic awareness, in which he realizes, in retrospect, that he is responsible for some tragic mistake (*hamartia*) that has led to a chain of ineluctable disasters. As Zuckerman decides to write the Swede's life, he imagines the Swede as a focal character and as the subject of introspection. In doing so, he turns him into the subject of tragic awareness: "I am thinking of the Swede's great fall and how he must have imagined that it was founded on some failure of his own responsibility. There is where it must begin. It doesn't matter if he was the cause of anything. He makes himself responsible anyway" (88). Indeed, introspection will consist in an effort to determine the nature of the tragic mistake, the nature of *hamartia.* In this respect, the Swede's interior monologue is a tragic lament oscillating between the earnest attempt at defending himself in the face of Rita Cohen, the accusing Fury, and the equally earnest attempt at establishing the extent of his responsibility for his own tragic fate.

And yet, while the Swede is construed by Zuckerman as an example of tragic *awareness*, he is simultaneously portrayed as a man who never succeeds in pinpointing the moment when he made the tragic mistake, or even in identifying the nature of his mistake. *American Pastoral* is the novel in which the influence of the tragic model is the most explicit and yet, it is also the novel that seems to question in the most radical way the very notion of *hamartia* and the related notion of tragic responsibility. As in *The Human Stain*, the well-read Zuckerman is writing the biography of a dead friend by using elements of characterization and plotting which he explicitly borrows from Aeschylus, Sophocles, or even Aristotle's definition of the tragic action. Yet when Zuckerman characterizes the persecuted tragic hero as a radically innocent man (as in *American Pastoral*) or when he characterizes his tragic persecutors as essentially mindless stalkers who prove incapable of converting persecution into an act of prosecution (as in *The Human Stain*), Zuckerman the contemporary writer is distorting and burlesquing the tragic hypotext, emphasizing its poetic power but also its hermeneutic weakness.

This is probably the reason why Zuckerman has woven another intertextual reference into the fabric of Levov's biography: the reference to the Book of

Job, which points to a vision of human suffering and human responsibility that differs from the tragic interpretation. John Tunis's baseball novel, *The Kid from Tomkinsville*, is found on the Swede's shelves and is playfully described by Zuckerman as "the boys' Book of Job" because it depicts virtue as consistently rewarded with failure and loss. I would argue that Zuckerman's biography of the Swede offers the reader two interpretative paths: either the hermeneutic technique delineated by ancient Greek tragedy or the interpretation of human suffering appearing in Job's protest. In the tragic vision of man's fate, the figure of the persecutor is the external embodiment of the self-persecuting dynamics of tragic self-awareness. But in the vision of man's fate inspired by the Book of Job, the figure of the persecutor is an avatar of Satan, or an avatar of the Comforters who urge the afflicted man to hold himself responsible for his own predicament. The Swede's internal voice shows a definite hesitation between the literary model of the tragic lament and the scriptural model of Job's angry protest that his suffering has no justification.

In *Nemesis* (2010), a similar hesitation between the tragic lament and Job's protest will be heard in Bucky/Mr. Cantor's voice: Like Job, Cantor lashes out at the injustice of God, but in other passages, like Sophocles's Oedipus, he laments over his own personal responsibility in the disaster. In fact, the sound of Job's vigorous protest has been echoing through Roth's fiction for a long time, notably when the meaning of physical pain is at stake: in *Novotny's Pain*, in *My Life as a Man*, or *The Anatomy Lesson*, the ailing character is a literary echo of the biblical figure of Job who is beset by dubious comforters and other persecutors who interpret Job's pain as the result of divine punishment, while Job denies that his pain has any meaning at all. It is suggested that paradoxically, the moral dignity of the ailing man does not reside in the acceptance of the moral or psychic significance of his pain, but on the contrary, that there is moral dignity in the obdurate capacity to resist the comforters' interpretation of pain as a meaningful sign. In this respect, being able to resist the psychoanalytical reading of pain as a psychosomatic symptom becomes the touchstone of moral dignity, as in *The Anatomy Lesson.*

In *The Human Stain*, the "persecuting spirit" is said to be still active in contemporary American society (2). In saying so, the contemporary novelist is paying a tribute to Hawthorne and the Hawthornian vision of persecution that unfolds in *The Scarlet Letter*. In his posthumous dialogue with Hawthorne, and in his portraits of persecutor figures, Roth elaborates upon the character of Chillingworth the parasitical persecutor, but he also modifies this figure in one crucial respect. In the *Scarlet Letter*, Hawthorne's Chillingworth is mostly a voyeuristic figure, who delights in symptoms of secret guilt and who favors strictly private, covert manifestations of Dimmesdale's secret. On the contrary, Roth's persecutors are *agents provocateurs* who provoke their victims into speech, like the tragic furies or, more aptly, like Satan when he provokes Job into a shocking expression of his outrage. Far from being the agents of secret and oblique revelations, Roth's persecutors are instrumental in renewing the power of a speech that proves to be revitalized by wrath.

WORKS CITED

Aristotle. *Poetics*. Trans. Malcolm Heath. New York: Penguin, 1996. Print.

Bakthin, M. M. "Epic and Novel." *The Dialogical Imagination.* Ed. Michael Holquist, Austin: U of Texas P, 1981. Print.

Bellow, Saul. *It All Adds Up: From the Dim Past to the Uncertain Future.* London: Secker and Warburg, 1994. Print.

———. *The Victim*. New York: Vanguard, 1947. Print.

Berger, Alan L. *Children of Job: American Second Generation Witnesses to the Holocaust*. Albany: SUNY P, 1997. Print.

Budick, Emily Miller. "The Haunted House of Fiction: Ghost Writing the Holocaust." *Common Knowledge* 5 (Fall 1996): 121–135. Print.

Conrad, Joseph. *The Shadow-Line*. Oxford: Oxford UP, [1916–1917] 2003. Print.

Dostoyevsky, Fyodor. *Notes from Underground* and *The Double*. Trans. Ronald Wilks. London: Penguin, 2009. Print.

Kartiganer, Donald. "Fictions of Metamorphosis." In *Reading Philip Roth*. Ed. Asher Z. Milbauer and Donald G. Watson, 82–104. London: MacMillan, 1988. Print.

———. "*Zuckerman Bound*: the Cerebrant of Silence." In *The Cambridge Companion to Philip Roth*, edited by Timothy Parrish, 35–51. Cambridge: Cambridge UP, 2007. Print.

Kauvar, Elaine. "Some Reflections on Contemporary American Jewish Culture." *Contemporary Literature* 34 (Fall 1993): 337–357. Print.

———. "This Doubly Reflected Communication: Philip Roth's Autobiographies." *Contemporary Literature* 36 (1995): 412–446. Print.

Kermode, Frank. *The Sense of an Ending*. Oxford: Oxford UP, [1967] 1968. Print.

Lee, Hermione. *Philip Roth*. London: Methuen, 1982. Print.

Milowitz, Steven. *Philip Roth Considered: The Concentrationary Universe of the American Writer*. New York: Garland, 2000. Print.

Novick, Peter. *The Holocaust in American Life*. Boston: Houghton, 1999. Print.

Ricoeur, Paul. *Philosophie de la volonté*. Paris: Points, 2009. Print.

Roth, Philip. *American Pastoral*. London: Vintage, [1997] 2005. Print.

———. *The Anatomy Lesson*. London: Vintage, [1983] 2005. Print.

———. *The Counterlife*. London: Vintage, [1986] 2005. Print.

———. *Exit Ghost*. New York: Houghton, 2007. Print.

———. *The Facts: A Novelist's Autobiography*. London: Vintage, [1988] 1998. Print.

———. *The Ghost Writer*. London: Vintage, [1979] 1995. Print.

———. *The Human Stain*. London: Vintage, [2000] 2005. Print.

———. "I Always Wanted you to Admire my Fasting; or, Looking at Kafka" (1973), *Reading Myself and Others*, 281–302. New York: Vintage, 2001. Originally published in *American Review* 17, May 1973. Print.

———. *I Married A Communist*. London: Vintage, [1998] 2005. Print.

———. "In Search of Kafka and Other Answers," *New York Times Book Review*, February 15, 1976. Print.

———. "Interview with the *London Sunday Times.*" By Ian Hamilton. *Reading Myself and Others*, 111–118. New York: Vintage, 2001. Originally published in the *London Sunday Times*, February 19, 1984. Print.

———. "Interview with the *Paris Review.*" By Hermione Lee. *Reading Myself and Others*, 119–149. New York: Vintage, 2001. Originally published in *The Paris Review*, 93, Fall 1984.

———. *Nemesis*. London: Vintage, [2010] 2011. Print.

———. *Novotny's Pain*. Los Angeles, California: Sylvester and Orphanos, [1962] 1980. Print.

———. "On *Portnoy's Complaint.*" In *Reading Myself and Others*, 13–21. New York: Vintage, 2001. Originally published in *New York Times Book Review*, February 23, 1969. Print.

———. *Operation Shylock*. London: Vintage, [1993] 1994. Print.

———. *Patrimony*. London: Vintage, [1991] 1999. Print.

———. *The Plot Against America*. Boston, New York: Houghton, 2004. Print.

———. *The Prague Orgy* (1985). London: Vintage, [1985] 1995. Print.

———. "Primo Levi by Philip Roth." Foreword to *The Periodic Table,* by Primo Levi, vii–xix. London: Penguin, 1987. Print.

———. "Some New Jewish Stereotypes." In *Reading Myself and Others*, 183–192. New York: Vintage, 2001. Originally published as "The New Jewish Stereotypes." *American Judaism* 11 (Winter 1961). Print.

———. "Writing About Jews." In *Reading Myself and Others*, 193–211. New York: Vintage, 2001. Originally published in *Commentary* (December 1963), 446–452. Print.

———. "Writing and the Powers That Be." In *Reading Myself and Others*, 3–12. New York: Vintage, 2001. Originally published in *La Trappola e la Nudità: Lo Scrittore e il Potere*, edited by Walter Mauro and Elena Clementelli. Milan: Rizzoli, 1974. Print.

———. *Zuckerman Unbound*. London: Vintage, [1981] 2005. Print.

Rothberg, Michael. "Roth and the Holocaust." In *The Cambridge Companion to Philip Roth*, edited by Timothy Parrish, 52–67. Cambridge: Cambridge UP, 2007. Print.

Shostak, Debra. *Philip Roth—Countertexts, Counterlives*. Columbia, SC: U of South Carolina P, 2004. Print.

Chapter Seven

"I told my wrath, my Roth did grow"

Anger in Operation Shylock

Alex Calder

William Blake's "A Poison Tree" (1794) begins with a confession: "I was angry with my friend: / I told my wrath, my wrath did end." This may be wise counsel, but not a promising line of plot development. In the opening pages of Philip Roth's *Operation Shylock: a Confession* (1993), the narrator's first impulse is indeed to tell his wrath. When the eminent novelist—for the narrator is Roth himself, we are meant to understand—learns that someone has been using his good name to advocate the return of Israel's Ashkenazim to their European homelands, he decides to have it out with the imposter and telephones the "false" Philip Roth in Jerusalem. Perhaps, as he dials, he contemplates the efficacy of such phrases as, "Now look here my good fellow"—but when the phone rings and the namesake answers, the narrator in a panic immediately hangs up. Had he the presence of mind to say, "Well this is Philip Roth . . . the one who was born in Newark and has written umpteen books. Which one are you?"—the whole of *Operation Shylock* might have rested there (28).

Story stops—or fails to start—when anger ends. That the obverse is true is evident in Homer's thrilling invocation, "Sing, O goddess, the anger of Achilles," and in the vehement passions of Shylock, Othello, and Lear—as well as in Nathan Zuckerman's milder observation in *The Counterlife* (1986): "People are unjust to anger—it can be enlivening and a lot of fun" (140). Blake's poem continues: "I was angry with my foe: / I told it not, my wrath did grow." Only now does the poet have a story to relate. Untold anger is, paradoxically, wholly on the side of storytelling. Many of us, when suffering from a slight, will return to our grievance in sleepless dissections of the wounding incident, inventing ripostes and courtroom speeches, plotting vindictive dramas of the tables turned. In "A Poison Tree," the speaker explains how he cossets his anger, watering it with fears, sunning it with "soft deceitful wiles" until "it bore an apple bright / And my foe beheld it shine." The poem's aura of narcissistic delight encourages us to see the foe, who might be any actual person, as a projection formed by the speaker in the ramping-up of his rage. Similarly, when Philip Roth does not speak his wrath and puts down the phone, when he begins to speculate and postulate and fret and fulminate about his foe, he grows a "Roth"—he pods a Pipik and makes his very own poison tree.[1]

Perhaps no other emotion matches anger in its capacity to generate story. Tales of love, like the happy families in *Anna Karenina,* are alike, but angry characters are angry in their own particular way. Consider, for a moment, the potential bandwidth of the emotion and the various modes and genres in which it is most commonly represented. Negatively construed, anger is regarded as a loss of proportion and self-control that harms others in its stormy wake. We see this most obviously in tragedy, where the intemperate fury of the protagonist will occasion feelings of "fear and pity" in the spectator. Yet characters in the grip of rage are at home in comedy too: I picture that scene in *Fawlty Towers* where Basil, thwarted by his car's malignant failure to start, pounds its hood with a tree. From childhood, we are taught not to "give in" to this sort of tantrum, yet an incensed person might conceivably be cheered on from the sidelines. "I'M MAD AS HELL AND I'M NOT GOING TO TAKE IT ANYMORE," yells the anchorman in *Network* (a declaration of this sort always works on public television). If that sentence were uttered by one's spouse, it might compel attention, but as a parental address to one's teenager, the very same words would misfire and provoke derision.

Anger never just flows: it is articulated through the veins and arteries of social hierarchy. Positively construed, anger can speak to an outraged sense of justice: it is militant and wakeful. Philip Fisher reminds us that there are many circumstances in which the problem with anger is that it is insufficiently felt (174). As for anger's less-than-civic wellsprings, those old insightful psychoanalytic explanations—anger as unprocessed grief, as defense, as aggression from the id, as the voice of a persecuting super-ego—are perhaps losing ground to explanations from socio-biology. Like animals, our puffs and prickles intimidate prey and predators; like addicts, we benefit from a hit of surging adrenalin. Even so, we have every reason to think of anger as thoroughly conditioned by historical and cultural circumstance. Perhaps readers have seen the Maori *haka* with its stamps and grimaces and glaring eyes? Early European observers, who saw only the savagery of a war-dance, read the anger wrong. The civil ferocity encountered by Captain Cook was part welcome, part challenge, yet this piece of theater emerged in a culture in which a warrior's rage was genuinely relished. The haka retains its traditional meanings in many circumstances but is now regularly transmuted into the rhetoric of the rugby ground, designed to raise a New Zealander's dander, lift the spirits—and intimidate the foe.

Anger, then, is nothing if not various—a cluster of emotion and affect rather than a single ray, incorporating and augmented by those finer discriminations of the spectrum for which the thesaurus gives us so many words: gall, outrage, rancor, fury, choler, dudgeon, pelt, fuff, kippage, *broiges.* Incidents from *Operation Shylock* might be found to illustrate them all; the book is an anatomy of contemporary anger. But anger in *Operation Shylock* is more than a collection of its types: anger is an organizing force throughout the novel, propelling the actions of doubles and registering what seems a relatively new formation of the choleric dispositions.

In *The Counterlife*, Nathan Zuckerman takes stock after hearing Mordecai Lippman expound his rabid, nutcase, amnesiac views on Palestinian removal from the Jewish homeland. "Following Lippman's seminar," reflects Nathan, "language didn't really seem my domain any longer. I wasn't exactly a stranger to disputation, but never in my life had I felt so enclosed by a world so contentious, where the argument is enormous and constant and everything turns out to be pro or con, positions taken, positions argued, and everything italicized by indignation and rage" (121). Nathan has encountered what we might term "stupire": a roiling, credulous kind of anger, expressing some incandescent combination of entitlement and paranoia. Stupire is likely to come across as "too ridiculous to take seriously and too serious to be ridiculous" (*Shylock* 55), and it can be difficult to handle because—as with Holocaust revisionism, as with libels about President Obama's origins—engaging with it turns out to require not the production of a truth card but a corrosively disproportionate expenditure of psychic or social resource. Around stupire, what ought to be simple questions of truth and falsity, fact and fiction, turn out to be more like questions of immunity and contagion. Claire's advice to her husband is to keep well away from his double, but Philip feels, on the one hand, a threatening "reactivation" (55) of the self-obsessed misery of his Halcion-induced breakdown, and on the other, "volatilely irritated" (35), "plagued," "preoccupied," "obsessed" (55) by Pipik, yet also revitalized to be vying with an adversary (37). He is dazzled by the apple hanging from the poison tree.

People have, of course, aired ludicrous opinions angrily—and contagiously—in public for generations, but stupire in the form I am attempting to describe perhaps only emerges with the atomization of broadcast media and an associated rise in the fluidity of cultural authority. Stupire's prototype is not the crackpot dictator speaking into a microphone to millions, but the ranter on talk radio, host indistinguishable from guest, sharing a mike with a micro-audience of like-minded listeners. Its institutional support network is broadcasting minus journalism, the news as a sort of echoing wiki-chamber. Its sounds (we shall hear more of them) are those of Pipik's "Anti-Semites Anonymous Workout Tape #2":

Did six million really die? Come off it. The Jews pulled a fast one on us again, keeping alive their new religion, Holocaustomania. . . . Auschwitz was mainly a plant to produce synthetic rubber. And that's why it was so evil smelling. They didn't send them to the gas chamber, they sent them there to work. Because there were no gas chambers, as we now found out. From chemistry. Which is hard science. Freud. That was soft science. . . . You can forget that . . . . Chicago has the biggest Polish population outside of Warsaw. The Poles are united by three things. The Roman Catholic Church. Fear of Russia. And hatred of the Jews. Why do they hate Jews? The Russian czars constantly sent their bad-ass Jews into Poland and they were money-changers, ghetto dwellers. Jews are very ugly people. . . . Notice the Jew, notice the Jew from the hips down, especially below the knees, they're all fucked up. . . . The bone thickens and their legs get bowed. . . . Look at Philip Roth, for God's sake. (253–255)

A careening confidence, an incessant flow of behind-the-scenes information, of hidden reasons for things—these anneal with older forms of anger in Pipik's "workout tape" to produce stupire. "Toxic babble," the narrator calls it, un-dismissively, and suggests that something about the tape will allow "readers of this confession to conjecture about [Pipik's] purpose and, in this way perhaps, to share something of the confusion of that week in Jerusalem, the extravagant confusion aroused in me by this 'Philip Roth' by whom I was beset" (253).

What might Pipik's purpose have been? Let us imagine that before it found its way into Philip's tape machine in his Jerusalem hotel room, it had been part of a package of cassettes issued to members of "Anti-Semites Anonymous" for the purposes of venting. Perhaps it is Pipik's demonstration tape, perhaps it is his confession, or perhaps it is Pipik's idea of a joke—a bit of "Jewish mischief"—that has him cracking up every time he imagines Philip's reaction. But in *Operation Shylock,* wondering about the adversary's purpose, putting oneself in the place of the foe, is the door to a mirror maze. Yet thinking about how Pipik's monologue sounds takes Philip in another direction: "What was *that* chilling thought stream about?" he asks later, and for a second wonders if Pipik might be "a pathological Gentile, stuck with the Jewish look and out to extract unbridled revenge on the whole vile subspecies as represented by me" (374). And then his thoughts turn: "Of his entire arsenal of stupid stunts, that sham—if such it was—remains the most sinister, demented, and alas, compelling . . . yes, aesthetically alluring to me in its repugnant, sickish, Céline-like way" (374). Looked at that way, Philip (for the first time) gains some distance. It can't be about me, he concludes: "All the dizzying energy, all the chaos and frenzy behind the pointlessness of contending with me, points to something else" (374).

Before turning to that "something else," it might be worth anticipating a possible misconception. So far, my examples of stupire have related to anti-Semitic tirades, Pipik's Diasporism, Rabbi Kahane's plan for Palestinian Removal, as well as suspicion about the birthplace and religious affiliation of President Obama. Yet if stupire's thickest seam is on the right, it is not without representation on the left. In the first season of *Treme*, for example, the character played by John Goodman is a Tulane Professor of English and blocked novelist who, without realizing that what he is doing is called blogging, most evenings uploads a semi-drunken video of himself ranting against the evils of the Bush administration's response to Hurricane Katrina. He inadvertently becomes a minor celebrity garnering nods of approval from acquaintances. But this character is not one of the show's recovery-builders. The anger is self-isolating and spirals towards despair. It is recognizable as stupire partly because it breathes the air of publicity, and partly because its objects and goals are obscured by the conflation of public with private reservoirs of irritation along with an attenuated relation of the irritation to its provoking cause. There can be no arguing with this kind of anger—it is both too diffuse and too hyperbolic—but even if, on occasion, stupire might seem like the anger of the merely stupid, the core of the affect is much closer to stupefaction, to the beggaring of one's beliefs, and exasperation at the possibility of effective political or ethical discourse.

Philip Fisher, in his very suggestive survey of the vehement passions, defines anger as "a territorial passion" (181). Anger, he suggests, discloses a perimeter around which any actual or potential diminishment of the world of "me and mine" meets resistance (181). The perimeter might have some flexibility; it might be a Gaza Wall. Consider one of Roth's more economical depictions of a state of anger. A priest distributing pro-Ukrainian Catholic literature outside the Demjanjuk trial attracts the attention of a Golem-like Jewish giant who shouts in protest: "Hitler and Ukrainian! Two brother! One thing! Kill Jew! I know! Mother! Sister! Everybody! Ukrainian kill!" (*Shylock* 305). To use a common spatial metaphor for anger, the priest *treads all over* this Ukrainian Jew's sensitivities regarding a long history of pogroms and anti-semitism. To use another, the priest is *out of line*. This simple scene is like a border dispute: the angered person registers an incursion which must be intercepted and ejected—and on this occasion the perimeter is maintained: the priest's offending pamphlets are tossed to the winds. A golem, at the time, say, of Rabbi Loew, Maharal of Prague, provides homeland security for a homeless people. But in Jerusalem, in the late 1980s, the actions of those securing the perimeters of the state of Israel, like the actions of those Palestinians attempting to restore an earlier border, are both more ambivalent and far less susceptible to control. There is no *shem* or magic formula that can be withdrawn from the Golem's mouth. Characters speak, and everything is italicized by indignation and rage.

And while Roth's attention is largely fixed on their speaking, with the trajectory and affect of these passions, he takes care to register the political background of the first intifada in several ways. There are the little metonymic glimpses from a hotel window: masked rioters, their pile of rocks, a convoy of buses as the IDF assembles (209). There is also the novel's opportunistic use of Israel's territorial divisions: trips to and from occupied Ramallah, the two hotels, the King David, where Pipik—self-appointed best hope of the Jews—has a room, and the American Colony, where the notoriously ambivalent Philip Roth stays in an Arab-run hotel in East Jerusalem, on the old pre-1968 border. The disputed perimeters of the city are literally and metaphorically grounds for anger. And they are especially hospitable to the febrile plotting, counter-plotting, and counter-counter-plotting, of the book's spy-masters, George Ziad and Louis B. Smilesburger, who each hope to find in "the uncontrollability of real things" an advantage secured by a preemptive operation against their foe (239). Complicating all this, and drawing on the always problematic legacies of societies founded on settlement, on the displacement of one group of people by another, is the figure of the Double.

In Gothic Literature, the psychology of the double is supported counterfactually and utilised spatially. The implausible creation of Edward Hyde, for example, is supported by credible props such as a laboratory, a flask, and a potion, and the elaboration of the story will require the possibility of his movement from a locked and secret room out into the world at large and back again. The props support a transformation we interpret psychologically as the release of anger and libido while the movements of the double through physical space are essentially those of projection and the return of the repressed. Something unruly from *inside* the self has been sent *outside* the self—and will return. Thus, when Philip is barricaded in his hotel room, and Jinx wants to enter with urgent news of Pipik's mad plot to kidnap and torture Demjanjuk's son, the physical spaces relay a paranoid itinerary that began when Philip, sitting in the courtroom, himself thought of torturing Demjanjuk's son to force a confession from the father. He then worries that another outraged Jew might have that same idea and act on it, and, in a flash, projects that thought on to Pipik, who must be the deviser of the kidnapping scheme. Later, Philip is about to flee the city when the memory of a "detestable cartoon" in the *Guardian* turns him back from the airport (248).[2] In the cartoon, Menachim Begin appears much as he might have been depicted in Pipik's workout tape: "a big-nosed Jew" shrugging nonchalantly atop "a pyramid of dead Arab bodies" (248). It is not anti-Semitism *per se* that has Philip change his plans, but the thought that "the *Guardian* will have a field day" if he fails to stop Pipik's scheme to kidnap Demjanjuk's son (248). Why would Pipik do this? It can only be, concludes Philip, a monstrous "publicity stunt . . . perform[ed] in order to vent his rage with me" (249).

"Publicity" is the rationalizing glue for most of the paranoid arcs traced in the novel's complex plotting. Soon after arriving in Jerusalem, Philip, perusing a file of news clippings, wonders if the Demjanjuk trial has prompted his impersonation by a double—perhaps because Pipik was "emboldened by the identity issue at the heart of the case," perhaps "because of the opportunities for publicity provided by the extensive media coverage" (51–52). Later he wonders if Pipik's whole Diasporism shtick might be a cunning plot to put himself as a pro-PLO Jewish writer on the cover of *Time* magazine. Towards the end of the novel, Smilesburger threatens that unless details of "Operation Shylock" are repressed, Mossad will unleash a ruinous campaign of negative publicity—poisonous whispers, besmirchments, slanders—from which the novelist will never recover. In all of these examples, worries about personal integrity and stability are projected outwards and return in an inflated form as public assaults on a reputation. And this is why the podding of a double draws counterfactually on not one but two main ingredients: Halcion and the news.

"Where is Philip Roth, . . . where did he go?," the narrator helplessly asks Claire, in the midst of his breakdown (22). One answer, crystallized in proximal story time as well as spatially, is that he is in Suite 511 of the King David Hotel. The psychological explanation, which the narrator is still half-convinced by, is that Halcion has been a sort of catalyst, allowing something unruly from inside the self to be sent outside the self. Philip reflects on the process by which the self as *this* becomes the self as *"that"*:

> I owed my transformation—my *deformation*—not to any pharmaceutical agent but to something concealed, obscured, masked, suppressed, or maybe simply uncreated in me until I was fifty-four but as much me and mine as my prose style, my childhood, or my intestines; half-convinced that whatever else I might imagine myself to be, I was *that* too and, if the circumstances were trying enough, I could be again . . . a frenzied, maniacal, repulsive, anguished, odious, hallucinatory *that* whose existence is one long tremor. (27)

Part of the fun of any double narrative is the author's skillful elaboration of very precise counterfactual details—the same missing jacket button leaving the same "nub of tiny threadlets" (76), the hair with the same parting seen as in a mirror—along with the seeding of numerous lines of implication. For instance, we have the teasing possibility that Philip's double is Zuckerman, Kepesh, Tarnopol, and Portnoy—"all of them in one, broken free of print and mockingly reconstituted as a single satirical facsimile of me" (34). This is one possibility; the author's job is to ensure it is suggestively entangled with others, enriching texture with an over-saturation of interpretative possibilities, but nonetheless basing his riffs on a genre formula which includes creation scene, first encounter with the double, dissolution of the double.

To the extent that *Operation Shylock* imagines a creation scene for its double, Halcion would be the equivalent of Dr. Jekyll's potion, while newspapers and television figure as the equivalent of his laboratory. The larger background is the riots in Gaza and the West Bank unfolding on the nightly news. The precipitating announcement comes from cousin Apter, who has heard about the other Philip Roth from watching the Demjanjuk trial on television. Aharon Appelfeld has also seen reports of Roth the diasporist in *The Jerusalem Post* and subsequently in a Hebrew newspaper, where the headline, "Philip Roth Meets Solidarity Leader" is accompanied by a photo of the author—a photo easily retrieved from their files (31).

Philip's first reaction is to contact the newspaper before the story makes the wire services, but even supposing they were to print a retraction, even supposing he were to take out a full page ad in *The Jersualem Post* or make an appearance on television himself, he realizes the story is nonetheless out of the box and has acquired a half-life of its own (55). "The ideas espoused so forcefully by the Philip Roth in that story were mine now," reflects the narrator, "and would likely endure as mine even in the recollection of those who'd read the retraction tomorrow" (35). Pipik has indeed "broken free of print" and is reconstituted as a compound "satirical facsimile" beamed back at Philip Roth like a demented pundit on the late night news.

When the doubles first encounter each other in person, Pipik is overjoyed to meet Philip: his attitude is that of the greatest fan, who, to repeat a telling phrase, knows his author "inside out" (73):

> I listened as he recalled every affront that had ever appeared in print, every assault that had ever been made on my writing and me . . . It was as though the genie of grievance had escaped the bottle in which a writer's resentments are pickled and preserved and had manifested itself in humanish form, spawned by the inbreeding of my overly licked oldest wounds and mockingly duplicating the man I am. (74)

If that were the case, those wounds suffered in print and on *The Carson Show* have spawned a Pipik who is armoured for triumph in the media. His voice, in the interview by telephone, when Philip was posing as the French journalist Pierre Roget, had seemed "more resonant . . . and more stentorian by far" (41) than his own, as if imbued with a pop idea of what a celebrated author should sound like, while Pipik's face—"the after to [Philip's] before in the plastic surgeon's advertisement"—is like a "Hollywooded version" of his own (72). Philip is incensed, but worse is to come. To add to the horror, the very thing "everyone knows" about Philip Roth—the inveterate masturbator from whom not even a plate of liver is safe—is reflected back twice its size when Pipik plays with his massive erection in front of a gaping Philip. *"There's reality. Like a rock!,"* Pipik taunts, lunging the "oversized pole" toward the novelist—but fortunately, the imposter with the implant sproings off the bed and is manhandled into the corridor, where he is, as a monstrous double should be, once again "at large" (205).

Once doubles are podded and on the loose, a plot's standard destination will be a series of encounters leading at last to a final struggle, pitching Philip against Pipik, like Sherlock Holmes and Moriarity locked in combat above the Reichenbach falls. *Operation Shylock*, though, goes through an elaborate series of gear changes that shift the story of the double into a story of double agents. Suffice to say, the double plot proper ends when Pipik leaves Israel for the US, and becomes a generalized threat always out there somewhere. "He's my terrorist for life," thinks Philip. "I'll be sighting him on rooftops for years to come, just as he'll be seeing me, sighted in the cross hairs of his rage" (281). The double agent plot is seeded when Philip impersonates his impersonator and travels to Ramallah with his old college friend, George Ziad, once an urbane cosmopolitan intellectual, now a Palestinian militant and an "overwrought cyclone of distress" (123):

> As we drove, embittered analysis streamed forth unabated . . . each sentence delivered with an alarming air of intellectual wantonness, the whole a pungent ideological mulch of overstatement and lucidity, of insight and stupidity, of precise historical data and willful historical ignorance, a loose array of observations as disjointed as it was coherent and as shallow as it was deep—the shrewd and vacuous diatribe of a man whose brain, once as good as anyone's, was now as much a menace to him as the anger and loathing that by 1988, after twenty years of the occupation and forty years of the Jewish state, had corroded everything moderate in him, everything practical, realistic, and to the point. . . . Now at the core of everything was hatred and the great disabling fantasy of revenge. (129)

Speaking of the Israeli Jews, George says: "'I spit upon them! I *spit* upon them.'" Yet he becomes one of the novel's Shylocks.[3] George's affect—"the gush, the agitation, the volubility, the frenzy barely beneath the surface of every word he babbled, the nerve-racking sense he communicated of someone aroused and decomposing all at the same time, of someone in a permanent state of imminent apoplexy" (122–123)—is of someone in the grip of stupire. His anger is primed by injustice in the Occupied Territories yet it is also fuelled by the limitless guilt of "a son trying in vain to staunch the bleeding of a wronged and ruined father" (123). Zee's rage has the capacity to constantly surprise itself yet never be caught napping. It outruns its ostensible cause, it damages his wife and son, and sets in train an operation that will boomerang in the counter-operation that gives the novel both its title and its missing eleventh chapter.

What is *Operation Shylock*? Let me describe what we know of it. Philip Roth, under the cover of his identity as an anti-Zionist sympathetic to Palestine, but working secretly for Mossad, visits Athens, where he meets rich Jews, "Hellenized" Jews, his own kind of Jew in fact, and does something that, were the details known, would cause an international incident and put Israel in the dock of outraged public opinion. The operation leaves a residue in the form of banknotes in an envelope—money, perhaps, that ought to have gone to the Palestine Liberation Organization, but has been diverted by a sting operation which Philip has presumably managed with the debonair aplomb of James Bond in *Casino Royale*. There are uncanny echoes of the book we have already read, with the visit to Ramallah, Smilesburger's check, and the whole question of Pipik as a pawn put in play by one intelligence agency or another.

We also know that Operation Shylock is the intersection of two operations, the first, made up by George, becomes the smokescreen for another, made up by Smilesburger. It is spy versus spy—and not, in essence, unlike the famous *Mad* magazine cartoon series, which generally concluded with the white spy lighting the fuse of a bomb in the black spy's overcoat pocket, while the black spy lights the fuse of a bomb in the white spy's pocket. But two key details nudge the comedy of doubles towards tragedy. If, as Blake suggests, nursed anger grows a poison tree, then *Operation Shylock* is its banyan, many branched and multi-trunked. In the course of the book, we have seen characters imagining their foes, Philip pods a Pipik, and George is tantalized by the shiny apple dreamt into existence for him:

And my foe beheld it shine,

And he knew that it was mine.

And into my garden stole

When the night had veild the pole;

In the morning glad I see

My foe outstretched beneath the tree.

Within the story-world of the novel, the plumply ripening anger of interlocking fabulists has only one place to go: George is knifed to death in front of his son; Pipik dies just after the first Iraqi SCUD missiles explode in Tel Aviv. Exit George. "*Exit Jew*" (276).[4]

A psycho-geography of anger in *Operation Shylock* might resemble a map of Israel: a country that has overrun its borders and fences in zones of hostility. Smilesburger comments:

The Jewish state, from the day of its inception, has been dedicated to eliminating a Palestinian presence in historical Palestine and expropriating the land of an indigenous people. The Palestinians have been driven out, dispersed, and conquered by the Jews. To make a Jewish state we have betrayed our history—we have done unto the Palestinians what the Christians have done unto us: systematically transformed them into the despised and subjugated Other, thereby depriving them of their human status. . . . I speak sincerely. They are innocent, we are guilty; they are right, we are wrong; they are the violated, we the violaters. I am a ruthless man working in a ruthless job for a ruthless country and I am ruthless knowingly and voluntarily. (349–350)

The historical situation Smilesburger describes is that of any settler society, be it Israel, the USA, Canada, Australia, South Africa, or New Zealand. All societies that are based on the foundational injustice of appropriating the land of an indigenous people have problematic legacies. But these are swept aside, not addressed, by their reduction to personalized moral binaries. Moreover, the many-faceted processes by means of which an old cross-cultural frontier develops into an ostensibly settled monoculture are blurred, not focused, through binary narratives of settlers "starting over" or "taking over," or—in an Israeli variant—of either "betraying" the Holocaust or deriving legitimacy from it. Settlers around the world have talked like Smilesburger, collapsing a middle ground into armed antitheses, and never shy of acknowledging an injustice so long as it promotes a *realpolitik* that knows no alternatives.[5] Since alternatives can be found—though never finally found[6]—the inevitable question for this reader is: does *Operation Shylock* reach toward them?

The more intractable a country's political situation, the more its public discourse might seem vulnerable to stupire: to heated daydreams of retribution, to hyperbolic magnifications, to wells of unappeasability, to the crackpot solutions of a Pipik or the tautological rationales of a Smilesburger. John Updike, in a much referenced *New Yorker* review of the novel, complained that Roth "has become an exhausting author to be with. His characters seem to be on speed, up at all hours and talking until their mouths bleed" (112). That is an impression masquerading as a diagnosis. The novel is to a large extent about how people build their poison trees. It is a journey into "that paranoiac no-man's-land where there is no demarcation between improbability and certainty and where the reality of what menaces you is all the more portentous for being inestimable and obscure" (*Shylock* 363). Yet it is not difficult to imagine why Updike formed the impression he did: the book is such a loud, quid-pro-quoing, turbulently argumentative approximation of stupire that its own affect might well strike some readers as "exhaustingly" rather than (as it seems to me) exhilaratingly contrived. Perhaps there is another way to come at this question: there are grounds for anger in *Operation Shylock*—the smirk of a war criminal, the misappropriation of one's identity, the unaddressed wrongs of a settler state—but in a novel so uproariously undermining of difference, can an anger that speaks for honor and against injustice be differentiated from stupire?

Of course it can. *Operation Shylock* is a novel structured around foils as well as doubles. Next to George Ziad, there is the anger of his wife Anna, exasperated by the "moral childishness" of her husband's "spurious loyalties" to "stupid ethnic mythologies" (160–161). "'Roots!'" she exclaims, "'A concept for *cavemen* to live by'" (161). Next to Philip-as-Pipik, enjoying the "lubricious sensation that is fluency" as he waxes on about Diasporism, the author has taken care to place Gal, the Israeli army officer who hates the government he serves and is "torn in two . . . by the rebellious and delinquent feelings of a loyal, loving son" (171). Demjanjuk is a double figure—"There he was. *There he was*," observes Philip without redundancy, by way of prefacing an account of his alleged crimes that is notable for a succession of sentences that fail to identify a subject.[7] Next to him, there is the outrage of the witness, Eliahu Rosenberg, a survivor of the camps, as he is caught in a logical contradiction that risks disqualifying his testimony.[8] And next to Philip Roth, there is Aharon Appelfeld, a novelist whose life and art have the fascination of being the obverse of Roth's own. Locked in his hotel room, as Jinx Possesski hammers at the door like the repressed returning, as she slips that sublime signifier—a yellow cloth Star of David—under the door, and with the real violence of the Intifada unfolding outside his window—his perimeters thus pressured and blockaded, the author in the book contemplates a question for his friend:

> *Living in this society, you are bombarded by news and political disputation. Yet, as a novelist, you have, by and large, pushed aside the Israeli daily turbulence . . . in order to contemplate remarkably different Jewish predicaments. What does this turbulence mean to a novelist like yourself? How does being a citizen of . . . this self-revealing, self-asserting, self-challenging, self-legendizing society affect your writing life? Does this news-producing reality ever tempt your imagination?* (217)

The author in the book withholds Appelfeld's answer. Jinx has—as it were—been interrupting the formulation of the question quoted above with alarmist cries, while the author in the book, realizing that the situation calls for "'silence and self-control,'" that it is time to "Stop. Breathe. Think," does just the opposite. He opens the door on all this turbulence—and it's "*Hellzapoppin*" inside *Operation Shylock* (221). But the author *of* the book knows what Appelfeld had to say in reply to his question. "True," says Appelfeld, "Israel is full of drama from morning to night, and there are people who are overcome by that drama to the point of inebriation. . . . Daily events do indeed knock on every door, but they know I don't let such agitated guests into my house" (Roth, "Conversation" 32–33). One writer opens a door; another prefers to keep it shut. There are many ways to tell one's wrath.

NOTES

1. I use the nickname Pipik to refer to Philip Roth's usurping namesake. Philip Roth is the name of the author in the text as well as the author of the text: I rarely mention the latter, and context will make it plain when I do.

2. Perhaps Philip is recalling a cartoon drawn by Les Gibbard in *The Guardian* in September 1982.

3. Philip is another: "You have followed me and bugged me and baited me..." he tells Smilesburger, and threatens "to bring an action" (347).

4. *"Exit Jew"* (276) is the final stage direction in *The Merchant of Venice.*

5. For an example of a "settlement studies" approach to these issues, see my chapter on the New Zealand "Pakeha-Maori" author, F. E. Maning, whose position is exactly like Smilesbuger's—yet his writing also brings alternatives into view—in: *The Settler's Plot: How Stories Take Shape in New Zealand,* Auckland: Auckland University Press, 2011, 61–96.

6. The problems of settlement are foundational and ongoing, more like a condition we address and a relationship we enter into than a problem to be fixed by once-and-for-all solutions.

7. The passage continues: "Once upon a time, drove two, three hundred of them into a room barely big enough for fifty . . . Pumped out carbon monoxide for half an hour" (60).

8. For an excellent discussion, see Kate McLoughlin's "'Dispute Incarnate'": Philip Roth's *Operation Shylock,* the Demjanjuk Trial and Eyewitness Testimony."

WORKS CITED

Blake, William. *Songs of Innocence and Experience.* Ed. Geoffrey Keynes. London: Oxford UP, 1970. Print.

Fisher, Philip. *The Vehement Passions.* Princeton: Princeton UP, 2002. Print.

McLoughlin, Kate. "'Dispute Incarnate': Philip Roth's *Operation Shylock,* the Demjanjuk Trial and Eyewitness Testimony." *Philip Roth Studies* 3.2 (2007): 115–130. Print.

Network. Dir. Sidney Lumet. Screenplay by Paddy Chayefsky. Perf. Faye Dunaway and William Holden. 1976. Warner, 2006. DVD.

Roth, Philip. "Conversation in Jerusalem with Aharon Appelfeld." *Shop Talk.* New York, Vintage, 2001. Print.

————. *Operation Shylock: A Confession* (1993). London: Vintage, 2000. Print.

————. *The Counterlife* (1986). *Novels and Other Narratives 1986–1991*. New York: Library of America, 2008. Print.

Treme: The Complete First Season. Creators, Eric Overmeyer and David Simon, 2010. Warner Home Video, 2011. DVD.

Updike, John. "Recruiting Raw Nerves." *The New Yorker* 15 March 1993: 109–112. Print.

Chapter Eight

"My Kinsmen, My Precursors"

Philip Roth, Epic, Influence, and Bardic Proclivities

Catherine Morley

Philip Roth is a born performer. Just look, for example, at the photographs that document his life, not least the unforgettable black and white shots of him in 1968, clowning around outside the Jewish center he attended as a boy. But his capacity for performance was nowhere more in evidence than at his 80th birthday celebration in Newark in March 2013. Led in by a marching band from Weequahic High School, Roth arrived at his lavish party to the sound of drums and brass and with more than a little chutzpah in his nifty footsteps.

As an academic festschrift followed by an evening of talks from the likes of Dame Hermione Lee, Edna O'Brien, and Claudia Roth Pierpoint, the event might have been expected to be a sober, serious affair. Instead, it felt more like a good old party, the atmosphere driven, above all, by the sprightly octogenarian who held court, regal in his bearing, before an eager throng of literary friends and scholarly fans—myself among them—eager to lay tribute, in the form of their scholarly monographs, before the seemingly appreciative and gracious literary monarch. I was, alas, not brave enough to present my own book.

The Roth@80 celebrations underlined the sense of the many faces of Philip Roth: the king and the dancing jester, the eloquent speaker and the empathetic listener, the internationally acclaimed writer and the boy from the back streets of Newark. But perhaps what the Roth@80 proceedings revealed more than anything else is the sense of Roth as an American bard. Not for nothing did Hermione Lee's paper trace the Shakespearean themes laced throughout Roth's work, focusing in particular upon the eloquent soliloquies of the inelegant Micky Sabbath. Of course, Roth's interest in Shakespeare extends across his entire *oeuvre*: for instance, one need only look to the title of *Exit Ghost* (2007).[1] But the Shakespearean theme surely reaches its peak in the American trilogy, in which each novel pits an individual against much larger social and cultural forces. As Nathan Zuckerman observes, following a series of conversations with his former English teacher in *I Married a Communist* (1998), "I felt I was being asphyxiated inside Shakespeare" (302).

But Roth's bardic propensities extend well beyond his engagement with a long line of influences, and even beyond his deployment of Shakespearean themes. Traditionally, the bard was a poet, and his role was to memorialize the history, myths, and stories of a nation, and to do so with attention to the generic tools at his disposal. Indeed, in *I Married a Communist*, Roth seems self-consciously to draw our attention to the formal and figurative aspects of the role, as Zuckerman contemplates a line from *Twelfth Night* in relation to his much-maligned childhood hero Ira Ringold:

> "And thus the whirligig of time brings in his revenges." Those cryptogrammic *g*'s, the subtlety of their deintensification, those hard *g*'s in "whirligig" followed by the nasalized *g* of "brings" followed by the soft *g* of "revenges." Those terminal *s*'s . . . "thus brings his revenges." The hissing surprise of the plural noun "reveng*es*." Guhh. Juhh. Zuhh. Consonants sticking into me like needles. (302)

The consideration of the language in terms of its audial impact, the matching of the sounds and the subject, the shift from a phonic hardness to a softness which is upended with the severity of the work "revenges," suggests a mind given over to the business of language-making and performance. Certainly the guttural "Guhh. Juhh. Zuhh" imparts a verbal sense of the motion and physical onslaught implicit in the Shakespearean line. That the sounds are likened to needles piercing Zuckerman's flesh is especially interesting, suggesting a relationship with Shakespeare that is somehow antagonistic, a battle of sorts. And here we come to the crucial aspect of Roth's relationship with his "kinsmen" and precursors who present something of an assault: they are a force against which the author must mount a desperate resistance.

This sense of antagonistic negotiation with a literary forefather is especially pertinent to Roth, who, throughout his writing, has presented a series of hostile relationships between fathers and sons. In generating a "genealogy that isn't genetic," Roth's writerly selves seek out literary fathers: mentors of sorts, to whom they wish to apprentice themselves (*Communist* 217). Indeed, Roth's textual preoccupations with literary paternalism indicate the American individual's necessary confrontation with the past—a past which, crucially, includes both the "American" and "pre-American" histories of the immigrant nation. In fact, Roth's recuperation in the American trilogy of Shakespeare, Milton, and the nineteenth-century writers of the American Renaissance, all of whom have become identified with the foundation of a national literature, might be seen as a kind of transnational literary patrimony, the building blocks of an inclusive and eclectic contemporary American epic, which celebrates the implicit and necessary hybridity of the American self and the American text.

Roth has described his fiction as "an expression of a moral consciousness . . . a conscience that has been created and undone a hundred times in this century alone" (*Reading* 137, 221). Evoking Joyce in his promise (through Stephen Dedalus) to "forge . . . the uncreated conscience of [his] race," Roth presents his writing as speaking for and to the Jewish people (Joyce 276). As part of the epic tradition of self-reinvention, Roth's writing aspires to present and recreate a more stable vision of this moral consciousness. His reference to the creation and undermining of a racial conscience contributes to the sense of unstable homelands and the fluidity of boundaries; indeed, due to its disparate nature in terms of the absence of an uncontested Jewish motherland, this conscience is necessarily multiple and shifting.

Tracing the invention of the second-generation American Jew, the American trilogy therefore situates Roth's meditation of literary paternalism both thematically and generically within the wider context of America's literary relationship with Europe. And by also situating this series of novels within a nineteenth-century American Renaissance tradition, Roth effectively renegotiates the relationship between the American and the European text. Thus, *American Pastoral* (1997) utilizes a prime instance of ambivalent literary paternalism from seventeenth-century England—John Milton's conflict with Shakespeare—and, in so doing, demonstrates the transnationality of Roth's American epic.

Meanwhile, *I Married a Communist* addresses most openly the question of influence—the pertinence of the literary past to the present moment—with a sustained meditation on the question of identity through Shakespearean allusion. As for the final text in the trilogy, *The Human Stain* (2000), it maintains this focus but within the context of an American tradition. It looks especially to Hawthorne as it explores the national fascination with the racial "other," questioning the terms under which the American racial conscience and consciousness have been forged.

Throughout the entire series, the pattern of literary paternalism is explicitly linked to genre and authorial gestures toward a national epic tradition. The trilogy as a whole is steeped in the kind of philosophical contemplation that has characterized American writing since its inception: a sustained consideration of national, racial, religious, and human identity. As a whole, the trilogy poses the question of what it means to be an American in the latter half of the twentieth century.[2]

Roth's rendition of the Jewish post-war acquisition and loss of an American Eden (specifically in *American Pastoral*) consciously alludes, both thematically and formally, to Milton's epic poem *Paradise Lost* (1667). It also evokes the soliloquies deployed by so many of Shakespeare's tragic heroes. The references to Milton and Shakespeare imply an extended panoply of inter- and intra-textual allusions and imitations: Milton's account of the love between Adam and Eve (Eve and Ira in *I Married a Communist*) closely resembles that of Aeneas and Dido (itself a reflection of Odysseus and Nausicaa), and reverberates with passages of Scripture and the Old Testament. Moreover, the various palimpsests complicate generic conventions, merging the tragic with the epic, ultimately serving to bring the epic to the level of the human and the everyday.

Roth presents a series of heroes, a "household Apollo," an irate giant, and an Athena-based classics professor with the ability to make himself invisible, as they negotiate the ordinary realities of post-war America (*Pastoral* 4). As we shall see, Roth reconsiders the basis of the national epic as located in the dramas of the everyday American experience. In grounding the epic in the quotidian, Roth exploits the overlapping characteristics of the genre with the tragedy. Both tend to present the hero as moving within a world too vast and multi-dimensional for him to comprehend and, in both cases, the hero is obliged, almost always unwillingly, to confront the mysteries of life and death, the relationship between past, present, and future, and the conflict between good and evil. While traditionally the tragedy presents, predominantly, the tangible and the concrete, the epic focuses upon questions of philosophical weight and significance to the predicament of mankind. Roth, however, merges these tendencies, contemplating the abstract and the philosophical through the lens of the tragic hero at the core of the narrative.

By layering *American Pastoral* atop a Miltonic intertext, Roth inherits the poet's interdependent yet antagonistic relationship with Shakespeare. Harold Bloom's essay on *Paradise Lost*, "Milton's Satan and Shakespeare" (1994) argues that Milton "best exploited the Shakespearean representation of character and its changes, even while working furiously to ward off the Shakespearean shadow" (169). The critic describes Milton's Satan as the "most Shakespearean" of all literary characters, the inheritor of aspects of Iago, Edmund, Macbeth, and the darker contemplative elements of Prince Hamlet. Yet Bloom also notes that Milton was interested not only in tragedy but in epic, refusing to allow elements of Shakespearean characterization into his portrayals of Adam, Eve, God the Father, or Christ (thus illustrating his ambivalence toward his precursor). Bloom takes Milton's tribute "On Shakespeare" (1632) as an example of the poet's hesitation to accept his literary inheritance through a seemingly less than genuine admission that Shakespeare's greatness cannot be surpassed: "Dear son of memory, great heir of fame / What need'st thou such weak witness of thy name? / Thou in our wonder and astonishment / Has built thyself a lifelong monument" (171).

As the son of memory, Shakespeare is Muse to Milton, without whom, at least according to Bloom, the latter could not have created the sexually jealous, self-deprecating yet utterly amoral Satan. Thus Shakespeare's enduring monument is his continual reinvention, in terms of theme and characterization, in the endeavors of his literary descendants. However, what allows Milton to break away from Shakespeare is his ability to be epic as well as tragic. Satan, unlike his Shakespearean counterparts, as tragic/epic villain is absolutely ambiguous in terms of his admirable articulacy and human pride, both godly and earthly. His elegant soliloquies and his lament at being cast from heaven invite our sympathies. As fallen angel he is banished from the heavenly kingdom, made human.

As in *Paradise Lost, American Pastoral* does not introduce the heroic Adam figure until the second section. Rather, it lays the background, the historical details out of which the story arises. The opening section, "Paradise Remembered," has as its focal point the forty-fifth reunion of the Weequahic Class of 1950. Paradise is constructed as the post-war, post-Depression United States, a land where young second-generation Jews did not share the "uncertainties" of their parents and were happy to be assimilated into the American way of life:

> Let's remember the energy. Americans were governing not only themselves but some two hundred million people in Italy, Austria, Germany, and Japan. The war-crimes trials were *cleansing the earth of its devils* once and for all. Atomic power was ours alone. Rationing was ending. Price controls were being lifted . . . the clock of history [was] reset and a whole people's aims limited no longer by the past . . .
>   And the upsurge of energy was contagious. Around us nothing was lifeless. Sacrifice and constraint were over. The Depression had disappeared. Everything was in motion. The lid was off. Americans were to start over again, en masse, everyone in it together. (40, emphasis added)

Roth's construction of paradise is laced with insinuations of control and influence. Second-generation Jews feel themselves to be free of the past. The United States *governs* most of Europe and Japan and administers retribution. Paradise seems to be based upon the attainment of control and power from either a god-like father figure or some suppressive force. The irony, however, is that such freedom is a fallacy; indeed, Roth demonstrates this through the intertextual sculpting of the narrative (an ironic American pastoral) which is very much governed by the literary past (in terms of theme, motifs, and form) associated with Europe. Furthermore, the idea that Jewish Americans, as well as all other Americans, were starting over "en masse" suggests two additional versions of enslavement: the individual's insidious assimilation into the American democratic collective, on the one hand, and the writer's enslavement to the collective literary past, on the other.

Roth's narrative converges on the life of Seymour "the Swede" Levov, "the household Apollo of the Weequahic Jews" (4). As a hybrid, earthly deity, the Swede's life is described as a combination of the epic and the tragic, initially embodying the American dream but quickly deteriorating into religious and ideological chaos against a background of mounting national frenzy. This turn is documented in the second section of the novel, "The Fall," in which the riotous sixties, the "demythologizing decade," produce "a countermythology . . . to challenge the mythic sense of itself the country had when the decade opened with General Eisenhower, our greatest World War II hero, still presiding" (*Reading* 81). So when Seymour's daughter Merry bombs the local post-office in an act of protest against American involvement in the Vietnam War, we learn that "The daughter transports him out of the longed-for American pastoral and into everything that is its antithesis and its enemy, into the fury, the violence, the desperation of the counterpastoral—into the indigenous American berserk" (86). Like Eve in Milton, Merry spirals the Adamic Seymour towards the Fall, unleashing a complicated anger at the nation and its unfulfilled promises, its betrayal of the immigrant ideal. Given the explicitly male nature of the classical epic, which concentrates on male quests and male protagonists, and pushes women, whether they be mortals or goddesses, towards the margins, Roth's focus upon Merry (later Eve and Delphine in *I Married a Communist* and *The Human Stain*, respectively) and her denial of the heroism of the male quest, her control over the cycle of human life, and the asceticism which is incomprehensible to her father, actually ascribes a rare, if ambiguous, power to the female. She is indeterminate and inscrutable, her stammered speech a version of speaking in revelatory tongues. She instills and reformulates the assimilated Jewish conscience; she makes man aware of his sinfulness, shattering the American illusion of purity. Merry, more than her successor Eve Frame, is an American incarnation of the Miltonic Eve figure. Neither mortal nor god in the coupling of her parentage, she resides on the cusp of Eden, the gatekeeper of the "counterpastoral."[3]

Meanwhile, Seymour 'The Love' Levov hurtles from the prelapsarian innocence of the pastoral sublime into a gory battlefield identified by the writer/narrator as characteristic of the national scene—a battlefield that also discloses the necessary conflict between the writer and his poetic ancestor.[4] Set within such a scene, the Swede loses his god-like characteristics, and his tale becomes "the tragedy of the man not set up for tragedy" (86). The final section of the book, "Paradise Lost," (which occurs over the summer of the Watergate hearings) concludes the narrative with a focus on partrimony, as we witness the ultimate demise of the Swede's happiness and his public humiliation by a larger-than-life Jewish father. Thus, what emerges from the narrative at a formal level, beyond the story of the Swede, is a concern with generic hybridity (an epic of a seemingly ordinary American life) and the weight of literary patrimony. That Lou Levov is allowed the final word in Seymour's narrative suggests a possible inability on the part of the writer (not unlike his protagonist), to step from beneath the shadow of the precursor.

Seymour, "the household Apollo," makes that Miltonic leap from the heavenly to the earthly, from paradise to hell. Generically, he straddles both the epic and the tragedy. And, the engagement with the Miltonic intertext intact, Roth makes his deviation from the original text, extending the dualistic anxiety implicit in Bloom's theory of poetic *misprision*.[5] Roth's textual evocation of Milton deliberately engages the earlier poet's generic combination of the tragic and the epic in order to respond to the call of an American Renaissance forefather—ironically, a call for a national literature distinguished from that of Europe with a guiding maxim to "insist on yourself: never imitate" (Emerson 199).

Layering *American Pastoral* and its Miltonic intertext upon *I Married a Communist* with its references to Shakespeare, Roth relocates "the Bard" temporally and geographically, effectively bringing him to the United States and to the present. *I Married a Communist* depicts the meteoric rise of Lincoln-lookalike Ira Ringold and his subsequent fall at the hands of his wife, Eve Frame, with the publication of her memoir "I Married a Communist" and the McCarthy witch-hunts. Murray Ringold, one of the text's narrators and brother to the protagonist, meets Nathan Zuckerman while attending a conference which—in its title at least—registers Roth's ambition: "Shakespeare and the Millennium" (3). And so Shakespeare is brought into the new millennium, both generically and thematically, in a tale of public betrayal in which Roth infiltrates and appropriates the themes and tropes of Shakespearean tragedy.

Roth hybridizes the plays. He makes them relevant to the American national scene. For example, in recalling the televised funeral of Richard Nixon, the narrator summons the words of Hamlet against Claudius: "Foul deeds will rise / Though all the world o'erwhelm them, to men's eyes" (279). Indeed, Murray refers not only to *Hamlet* and *Macbeth* but also to *King Lear* in describing the venomous Sylphid as akin to Goneril and Regan. As Nathan drives the decrepit, sleeping Murray home after the tale has been told, he, too, regresses to a classroom reading of *Macbeth* in which the sleeping man, the storyteller, had assumed the roles of both Macbeth and Macduff. These re-inventions of Shakespeare consciously depict identity, genre, and the palimpsests of patrimony as hybrid and complicated, the necessary condition of the contemporary American epic.

At a generic level, the uneasy engagement with Shakespeare—anxiety of asphyxiation as articulated by Nathan—is assuaged through fusion and overlap. Roth's employment of Shakespearean themes, symbolism, and motifs is, at one level, part of his continued consciousness of the presence of great literary progenitors. On another level, by bringing Shakespeare (and Milton in *American Pastoral*) to the modern epic, Roth, through the theme of paternal influence, looks to this literary engagement with precursors as an implicit feature of the contemporary epic of America. Roth perceives the anxiety of literary influence as part of the epicist's remit. This allows the author control over his text and facilitates an innovation in the genre pertinent to the experience of the contemporary text.

Traditionally, the epic involves the return of a hero to a homeland. Given the fact that the rudderless Jews of Roth's texts have no real homeland to which they might return, the reconstitution of heroic return with an anxiety associated with the re-visitation of literary fathers is more apposite. The self-consciousness characteristic of contemporaneity is nowhere more apparent than in the writer as he struggles with the bewildering realities of modern life and the weight of literary history. Roth's own fictional corpus of texts such as *Operation Shylock: A Confession* (1993) and *The Facts: A Novelist's Autobiography* (1988) are prime examples. Thus, Roth replaces the epic hero, the Everyman, with the figure of the writer, and the often metatextual self-consciousness of his enterprise becomes the ironic subject of the contemporary epic. However, anxieties and fears of betrayal by the literary forefather—a betrayal characterized by displacement and usurpation—vex this new notion of return.

Partly composed from the wrath of Roth at Claire Bloom's negative characterization of him in her memoir, *I Married a Communist* is driven by a steady anger at betrayal. The hero, formerly a national darling, finds himself before the House Committee on Un-American Activities, betrayed by his wife and betrayed by the very society that had previously nurtured him. The narrator, however, looks at Ira's betrayal as a literary phenomenon, and places it within a much wider literary and biblical context:

> What does it is betrayal. Think of the tragedies. What brings on the melancholy, the raving the bloodshed? Othello—betrayed. Hamlet—betrayed. Lear—betrayed. You might even claim that Macbeth is betrayed—by himself —though that's not the same thing. Professionals who've spent their energies teaching masterpieces, the few of us still engrossed by literature's scrutiny of things, have no excuse for finding betrayal anywhere but at the heart of history. History from top to bottom. World history, family history, personal history. It's a very big subject, betrayal. Just think of the Bible. What's that book about? The master story situation of the Bible is betrayal. Adam—betrayed. Esau—betrayed. Moses—betrayed. Samson—betrayed. Samuel—betrayed. David betrayed. Uriah—betrayed. Job—betrayed. Job betrayed by whom? By none other than God himself. And don't forget the betrayal of God. God betrayed. Betrayed by our ancestors at every turn. (185)

Seemingly solipsistic (as, indeed, the origins of *I Married a Communist* would suggest), the novel pushes narrative attention away from the hero or the writer and toward a broader socio-cultural critique, setting Ira as one in a long line of heroes betrayed, ultimately, by godly, unknown forces.

The reference to the Bible here could hardly be more significant. Northrop Frye's famous literary anatomy describes the Bible as the central epic form in Western culture: "a definitive myth, a single archetypal structure extending from creation to apocalypse" (315). Roth's inclusion of it here suggests an aspiration to raise the contemporary literary text into a culturally significant, culturally formative work on a similar level. Beginning with Ira Ringold's tale and working through Shakespeare to the Old Testament, Roth ironically renders his characters analogous to a series of biblical and Shakespearean figures, which have become mythological archetypes of Western culture and civilisation. Thus Roth presents his all-too-human Everyman (Ira/Seymour/ Coleman) as the archetype of the modern American citizen, the personification of a culture, ever conscious of the past and ever divided in selfhood.

Deliberately imitating the epic patterns laid down by Virgil and Milton, Roth's construction of his Jewish-American heroes in the mold of various charismatic American presidents illustrates this shift of focus from the individual hero to the foundation of a nation.[6] Of the Swede, Zuckerman remarks: "Kennedy, John F. Kennedy, only a decade the Swede's senior and another privileged son of fortune, another man of glamor exuding American meaning, assassinated while still in his mid forties . . . He is our Kennedy" (*Pastoral* 83). Further, of the great Iron Rinn, spokesman for the American Negro and Communist Movement, we learn: "[E]ight beds there and Ira in his robe and pyjamas and slippers, looking more like Lincoln with each passing day. Gaunt, exhausted, wearing Abraham Lincoln's mask of sorrow . . . If it weren't for that resemblance, none of this would have happened to him" (*Communist* 283). Finally, *The Human Stain's* Coleman Silk is analagous to Bill Clinton, hailed by the electorate on his ascension but publicly denounced for his "fall":

> The summer that Coleman took me into his confidence about Faunia Farley and their secret was the summer, fittingly enough, that Bill Clinton's secret emerged in every last mortifying detail . . . the summer of an enormous piety binge, a purity binge . . . what Hawthorne (who, in the 1860s, lived not many miles from my door) identified in the incipient country of long ago as "the persecuting spirit." (2)

Crucially, this shift into the sphere of the public and the national is always accompanied by an inextricable sense of the literary. The text is implicated in the mechanisms and foundations of a culture. Thus Roth's reference to Hawthorne alongside Coleman and his "secret" (that he is, in fact, an African-American passing for a white Jew) not only instigates a dialogue with Hawthorne in terms of his symbolism of Manichaean polarities, but also addresses the question of national founding in its reference to the Puritans.

The "piety/purity binge" would initially seem to refer to Coleman's affinity with Clinton in terms of their private, sexual lives. However, the persecuting spirit, in this instance, also refers to the national suppression of the racial other and to Coleman's containment of his black identity. It sets the issue of race and ethnicity right at the heart of American literary and political culture. For while the evocation of Hawthorne returns the issue of literary patrimony to the contemporary epic, revivifying the themes of the nineteenth-century writer, its purpose is to register anger at the nation's installation and perpetuation of such divisive dualisms. And so the systematic characterization of Roth's Jewish heroes as revered all-American presidents (with the exception, perhaps, of Clinton) is a direct and deliberate reappraisal of the American citizen and of the notion of a shared American conscience.

In casting Ira Ringold in the physical frame of Abraham Lincoln, Roth initiates a chain of historical and political associations concerning the nature of American citizenship and social inclusion. The very mention of Lincoln necessitates a consideration of American race relations, especially race relations as crucial to the formation and characterization of a people. Throughout the trilogy, Roth's invocations of political or literary paternalism confront this issue of national foundations and the implicit (and explicit) dualism at the heart of the American identity. But there is another dimension, too. Though outwardly Lincolnesque and frequently compared with Thomas Paine, Ringold is more obviously based upon the African-American actor Paul Robeson.[7]

The connection between the black actor and the fictional Jewish radio-star is partly implied by Ira's ease within the former Jewish ghetto of Newark (now occupied by African-Americans): "I'd never before imagined, let alone seen, a white person so easy going and at home with Negroes . . . [H]e went into Newark's Third Ward where the Negroes had come to occupy the streets and houses of the old Jewish immigrant slum. Ira spoke to everyone he met" (91–2). The habit of speaking with everyone he meets heightens Ringold's presidential affinities, though his political sentiments radically sever him from such a role.

At a later stage of the narrative, Ira is to be found deep in conversation with an African American cleaner, Wondrous, expounding the virtues of Paul Robeson. What emerges, however, is that the details of Ringold's political indoctrination are closely modeled on the facts of the actor's own political past. It is an Irish steelworker, Johnny O'Day, who "bolshevizes" Ira during the Second World War with his "pseudo-scientific Marxist lexicon" (123). O'Day stirs Ira into communistic activities and becomes, in many ways, a father to Ira and, by virtue of the filial relationship between Nathan and Ira, a grandfather to the young Zuckerman in terms of his revolutionary knowledge and education. Many readers will spot the link to Robeson, who in 1926 met the Irish-American journalist Frank Harris on the French Riviera. It was Harris who introduced the actor to Claude McKay, the associate editor of the Communist newspaper *The Liberator*, instigating Robeson's first contact with Communism. And so, creating a presidential figure from a character castigated by the American people, Roth works toward a necessary hybridity of character and citizenship, and of fact and fiction, to emphasize the implicit fallacy of American purity.[8]

The Human Stain, the final installment of the trilogy, is set against the backdrop of the Clinton-Lewinsky scandal and the president's controversial impeachment trial. Coleman Silk, a Jewish classics professor at Athena College, is forced to resign from his tenured position by a young French female professor, Delphine Roux. Zuckerman's presence in the New England college town of Athena is a return to his own past. Athena, formerly the home of E. I. Lonoff of *The Ghost Writer* (1979) to whom he had once apprenticed himself, is the town in which he had decided to take on the task of the writer. The classical allusions of *The Human Stain* are evident from the outset, with the epigraph from Sophocles's *Oedipus the King* describing the rite of purification through banishment or vengeance. The book is concerned with both tragic resolutions. In a thematic embodiment of the generic issues involving spectral literary precursors, the classics professor is already dead at the beginning of the book but is subsequently resuscitated by the processes of narrative.[9] Within that narrative, the dead come upon the protagonist himself who is haunted by a past he had sought to leave behind, haunted by "spooks."[10] As a professor of classical Greek and Roman literature, Coleman, like the writer, brings the literature of the past to bear on the present, causing the epic of antiquity to return in a contemporaneous manifestation. Moreover, the book finds its voice as an epic of wrath, driven forth by a fury against a society that, in the summer of 1998 had "revived America's oldest communal passion . . . the ecstasy of sanctimony" (2).

Formulating itself thus, the novel opens with a reading of *The Iliad*, the original epic of wrath, made relevant to the contemporary national situation:

> "'Divine Muse, sing of the ruinous wrath of Achilles . . . Begin where they first quarrelled, Agamemnon the King of Men, and great Achilles.' And what are they quarrelling about, these two violent mighty souls? It's as basic as a bar-room brawl. They are quarrelling over a woman. A girl, really . . . A quarrel, then, a brutal quarrel over a young girl and her young body and the delights of sexual rapacity: there, for better or worse, in this offense against the phallic entitlement, the phallic *dignity*, of a powerhouse of a warrior prince, is how the greatest imaginative literature of Europe begins, and that is why, close to three thousand years later, we are going to begin there today." (4–5)

Partly released from the anxieties of the earlier fiction, fearful of literary usurpation, Roth actively appropriates and renders with irony the context and the content of one of Europe's founding epics. Additionally, he not only makes the text relevant to America of 1998, but also negotiates a destabilizing interchange between *The Iliad* and the foundational mythos of America. By moving backward from the political hothouse of the impeachment summer, to baseball, back to Hawthorne and the Puritans, and then to the battle of Achilles and Agamemnon in the first four pages of the novel, Roth illustrates the increasingly tawdry manifestation of the myths behind the American national identity. Founded upon Puritan religiosity, the nation now finds itself defined in terms of a presidential sex scandal. Maintaining a dialogue with his literary patrimony of Homer and Milton (indeed, rendering it a continued thematic strand throughout the narrative), Roth utilizes the themes and tropes of these predecessors (purification rituals, biblical and Miltonic notions of original sin, Puritan polarities, etc.) to forge an epic of contemporaneity. Layered upon the palimpsests of the past, Roth's epic series engages, consumes and demythologizes the foundational myths of the United States.

Roth's intention to de-sanctify myths of national, racial, and literary establishment with his ironic reading of Homer is localized and politicized with the reference to the cherished American national sport, baseball: "Ninety-eight in New England was a summer of exquisite warmth and sunshine, in baseball a summer of mythical battle between a home-run god who was white and a home-run god who was brown, and in America the summer of an enormous piety binge, a purity binge" (2). While baseball returns the writer to the themes and ambitions of his own earlier fiction—one thinks of the national reflection and demythologizing of America in *The Great American Novel*, from which this piece takes its partial title—Roth here addresses an issue which has been a crucial indicator in the evolution of the national game: race.[11] Setting racial separatism amid Homer and Hawthorne and characterizing the players as gods, Roth situates the issue as central and crucial to the formulation of the nation.

In accepting the American invitation to individualism, Coleman sacrifices his racial community, passes for white, and relinquishes all traces of his black identity. His rejection of his ethnicity is complex, however, as he does not take on the more obvious identity of the American Anglo-Saxon Protestant, but that of the American Jew, surrendering one hyphenated selfhood in favor of another. This, however, is not the end of Coleman's reinvention. He steeps himself in the classical mythology of Europe, simultaneously unable and, indeed, unwilling to let go of a Whitman-*esque* celebration of the self unfettered by history, race, or ideology:

[F]ree to pursue the highest aim, the confidence right to his bones to be his particular I. Free on a scale unimaginable to his father. As free as his father had been unfree. Free now not only of his father but of all his father had to endure . . . Free on the big stage . . . free to enact the boundless, self-defining drama of the pronouns we, they, and I. (109)

This denunciation combined with celebration is the necessary condition of assimilation to America and is crucial to Roth's paternal ambivalence. As the national text of original purity is an impossibility, so too is the ancestral freedom Coleman seeks. In his quest for an identity of purity, free of historical ties, Coleman rejects all categories of identity. This embrace of a polyphonic selfhood renders him the American individualist *par excellence*. He endeavors only to be "Coleman, the greatest of the great *pioneers* of the I . . . never for him the tyranny of the we that is dying to suck you in, the coercive, inclusive, historical, inescapable moral *we* with its insidious *E pluribus unum*" (108). Seeking to escape his origins, ensuring the prevention of "his prospects to be unjustly limited by so arbitrary a designation as race," Coleman Silk, the outward "essence of singularity," casts off his past and his racial identity to taste the American promise of freedom (203, 120). Freedom, in this instance, is doubly weighted given Silk's ancestral stock. For Coleman, unlike Swede Levov, there is no recoverable prelapsarian moment: his ethnicity makes it impossible.

By creating a character who adopts the persona of an American Jew, Roth makes a very deliberate and bold statement of protest against the persistence of racial othering and tiers of "acceptance" in the United States, which make it more desirable to be an American Jew than an African-American. The American Jew, it seems, is more assimilated into the mainstream culture than his fellow African-American citizen, partly because he has, to an extent, "overthrown his origins."[12] Thus Roth, speaking through Zuckerman, casts doubt on an American dream which invites the individual to reinvent himself as a singular being, devoid of the inherent multiplicity of the immigrant American: "Was he merely being another American and, in the great frontier tradition, accepting the democratic invitation to throw your origins overboard if to do so contributes to the pursuit of happiness?" (334). While such considerations have always been part of Roth's agenda, the presentation of a character like Coleman is, perhaps, a deliberate gesture toward exposing the aestheticizing tendencies of American inclusion and purity. On the other hand, it is (possibly) an exercise in self-examination and self-critique, addressing the American writer's collusion in the overwriting of race.

At the time of *The Human Stain*'s publication, Roth, in an interview for *New York Times*, made clear the context in which he wished the novel to be understood: "In 1998 you had the illusion that you were suddenly able to know this huge, unknowable country, to catch a glimpse of its moral core.

What is being enacted on the public stage seemed to have the concentrated power of a great work of literature. The work I'm thinking of is *The Scarlet Letter*" (McGrath). The concentrated power of *The Scarlet Letter* operates generally throughout *The Human Stain* in terms of the public censoriousness about the Clinton-Lewinsky affair. More particularly, however, the earlier text resonates with many of the internal incidences throughout the contemporary novel. For instance, Hawthorne's "A Flood of Sunshine" chapter depicts Hester Prynne casting aside both her outward identity and her past through the removal of the letter from the breast:

> [S]he undid the clasp that fastened the scarlet letter and, leaving it from her bosom, threw it to a distance among the withered leaves . . . The stigma gone, Hester heaved a long deep sigh, in which the burden of shame and anguish departed from her spirit. O exquisite relief! She had not known the weight until she felt the freedom! (152)[13]

Similarly, Coleman, on the assertion of his new, white identity, the fluid and subtle "Silky Silk," "lost to all his people," perceives himself as free not simply of race but also of the past: "Ancestor worship—that's how Coleman put it. Honoring the past was one thing—the idolatry that is ancestor worship was something else. The hell with that imprisonment" (144). Coleman's declaration of his independent identity as an escape from an imprisoning past reflects an American idealism critically analyzed in terms of Roth's wider, textual dialogue with his nineteenth-century neighbours which attests to the limitations and the ultimate impossibility of such freedom.

This conversation with Hawthorne in particular, however, is most obviously centered on the subject of American individualism with Coleman's search for a purity of self. The narrator inquires into the costs of individualism, admiring Coleman's will to self-determination. However, he also detects within it a fatal asceticism, a vision of the self as an entity of purity that recalls the ancestral Puritanism (and contemporary censorship) that both Roth and Hawthorne seek to escape.

A colleague eulogizes and mythologizes Coleman at his funeral, describing him in terms of the Transcendentalist ancestry that he would, almost certainly, have seen as a form of imprisonment:

> Here, in the New England most identified, historically, with the American individualist's resistance to the coercions of a censorious community—Hawthorne, Melville, and Thoreau come to mind—an American individualist who did not think that the weightiest thing in life were the rules, an American individualist who refused to leave unexamined the orthodoxies of the customary and of the established truth, an American individualist who did not always live in compli-

ance with majority standards of decorum and taste—an American individualist *par excellence*. (335)

Yet Coleman Silk, the resistant "individualist *par excellence*," the European Classicist in the American Berkshires, is a pariah, so entrenched in American tradition yet so utterly outside it, fostered by American society but ever marginal. He epitomizes the extremes of individualism. His oppositional will to freedom is self-detrimental and erring: "The man who decides to forge a distinct historical identity, who sets out to spring the historical lock, and who does so, brilliantly succeeds at altering his personal lot, only to be ensnared by the history he hadn't quite counted on . . . The we that is inescapable" (335). Coleman's absorption of the dream of individualism denies the existence of a past, of the inescapable human stain.

Like the "spooks" in his classroom, Coleman is himself a spook, a ghost moving through life like the willful Hester and ever-paranoid Dimmesdale, described by Hawthorne as "each a ghost and awe stricken at the other ghost!" (142). It is, in the end, the female, Faunia (aided by Roth), who articulates the true nature of the American condition, the fantasy of purity and individualism: "The human stain . . . It's in everyone. Indwelling. Inherent. Defining . . . The fantasy of impurity is appalling. It's insane. What's the quest to purify, if not more impurity. All she was saying about the stain is that it's inescapable" (335). Coleman's story may be tinged with aspects of the Greek tragedy so dear to his heart, but Coleman Brutus is, ultimately, an American and his story a truly American tale of becoming: a quest for self identity.

In the shadow of the American Renaissance, Roth resumes the perennial struggle of the individual against the collective community. He maintains the American tradition of inventing the American self, a characteristic of the incipient Puritan country carried through to the slave narratives of the nineteenth century. Merging the Puritan confession with the formerly suppressed narrative of the African-American racial other, Roth, like Hawthorne before him, perceives the American ideology of purity and righteousness as that which is most detrimental to the sanctity of the individual, to the American identity in all its hybrid possibilities. Such is the bard's epic of contemporary America.

NOTES

1. In an interview with Mark Lawson for BBC Radio 4's *Front Row*, Roth noted that the title came to him having re-read *Macbeth*. The stage direction "exit ghost" also appears in *Julius Caesar* and *Hamlet*.

2. Roth articulates this in an interview with Al Alvarez for *The Guardian*: "The stuff that's happened in the last 40 years—the Vietnam war, the social revolution of

the 1960s, the Republican backlash of the 1980s and 1990s—have been so power-fully determining that men and women of intelligence and literary sensibility feel that the strongest thing in their lives is what has happened to us collectively: the new freedoms, the testing of the old conventions, the prosperity. That's what I was writing about in the trilogy that followed *Sabbath*—*American Pastoral, I Married a Communist* and *The Human Stain*: people prepare for life in a certain way and have certain expectations of the difficulties that come with those lives, then they get blindsided by the present moment; history comes in at them in ways for which there is no prepara-tion. 'History is a very sudden thing,' is how I put it. I'm talking about the historical fire at the center and how the smoke from that fire reaches into your house."

3. This ambiguous sense of power placed in the female, that is the power to reveal the nation to itself, is later reiterated in *The Human Stain* with Coleman Silk and Na-than Zuckerman's discussion of Monica Lewinsky: "this girl has revealed more about America than anybody since Dos Passos. *She* stuck a thermometer up the *country's* ass. Monica's *U.S.A.*" (148).

4. Merry's return from the city, from Newark, at the end of the novel exempli-fies the shift from arcadian idyll to the berserk, with the dinner party scene at which Jessie Orcutt stabs Lou Levov in the face with a fork. The scene, in its comic horror, microcosmically mirrors the wider descent from post-War peace to the pandemonium of the Vietnam years in the United States. It also, however, demonstrates the writer's antagonistic relationship with the paternal poetic precursor. Lou's survival of the at-tack attests to the ultimately inescapable weight of such figures.

5. According to Bloom's theory of poetic influence, poets inevitably "misread" their precursors; "poetic misprision," his term for this kind of creative misreading, is the first step in the "belated" poet's assertion of originality. See Bloom's *The Anxiety of Influence: A Theory of Poetry*.

6. See A. J. Boyle regarding the construction of Aeneas as the Caesar Augustus who commissioned his creation and Christopher Hill's *The Experience of Defeat: Milton and Some Contemporaries* for Milton's construction of his characters as Charles I and Oliver Cromwell.

7. The name "Ira," whilst obviously denotative of wrath and anger, was also that of an admired forefather of Robeson—the African-American actor Ira Aldridge. Aldridge, in fact, preceded Robeson in playing Othello. See Martin Duberman's *Paul Robeson*.

8. There are many such overlapping details between Robeson and Ringold: a shared sense of great physical presence, Robeson and Ringold's anglophilia, tempera-mental affinities between Robeson's wife Essie and Eve Frame and so on. Perhaps the most important biographical detail, however, is Robeson's famed performances as Shakespeare's Othello—the Moor betrayed by his ancient and the state that had formerly adopted him. Layering Ringold, a fictional character, upon an historical per-sonage who had brought to life a further fictional character, Roth re-invokes the Shake-spearean theme of seeming versus reality while also placing the American national issue of racial foundation and separatism within the context of literary patrimony.

9. Indeed, all of the protagonists, Coleman, Seymour and Ira, by the time we encounter them, are dead.

10. The whole story of Coleman's downfall begins with his unwitting use of the word "spooks" to refer to a pair of absentee students. The students turn out to be African-Americans. In light of this alleged racism, Delphine Roux begins a college witch-hunt causing Coleman to lose his job and ultimately divulge the secret of his own ethnic identity to the writer, Nathan Zuckerman.

11. *The Great American Novel* explicitly confronts the tendencies within national myths (such as that which surrounds baseball in the United States) to aestheticize and, therefore, distort, social realities. In the story of baseball's boundless enthusiasm (baseball as the great tool of democracy), Roth sends the manager of the Rupert Mundys off to the South Sea Islands (in typical Melville fashion of *Omoo* and *Typee*) to "Americanize" the natives.

12. Posnock's article "Purity and Danger: On Philip Roth" observes that Roth carefully chooses the historical moment when Coleman elects for an American Jewish identity: 1953, Greenwich Village. He argues: "From that time and place emanated the rising cultural significance of Jewish intellectuals, writers who challenged genteel decorum by flaunting 'the disputatious stance, the aggressively marginal sensibility, the disavowel of community ties' . . . To be part of the 'post immigrant generation' was to be granted a ticket out of the ghetto, set free to think critically, without the baggage of other ethnic groups with their 'Old country link and a strangling church' or of WASPs with their blind loyalty to the American way" (94–95).

13. Further affinities might include Coleman's expulsion from the faculty by the unforgiving Roux with "The Procession" chapter and Chillingworth's similarities with Les Farley and Delphine Roux, to name just a few. Posnock notes Roth's "troping" of "The Minister in a Maze" chapter that narrates Dimmesdale's inner "revolution." See Posnock's "Purity and Danger," p. 97.

WORKS CITED

Alvarez, Al. "The Long Road Home." *The Guardian*. Guardian News and Media Ltd., September 11, 2004. Web. March 7, 2016.

Bloom, Harold. *The Western Canon*. London: Macmillan, 1994. Print.

———. *The Anxiety of Influence: A Theory of Poetry*. Oxford: Oxford UP, 1973. Print.

Boyle, A. J., ed. *Roman Epic*. London: Routledge, 1993. Print.

Brauner, David. *Post War Jewish Fiction: Ambivalence, Self-Explanation and Trans-Atlantic Connections*. Basingstoke: Palgrave, 2001. Print.

Duberman, Martin. *Paul Robeson*. London: Bodley Head, 1989. Print.

Emerson, R. W. *Essays, First Series*. Ed. Larzer Ziff. London: Penguin, 1982. Print.

Frye, Northrop. *Anatomy of Criticism*. New Jersey: Princeton UP, 1957. Print.

Hawthorne, Nathaniel. *The Scarlet Letter* (1850). London: Wordsworth Classics, 1992. Print.

Joyce, James. *Ulysses* (1922). Ed. Declan Kiberd. London: Penguin Classics, 1992. Print.

Lee, Hermione. *Philip Roth*. London and New York: Methuen, 1982. Print.

McGrath, Charles. "Zuckerman's Alter Brain: An Interview with Philip Roth," *New York Times*. New York Times, May 7, 2000. Web. March 7, 2016.

Parrish, Tim. "Becoming Black: Zuckerman's Bifurcating Self in *The Human Stain*." *Philip Roth: New Perspectives on an American Author*. Ed. Derek Parker Royal. Westport, CT: Praeger, 2005. 209–224. Print.

Posnock, Ross. *Philip Roth's Rude Truth: The Art of Immaturity*. New Jersey: Princeton UP, 2006. Print.

———. "Purity and Danger: On Philip Roth." *Raritan* 21 (Fall 2001): 85–101. Print.

Roth, Philip. *The Human Stain*. London: Vintage, 2000. Print.

———. *American Pastoral*. London: Vintage, 1997. Print.

———. *I Married a Communist*. London: Jonathan Cape, 1998. Print.

———. *Patrimony: A True Story*. London: Vintage, 1991. Print.

———. *Reading Myself and Others*. London: Penguin, 1975. Print.

———. *The Ghost Writer*. London: Vintage, 1979. Print.

———. *The Great American Novel*. New York: Vintage, 1973. Print.

Royal, Derek Parker. "Pastoral Dreams and National Identity in *American Pastoral* and *I Married a Communist*." *Philip Roth: New Perspectives on an American Author*. Ed. Derek Parker Royal. Westport, CT: Praeger, 2005. 185–209. Print.

Shostak, Debra. *Philip Roth—Countertexts, Counterlives*. Columbia: U of Southern Carolina P, 2004.

Chapter Nine

"I was the prosthesis"

Roth and Late Style

Adam Zachary Newton

*The naive is a childlikeness, where it is no longer expected, and precisely
for that reason, cannot be attributed to real childhood in the strictest sense.*

—Friedrich Schiller, *On Naïve and Sentimental Poetry*

No, they are not quite Philip Roth's *Four Last Songs*—the valedictory composition by Richard Strauss first heard as incidental background music in *Exit
Ghost* (2007) when the aging Nathan Zuckerman wonders whether his arrival
at a couple's apartment "had prompted one or the other of them to play such
dramatically elegiac, ravishingly emotional music written by a very old man
at the close of his life" (485). And however tempting the comparison, they
don't quite correspond to the Adornian account of *Spätstil* in Edward Said's
unfinished set of reflections, *On Late Style*, which specifies "a nonharmonious, nonserene tension, and above all, a deliberately unproductive productiveness going *against*" in "constitutively alienated and alienating" works
of "intransigence, difficulty, and unresolved contradiction" (7). One of John
Updike's last published essays, "Late Works," is probably more proximate
to the mark in its claim that no less than by death, authorial posteriority is
haunted by the simple anteriority of "the author's previous works . . . with the
inexorable consistency of his own handwriting" (60).

So, how *should* one assess these final works termed "Nemeses"—the only
such designated grouping in the author's front matter cataloguing, and a portentous one at that? According to their author, these four last novels "all have
in common" a centralized focus on what he calls "the cataclysm [:] four men
of four different ages, brought down"—although he is quick to acknowledge
that such a précis might describe many of his longer novels of the 1990s and
early 2000s, as well (Pierpont, 319).[1] As two recent articles have already
proposed Said's poignant account of late style as gloss,[2] I will proceed oth-

erwise here, concentrating not on those books featuring an aging narrator/
protagonist, his phantasmal eros, and the rebuke of fate or destructive power
of shame, but rather on the two Nemeses that have received rather less critical
attention to date, *Indignation* (2008) and *Nemesis* (2010).

Late Roth, we discover, is short, or at least shorter, Roth: Roth *diminuendo*.
But because the now-long (six decades) career began with short form (*Goodbye, Columbus and Other Stories* from 1959), one might reasonably speculate
that it has elected either to cycle back—rounding the ninety feet from third
base to home—or to do something else, something novel instead.[3] Now,
reduction can mean the refiner's fire where intricate largeness is subject to
intense compression, as in Tolstoy's *The Death of Ivan Ilyich* (one of *Everyman*'s intertexts). Alternatively, as in *Indignation* and *Nemesis*, it can mean
eschewing maturation on the plane of story, fullness of accomplishment, a
realized and seasoned life. It can settle, instead, for the supplementary, the
auxiliary, the foreshortened. Echoing the final sentence of *The Plot Against
America*, I will call this supplementary something, "the prosthesis."

In *Everyman* (2007) and *The Humbling* (2009), reduction means the winding down or finishing off of an aging character—like *Sabbath's Theater* but
with the canvas contracted. In *Indignation* and *Nemesis*, we find Rothian
repoussoir—like a truncated *Plot Against America*, gesturing back, in the
context of some larger social or political crisis, to the periods of Roth's youth
(the 1940s and polio) and adolescence (the 1950s and the Korean War). It is
certainly true that nostalgia has suffused the late fiction: in *Patrimony*, in the
Newark Trilogy, in *Sabbath's Theater*, and *The Plot Against America*. And
a precedent of sorts might be traced as far as the forties baseball fable *The
Great American Novel* (1973).

What I want to explore in specific regard to *Indignation* and *Nemesis*, however, is the way the nostalgia gets cultivated, massaged, staged—much like
the very word itself, which "is only pseudo-Greek, or nostalgically Greek,"
coined at the end of the 17th century and in specific connection with me-
dicinal malady and cure (Boym 3). I asked above about assessing—more ac-
curately, *placing*—the Nemeses within the completed arc of Roth's achievement. For, late style Roth is also coda or epilogue Roth: post-*Sabbath's
Theater*, post-American trilogy, post-*The Plot Against America*. Critics have
both esteemed and clucked over them.[4] In a particularly trenchant meditation, for example, acknowledging that "that the ideal of a pure, unadulterated
reception becomes less and less tenable" once an author codifies his own
work, Ben Jeffrey adjudges the tetralogy to be a series of "weak stories,"
characterized by "thematic dread and formal weaknesses" ("What's Next").
"The Nemeses provide a frightening examination of talent losing its means,
and being aware of it," he adds, citing Adorno, too, albeit to rather different
effect than does Said: "late works are the catastrophes."[5]

By these lights, Roth's final four suggest "uncanny replicas" of the real and formerly sovereign thing: "a deliberately poor imitation of a Philip Roth book." While the Nemeses may extend the Rothian corpus, add to and even simulate it, in themselves, they remain an artificial appendage, "thinner, flatter, purged of scenery; lacking a third dimension" ("What's Next"). One wonders, however, whether prostheses need to be conceived as less-than—thinner, flatter, more schematic—solely by dint of artifice? (And what, by the way, could be more device-driven or than a book like *The Breast* or *Deception*?) Cannot the lesser stake a claim in its own right? As exercises in willed reduction, might *Indignation* and *Nemesis* still "hold out the promise of some new way of understanding their author" (Jeffrey)? Moreover, can an apparent replica or "deliberately poor imitation" still succeed as a compressed and pointed *rewriting*?

Accordingly, I am not persuaded that the Nemeses represent patently defective markers of lack, with the author's artistry similarly "brought down" alongside the catastrophized lives of his four protagonists. I prefer the jury stay out instead, while we entertain some recuperative speculations: that the prosthesis may possess its own vivacity, the lateness its own "productively unproductive" style of invention, the nostalgia—befitting what Polish modernist Witold Gombrowicz would call "memoirs from the time of immaturity"[6]—its own suitability.

GENEALOGY

An account of internal influence would link these books to predecessor texts in the Roth canon, like *Portnoy* or *Goodbye, Columbus* for their youthful protagonists, to the American trilogy for its counter-trio of father figures, or to *Sabbath* and *The Plot,* for the core of grief and death in the one and of nostalgic hankering after childhood Newark in the other. From canon to Canon, and through a literary filiopietism that might well satisfy Gabiel Josipovici or even Friedrich Schiller, the Nemeses extend backwards Roth's penchant for strong readings of the canon by deliberately invoking classical or premodern literary traditions which they then cleverly revise: medieval morality play in *Everyman*, Sophocles and Shakespeare in *Exit Ghost* and *The Humbling*, Homer and Euripides in *Indignation* and *Nemesis*. Of the last two, for instance, critic William Deresiewicz observes,

And like *Indignation*, [*Nemesis*] is a kind of Attic tragedy in prose: hubris, hamartia, nemesis; spare plot, fallen hero, endless suffering. Axler and Zuckerman are old; the one dies and the other exits because they lose the strength to start again and so run out of ways to change. But Marcus and Bucky belong to Euripides; like Pentheus in *The Bacchae*, they refuse to release their rigid self-conceptions and so, like him, are torn apart. (26–27)

At the same time, the novel betrays "a depthless kind of naïveté—a more intelligent and literary version of the effect connived at by the '50s-nostalgia genre" ("Portnoy Agonistes" 27). Yet, the canonical overlay itself is any-thing but naïve—at least in Schillerian sense of a devotion to sensuous truth, simplicity, and unmediated perception, aesthetic activity as a kind of participation mystique (or so deemed Carl Jung[7]) as over against a decidedly more modern, self-alienated, and *sentimentalische* mode. To this degree, the Greeks were "naïve" but not *nostalgic*, an affective disorder only we moderns typically contract, for "Unser Gefühl für Natur gleicht der Empfindung des Kranken für die Gesundheit [our feeling for nature resembles the feeling of the sick for health] (Schiller 727).

Roth has been a sentimental writer from the get-go; both the pastoral idyll of Short Hills and the urban reframing of Gaugin in *Goodbye, Colum-bus* drive such counter-naïveté pointedly home. And while his continuing preoccupation with craft might suggest greater affinities with Josipovici's notion of trust as something we ascribe to both maker and material, Roth's continuing play with the politics of author- and readership fairly obviously aligns him with "the journey of the post-Romantic artist" in concert with the "temptations of suspicion" (*On Trust*, 5). And yet such temptations are not exclusively the terrain of postmodernism (just as Josipovici will treat the likes of like Beckett, Proust, and Wittgenstein[8]).

Indeed, in this essay, I want to propose an alternate genealogy for Roth's late work that if not directly influenced by, still shares a commitment to, the second-ary, unsublimated terrain of the sub-adult explored by the Polish modernists Bruno Schulz and Witold Gombrowicz.[9] "[As] immature, ridiculous green-horns fighting for our expression on the plain of concreteness and dealing with our meaninglessness," wrote Schulz in a 1935 review of Gombrowicz's novel *Ferdydurke,* "we are closer to the truth than if we were solemn, sublime, ma-ture, and completed" (Schulz 421). Likewise, both writers allow us to reframe the critique of late Roth as imitative or subordinate, since in Schulz and Gom-browicz these qualities disclose productive energies, not deficits. Finally—and this is especially true of Schulz—there is the uncanny power of the prosthetic: supplementary yet mobile, the sign of contiguity not lack.

SHOP TALK

Reflecting on his life and work in the spring of 2011, Roth recounted the amount of research—"studying" is his preferred term—on the science of amputations and prostheses in the 1940s for his 2004 novel, *The Plot Against America* (*Web of Stories* 105). It is a matter of biographical record that the young Roth had a dying aunt during that novel's time period whose boarding in the Roth family home served him as a compositional model for having to "be in the room with somebody who's in terrible trouble"—namely, the fictional amputee-veteran cousin Alvin (*Web of Stories* 105).[10] Still, for the particulars of missing limb, ill-fitting replacement, and suppurating stump, Roth insists, "I have to invent what happens. Well, it's a pleasure to invent what happens . . . And I was, of course, as fascinated as I was when I was studying gloves for *American Pastoral*" (*Web of Stories* 105).

Prostheses embody loss, artificially compensating for the missing or amputated body-part. Yet, the made object possesses an intrinsic power and "fascination" in its own right. Prosthetic limbs thus bear a kind of family resemblance to gloves, as mechanically reproducible sheath or covering is to a mechanically generated "replica" (or simulacrum). "Takes great skill to cut a glove right," says Swede Levov to Rita Cohen while escorting her around the glove manufactory, which she, in return, captures as "the romance of the glove business" (130). And as Zuckerman explains, "trade talk was a tradition in glove families going back hundreds of years" (121). By analogy, we understand also the romance of research, so crucial to the American trilogy and *The Plot Against America* but also central to the polio plot of *Nemesis*, the author's final creative intervention in historical fact and record.[11]

In explaining how he turned to writing short novels into his sixth decade as a writer, Roth also points to the determinative question of craft, the source, we recall, of authorial *fascination*: "how do you pack a punch in a third of the pages? I know how you do it with a novel. The power of the amplification provides you with the punch" (*Web of Stories* 30). Obviously, the kind of book Roth sets out to write in the Nemeses demands a different strategy, although the boxing metaphor—a consistent trope of Roth's—retains its salience.[12] When Nathan Zuckerman recalls an out-of-class conversation about baseball, boxing, and books with his high-school English teacher Murray Ringold and his brother Ira, he adduces this *ars poetica*: "Not opening up a book to worship it or to be elevated by it or to lose yourself to the world around you. No, boxing with the book" (*Communist* 27). Reading is sweet science. How, then, to box with *Indignation* and *Nemesis*?

NAÏVE AND SENTIMENTAL, SENESCENCE AND JUVENILITY, BRUNO SCHULZ

Let us start, a few years back, with those cameo portraits of a minor character type that start appearing in the major novels of the early 1990s,[13] a certain kind of stunted, neotenous, or even post-social character, who seems to presage an increasingly prominent swerve towards nostalgia in the late work. First, there is "tiny cousin Apter" in *Operation Shylock*, "chained to his childishness . . . someone whose whole life lies in the hands of the past":

> This cousin Apter—twice removed on my mother's side—is an unborn adult, in 1988 a fifty-four-year-old who had evolved into manhood without evolving, an under-life-size, dollish-looking man with the terrifyingly blank little face of an aging juvenile actor. There is imprinted on Apter's face absolutely nothing of the mayhem of Jewish life in the twentieth century, even though in 1943 his entire family had been consumed by the German mania for murdering Jews. (18)

Next, there is one hundred-year old Fishl Shabas in *Sabbath's Theater*, a survivor in a wholly different, cozily Jewish American sense: "'The accent and syntax the same, but no longer the muscular voice for shouting from the street into the houses and all the way back to the yards, 'Veg-etables! Fresh veg-e-tables, ladies!' In the tonelessness, the hollowness, you heard not only how deaf he was and how alone he was but that his was not one of his life's great days. A mere mist of a man" (382).

Each (for this particular reader at least), suggests a family resemblance with certain subsidiary figures in the work of Bruno Schulz. Albeit apperceived through post-Holocaust eyes, the shrinkage, dependency, and infantilism cousin Apter embodies, for example, are trademarks that Schulz often assigned to a gallery of strange, desocialized, and melancholy characters in his own fiction from the mid-1930s. Apter differs markedly from Fish, who, by comparison, stands out as simply an icon of senescence, an improbable relic of the Jersey shore of Sabbath's youth, a living testament, not to the whipsaw of history or the antagonism that is the world but rather to benign anachronism, to "*The incapacity to die. Sitting it out instead . . .*: the perverse senselessness of just remaining, of not going" (384).

Centenarian Fish exudes his own quasi-Schulzian air, though. Described as "a mere mist of a man," he evokes oblique shadows of Uncle Mark, "small and hunched, with a face fallow of sex, sat in his grey bankruptcy, reconciled to his fate" or cousin Emil, with his "mist of a face," both minor family members in stories from *Cinnamon Shops* (I point here only to the affinity with no claim about direct influence). Of the latter relative, Schulz's narrator writes, "it seemed as if it were only his clothes that had been thrown, crumpled and empty, over a chair. His face seemed like the breath of a face —a smudge which an unknown passerby had left in the air" (14).[14] Roth's nostalgia for Newark, for family, becomes more and more localized in the fiction after the eighties' Zuckermania and early nineties' *dédoublement*: in *Patrimony*, *Sabbath's Theater*, *American Pastoral*, and most dramatically in *The Plot Against America* and also *Indignation* and *Nemesis*, the two smaller fictions also motivated by historical record and defining national event. Not unlike Schulz's Drohobycz, the micro-theater of Weequahic and its environs licenses generative, demiurgic mythos of its own, just as retrospect, nostalgia, recollected childhood and youth open a whole world of what Schulz calls "spiritual genealogy" (370).

Nemesis renders such a world—encroaching upon the borders of which are a whole world at war and the threatened proximity of polio—in this paean to summertime juvenescence:

> Yet in spite of everything uninviting about the night, there was a string of boys on rattly old bicycles coasting full speed down the uneven cobblestones between the trolley tracks on Avon Avenue and screaming "Geronimo!" at the top of their lungs . . . boys cavorting around and grabbing at one another in front of the candy stores . . . boys in the middle of the street lazily tossing fly balls to one another under the streetlights. (350)

Admittedly, cousins Apter and Fish do not quite personify what Ross Posnock has in mind when he treats "Roth's long commitment to a mature immaturity" (62, 87).[15] But in their arrested or retrograde development, such characters (are they always cousins?) gesture toward what will become a fuller valedictory investment in the familial-national past concentrated in nineteen-forties and nineteen-fifties Newark and its environs.

What such cousin-characters also have in common, what also makes them also distant relatives of Bruno Schulz's family imaginary, are varieties of reduction. No grandiosity on the order of Mickey Sabbath or Simon Axler (lynchpin of *The Humbling* and a role almost too-perfectly assigned to Al Pacino in the 2014 film version) for them. No extravagance of the sort acted out by late-stage Zuckerman and Kepesh, for whom sexual adventure, no less than finely calibrated voice, remain the dominant rhetoric of self-expression: just contraction in size, sovereignty, selfhood. Apter and Fish, let us say, are the "short novels" to the largeness of mimesis and exaggeration of character on display in Roth's second-to-last decade's run of great fiction.

In *Indignation* and *Nemesis*, Rothian late style signifies its own kind of foreshortening. The addition-that-is-prosthesis now becomes either telescoping in exploit (Bucky and Marcus and localized to college campus and playground) or temporal regression (late adolescence). Moreover, if we look for a parallel figure to Apter and Fish in the final work, we come upon one whose more-than-Winesburgian grotesqueness shades arrested development into outright imbecility: his name is Horace. And yet, one suspects that *Nemesis*, the novel in which he appears, nevertheless desires its readers to accord him something of the benefit of the doubt elicited by the marginal figures in earlier novels, an exaggerated naïf described as follows:

Horace was the neighborhood's "moron," a skinny man in his thirties or forties—no one knew his age for sure—whose mental development had stopped
at around six and whom a psychologist would likely have categorized as an
imbecile, or even an idiot, rather than the moron he'd been unclinically dubbed
years before by the neighborhood youngsters. He dragged his feet beneath him,
and his head, jutting forward from his neck like a turtle's, bobbed loosely with
each step, so that altogether he appeared to be not so much walking as stagger-
ing forward. (322–323)

Horace is Eugene "Bucky" Cantor's photo-negative in *Nemesis*: the pathos
to his ethos, the congenitally backward to his aspiringly valiant, the feeble-
minded to his barrel-chested, the rebarbative to his admirable, the lesser to his
protagonistic, the naïf to his elected gallantry. And yet, according to the novel's
inexorable logic of necessity—the eventuation of "pointless, contingent, pre-
posterous, and tragic" (430) nemesis—they are both ultimately aligned through
unluck and bodily affliction: Horace's mentally disabled to Bucky's poliomy-
elitic. Cataclysm takes no prisoners, as "biography is chance, and, beginning at
conception, chance—the tyranny of contingency—is everything" (427).

MIMESIS, PROSTHESIS, AND WITOLD GOMBROWICZ

Like *Everyman* and *the Humbling*, *Indignation* and *Nemesis* form an obvious
pair among the Nemeses. Moreover, the syncopating rhythm between juvenil-
ity in the one and senescence in the other reads as deliberate, suggesting that
the four separate plots were composed with some sort of abstract connectivity
in mind.[16] It may thus be only fitting that in some mythological accounts, the
Greek goddess Nemesis was believed to have engendered an egg from which
hatched two sets of twins.[17] The balance thus struck between a narrating first-
person in *Indignation* (through "morphine-induced recollection") and the reverential documentor of *Nemesis* also make the novels paradigmatic for the long
arc of Roth's project of voice and consciousness, which has toggled between
amped-up autobiography on the one hand and imaginative witness on the other:

If you ask how this can be—memory upon memory, nothing but memory—of
course I can't answer, and not because neither a "you" nor an "I" exists, any
more than do a "here" and a "now," but because all that exists is the recollected
past, not recovered, mind you, not relived in the immediacy of the realm of sensation, but merely replayed. . . . Is this really to go on and on—my nineteen little
years forever while everything else is absent, my nineteen little years inescap-
ably here, persistently present, while everything that went into making real the
nineteen years, while everything that put one squarely in the midst of, remains
a phantasm far, far away? (131)

This is Marcus Messner, deceased narrative voice of *Indignation*, struggling with the dilemma of story and discourse this more sentimental than naïve novel has handed him: a dead man talking. Yet, more precisely put: an almost-man. Decades ago in his *oeuvre*—five in the case of narrated Neil Klugman, four in the case of narrating Alex Portnoy—Roth conducted his novelistic "scrutiny of things" (as Ira Ringold defines one of literature's signal properties to his English class), through the lens of critical immaturity (*Communist* 185). While it is true that Marcus is given the same task of defending one's life that defines so many of Roth's major characters, with a voice aggrieved and tenacious and with hands that hammer and fingers that point, he *is* only nineteen—just as Bucky Cantor is twenty-three and (for the purposes of a genealogy internal to Roth's output), the focalized consciousness of Philip Roth in *The Plot Against America* is seven.

Had he read Polish or survived the Korean War, Marcus Messner might possibly have become an enthusiastic reader of Witold Gombrowicz, whose programmatic exploration of what he called "the extraordinary significance of form in both social and personal life"—of the twin operations of "giving someone a mug" and "fixing a bum on someone," distorting and infantilizing the Other—discloses obvious Rothian affinities (4–5). As things stand in the novel, however, Marcus's chosen culture hero is the "immoralist[,] self-confessed socialist" Bertrand Russell; the story and fate in which he finds himself emplotted ring multiple tragicomic variations on the deformations he must endure through mug-wearing and bum-fixing.

The extraordinary significance of form in both social and personal life: as leading lights in Polish modernism before Europe's own world-altering crisis of form, Gombrowicz and Schulz constructed different versions of this subversive mimesis. Roth's articulation of it, we know, is distinctly American (Newarkian middle-class) and post-war. Although Deresiewicz laments Roth's failure to inhabit youthful character and consciousness in *Indignation* and *Nemesis* as "another demonstration of the fallacy of imitative form," the latter formulation so uncannily recalls the common terrain for Gombrowicz and Schulz that—without, again, claiming deliberate literary influence—we might simply pause to consider the politics of imitative form in the first place.

Indeed, the very collocation of high (classical tragedy) and low (adolescent melodrama) in both novels indicates a stylistic choice about imitation as something other than fallacy or the product of waning authorial powers. It likewise suggests its own working out of naïve vs. sentimental and trust vs. suspicion, albeit against rather than with the grain of the mature and reverential norm we might associate with Schiller or Josipovici, who look (nostalgically) back to foundational discursive traditions like the Hebrew Scriptures and Greek epic and tragedy, in which a twinning of craft and trust was the *sine qua non*, and the reflective pressure of self on self (as I express it above) was noticeably absent.

Thus, the Deuteronomic *Nemesis* rewrites not only its 1940s antecedent *The Plot Against America* but also—through its geographical focus in equatorial Newark, a brief idyll in the Poconos (prelapsarian Short Hills), and its class-romance—the Genesis that is *Goodbye, Columbus*.[18] Against the "back to school" motif that characterizes both Gombrowicz's *Ferdydurke* and Schulz's *Sanatorium pod klepsydrą* (1937),[19] juvenilization in the college plot of *Indignation* on one hand (reaching its acme in the "White Panty Raid"), and situational constriction in *Nemesis* on the other (Bucky's mythic fortitude, "exacerbated sense of duty" and "masculine development" [443, 314] measured against his body's less-than-hero's size, the playground that constitutes the extent of his authority, and the tenement origins of his biography that situate him unnervingly proximate to the Hebrew Orphan Asylum), imitative form seems more than apposite.[20]

"[With] the cast-iron, wear-resistant, strikingly bold face of a sturdy young man you could rely on" (309), Bucky, too, has both an idealized mug and a brutally deforming bum fixed on him at the terminus of Roth's career: that he is ultimately diagnosed to be a "healthy infected carrier" of polio who has quite possibly contributed to the deaths of the children in his charge; that he contracts the disease himself to permanently deleterious effect—with withered arm, useless hand, and debilitated leg that causes a dip in his gait (eerie echo of Horace) and requires an orthotic brace (cousin to prosthesis); and most of all that "he has the aura of ineradicable failure about him . . . not just crippled physically by polio but no less demoralized by persistent shame" (429), demonstrates both the unreasoning cruelty of nemesis, and—because Bucky is a character in a novel by Philip Roth—the hyper-magnified burden of his own tormented agency as calamity's supposed "invisible arrow" (442).[21]

At the beginning of Roth's career, in such stories as "The Conversion of the Jews" (1959) and "Eli, the Fanatic" (1959), individual rebellion becomes an almost sacred duty within the porous boundaries of community; in his final testament, such porosity comes to signify the risk of infection, as human mortality is rendered as the journal of a plague year:[22]

> he took off his glasses and went up on the high board and for half an hour concentrated on doing every difficult dive he knew. When he was finished and came out of the water and put on his glasses, he still hadn't gotten what had happened out of his mind—the speed with which it had happened or the idea that he had made it happen. Or the idea that the outbreak of polio at the Chancellor playground had originated with him as well. All at once he heard a loud shriek. It was the shriek of the woman downstairs from the Michaels family, terrified

that her child would catch polio and die. Only he didn't just hear the shriek—he was the shriek. (418)

Syntactically and symbolically, the sentence exactly recapitulates the final sentence of Roth's late, great novel of 1940s Newark in existential crisis, "I was the prosthesis" (362). And if the Nemeses could be said to begin with this expostulation from *Everyman*, "There is no remaking reality," then in these introjected screams and prostheses we can read the counter-text (5, 78).

Mimesis *is* nemesis, argued Gombrowicz; or at least it proceeds according to a law of unintended consequence that reads as downfall (for that is what immaturity partly embodies or effects). Similarly, for Schulz, demiurgic matter ineluctably descends to the level of the flea market—except that therein lies one of its most liberating properties: if the aesthetic category of imitative form is a cut below artistic perfection where the seams are hidden, the resulting "clumsy stiches" (Schulz 419)—a coarseness of material or faultiness in execution—nevertheless works against any fetishized inviolability of the work.[23] When something debatably less than a well-wrought urn or even a jar in Tennessee, mimesis also means prosthesis: "A misplaced sense of responsibility can be a debilitating thing," says Dr. Steinberg, unwittingly encapsulating the plot's implacable logic (355).

Lesser, in the double sense of both the minor or reduced and the subordinate or sub-adult, is so very clearly the burden of both these novels that they return us to Edward Said's thought that what characterizes late style is the quite deliberate stepping away from, or stopping short of, transcendence and resolution—especially as this particular Prospero bids farewell to his magic. As Bruno Schulz expresses it, there is an authenticity to be found in the prosthetic and rudimentary, the "zone of subcultural contents [and] backyard inventory of things, the rear building of the self" (418–419). The "uncanny replicas" and "deliberately poor imitation of a Philip Roth book" lamented by Jeffrey and other critics may thus actually number among the Nemeses' semi-virtues. This also allows us now to retrieve the question of lateness with which this essay began together with the valedictory gesture that directs our gaze backwards.

NOSTALGIA

One review of *Nemesis* notes that, "what heat his previous novels give off is the heat of friction, of conflagration. His newest, *Nemesis*, stands out for its warmth. It is suffused with precise and painful tenderness" (Cohen). Part of the novel's artistry—like *Madame Bovary*, oddly enough the model Roth cites for its discursive design, which is actually new in his work[24]—lies in the emergent distinction between narratorial consciousness and protagonist, what Mikhail Bakhtin identified as the "gift-giving capacity" for aesthetic consummation of the former and the necessarily flawed "axiological position" of the latter. That the narrator's personal identity is revealed to readers in the final pages, I also take to be a token of authorial generosity in parallel with his chronicler's reportorial modesty.[25]

As indicated, *Nemesis*'s narrator is known to Bucky: his name is Arnold Mesnikoff. In that capacity, he is the only narrative voice in the four last novels to approximate the role played by Nathan Zuckerman in the Newark trilogy: the acquaintance/witness for a figure made larger-than-life through reportorial agency after being brought down by cataclysm:

> Talking like this seemed to him to be neither pleasant nor unpleasant—it was a pouring forth that before long he could not control, neither an unburdening nor a remedy so much as an exile's painful visit to the irreclaimable homeland, the beloved birthplace that was the site of his undoing. . . . the fact that I had been one of the kids hanging around Chancellor that horrible summer—that I was the best friend of his playground favorite and, like Alan and like him, had come down with polio—made him bluntly candid in a self-searing manner that sometimes astonished me, the auditor whom he'd never before known as an adult, the auditor now inspiring his confidence the way, as kids, I and the others had been inspired by him. (428–429)

And this is his bitter judgment:

> That the polio epidemic among the children of the Weequahic section and the children of Camp Indian Hill was a tragedy, he could not accept. He has to convert tragedy into guilt. He has to find a necessity for what happens. . . . I have to say that however much I might sympathize with the amassing of woes that had blighted his life, this is nothing more stupid than hubris, not the hubris of will or desire but the hubris of fantastical, childish religious interpretation. We have heard it all before and by now have heard enough of it, even from someone as profoundly decent as Bucky Cantor. (439)

If *Indignation* borrows some of its timbre and educational critique from *The Catcher in the Rye*, with Marcus Messner's self-righteousness supplying an ideal vehicle for the Salinger brand of sentimental/suspicious adolescent reflection, *Nemesis* calculatedly courts the naïve—at story and discourse levels alike. If Marcus Messner is a *shames* (his last name is German for "sexton"[26])—punctilious and wardenly to a fault, then Bucky Cantor is a *hazzan*—a pied piper, if not exactly sweet singer, for Jewish solidarity. While his stolidness of personality ("largely humorous . . . with barely a trace of wit" [441], we are told) may be no more his fault than his congenitally poor eyesight and short stature, the novel wants, unironically, to accord him the heroism he desires. He *really is* a "good boy," in Arnold Mesnikoff's melancholy reckoning, and thus significantly other than his off-rhyme non-neighbor Portnoy—more scion of hard-working Jewish grandparents than ethno-cultural petri dish for over-protective Jewish mothering: "There's nobody less salvageable than a ruined good boy . . . The guilt in someone like Bucky may seem absurd but, in fact, is unavoidable. Such a person is condemned. Nothing he does matches the ideal in him. He never knows where his responsibility ends" (443).

In his practiced valor and doughtiness—the novel's very last line avers, "to us he seemed invincible" (446)—twenty-three year old Bucky Cantor splits the difference between *Everyman*'s "Hold your ground and take it as it comes" and cousin Fish's wholly fortuitous "sitting it out instead: the perverse senselessness of just remaining, of not going" (384). The line is the very quintessence of laudable naïveté. For obviously, it's Mesnikoff's more refracted desire that's recorded here as much as, or perhaps even more than, Bucky's own. And as his now-thirty-nine year-old self wishes us to know, there is also a certain gallantry in just listening and recording, "the auditor now inspiring his confidence the way, as kids, I and the others had been inspired by him" (429).

We already know something of his own quiet heroism when he tells us that personal experience as a polio victim and graduate training in architecture melded to create a business devoted to wheelchair accessibility, modifying existing structural limitations to accommodate human disability—not unlike the function of prosthetics. Although narratively contrapuntal, one difference between Mesnikoff and Mr. Cantor (as he continues respectfully to call him) is just that "tyranny of contingency." One of them was a Chancellor Avenue playground boy who happened to contract a disease that left him seriously but not fatefully impaired; the role chance plays in the biography of the other—including more debilitating injury—scripts a decidedly different set of consequences: the difference, in other words, between prosthesis and shriek. Moreover, "[h]e was the very antithesis of the country's greatest prototype of the polio victim, FDR, disease having led Bucky not to triumph but to defeat" (429).

The "nemesis" of the title plainly signifies polio, "an infirmity that never ends" (438). But it also can be taken as speaking to the plot of counterlife at the core of so much of Roth's mature writing, the self-reflecting-self as its own implacable and retributive agent: "Maybe Bucky wasn't mistaken . . . Maybe he *was* the invisible arrow" (444). In the anagnorisis scene between erstwhile schoolboy and physical education teacher, the effects of polio are shown to have altered everything—all the "obstinacy and gutsy, spirited, strong-willed fortitude" (315) that once prompted his grandfather to rename ten-year old Eugene, "Bucky."

> The sharp planes of his face were padded by the weight he'd gained, so he was nowhere as striking as when the head beneath the tawny skin looked to be machined to the most rigorous rectilinear specifications—when it was a young man's head unabashedly asserting itself. That original face was now interred in another, fleshier face, a concealment people often see when looking with resignation at their aging selves in the mirror. No trace of the compact muscleman remained, the muscles having melted away while the compactness had burgeoned. (428)

His withered arm and withered leg present as metonymies for a wholesale withering away and truncation of personality: "Mostly Bucky considered himself a gender blank—as in a cartridge that is blank—an abashing self-assessment for a boy who'd come of age in an era of national suffering and strife when men were meant to be undaunted defenders of home and country" (429). Perhaps even more than Horace, Bucky stands out finally in the novel as a figure of deforming reduction and shriveled manhood, the very antithesis of not only FDR but also the image of him reflected back in a letter sent by his then-fiancée Marcia in 1944, in which the phrase "my man" is repeated two-hundred and eighteen times "in perfect Palmer Method cursive" (431).

The final, short section of *Nemesis* is entitled "Reunion." Its prose registers a profound decency, which is the phrase Mesnikoff uses to describe Bucky Cantor. To that extent, even though its elegiac frame recalls Roth's memoir of his dying father, the sentences remain perhaps just this side of the "notably pure" style of fiction that Robert Pinsky astutely identified in his review of *Patrimony*: "intellectual, ironic and practical in a European way, never straining for the seedy romantic lyricism of some American novelists" ("Letting Go"). Arnie Mesnikoff's register, certainly in this last section where it strikes a balance between the still laudably naïve and determinedly realist, is, I believe, a principled choice on Roth's part—even if the word "naïve" itself is reserved for Bucky's patronizing, bitterly tinged description of the long-lost Marcia.

In the final ode to Mr. Cantor's pre-polio athlete's self, one suspects we are to take the following earnest string of adjectives, in their staunch scout-oath fashion, sincerely and at face value: "he was, to all of us boys, the most exemplary and revered authority we knew, a young man of convictions, easygoing, kind, fairminded, thoughtful, stable, gentle, vigorous, muscular—a comrade and leader both" (444). The ode itself is a gorgeous prose poem—technically speaking, the author's true envoi to fiction-writing.

By contrast, after the first one-hundred page section of *Indignation* narrated by Marcus Messner himself, the novel concludes with a four-page addendum whose anonymous narrative voice, dutifully relating the circumstances of Marcus's death and of his parents' grief, is by turns acid, laconic, histrionic (in the single paragraph of free indirect style that retrieves Marcus's titular umbrage), and in its final paragraph-long sentence, scathingly Rothian ironic. As Derek Parker Royal has also remarked, Marcus already dramatized himself as less a character than a voice, which is, by turns, grim, sardonic, outraged, and artless—naïve in the cliché sense ("What to Make"). While the indignation he vents may recall the histrionics of Alex Portnoy, the reduction to voice—and just as significantly, to "memory alone" (131)—suggests a deeper novelistic investment: "Retelling my own story to myself round the clock in a clock-less world, lurking disembodied in this memory grotto, I feel as though I've been at it for a million years. Is this really to go on and on?" (131–132).

LATE STYLE REVISED

Royal construes this mimetic ploy as "the logical conclusion of various premises" in Roth's later fiction "that emphasize the inextricable links between memory, the narrating voice, and the creation of the subject" ("What to Make" 134). Thus, along with a number of other similarities *Indignation* shares with *Portnoy's Complaint*, Royal identifies "not only an indignation over the unjust treatments of their protagonists, but a form of literary indignation over the constraints of traditional realistic narrative" (136). If Roth's public comments about the work don't quite play up the device of a disembodied narrator—an analogue to the Flaubertian "trick" he deploys at the end of *Nemesis*—they do acknowledge that the technical problem he posed for himself in *Indignation* was "to get [Messner] into the War, and the whole book consists of my working out his fate so that he ends, winds up in, in the War" (*Web of Stories* 156).

That assertion that jibes with an *ars poetica* he supplies for his authorial practice generally: "I advance my understanding of the book by writing it," which not only militates against programmatic arguments about compositional unity but also leaves room for boxing with the book (Web of Stories 56). But if *Indignation* is read primarily as a late exercise in an overarching and persistent Rothian commitment to "the construction of the subject" (Royal's phrase), the question of late style itself either recedes or blurs into judgments about sustained vision and/or artistic decline ("What to Make" 136). *Pace* unifying schemas for Roth's thirty-one books, the idea that late works evince "a nonharmonious, nonserene tension, and above all, a deliberately unproductive productiveness going *against*" may yet capture some thread connecting these two texts besides that between fiction and memory or between voice and the constructed subject. That would be the deeper novelistic investment intimated above.

I've suggested that as youthful figures, Marcus and Buddy allow Roth, in career twilight, to restage an appeal stimulated by the minor and embodied in both the naïf and the naïve. I've invoked Schulz and Gombrowicz as Roth's modernist precursors outside the mainstream of Flaubert, Joyce *et alia*, because of the counter-terrain or district each proposes to the official topos of mature, fully adult, and finished forms. Thus, along with *Indignation*'s and *Nemesis*' conspicuous reduction of form, their stories—nostalgically backdated to periods of the author's youth in Newark (and thus in added contrast to the plots of the two other Nemeses)—mark both works as expressions of late style.

It would be too facile to propose a dialectic of naïve and sentimental, trust and suspicion, as pitched *between* or *balancing* the two novels, with *Nemesis* bodying forth the one, and *Indignation* the other. Rather, I think it fairer to say that each rehearses such tension within itself and to discernibly contrastive effect. *Indignation* intermeshes the two around the axiom that Marcus' father catechistically repeats, "the tiniest misstep can have tragic consequences" (108), which the novel all but mechanically proceeds to bear out. The sheer truthfulness of that maxim along the paralyzing fear it thereby licenses encapsulates the very entanglement of suspicion and trust. Narratorially speaking, *Nemesis* secures the edge as a drama *about* trust enacted on at least three planes: by Bucky Cantor in relation to an elevated ideal of his own capacities, by Arnie Mesnikoff in respect to the particulars of Bucky's story, and by readers in their counterpunching engagement with the book.

As if on order, each novel secretes its own pearl about late style. But I emphasize the "as if"; a writer of prodigious intertextual and technical gifts, Roth for the most part eschews the impulse, à la Joyce or Nabokov, to encode or encrypt. Marcus' disreputable roommate in his early days at Winesburg College is a certain Betram Flusser: mimic, farceur, slovenly, acerbic, antinomian, "a gargoyle" (203), given to compulsive late-night reiterations of Malvolio's line from *Twelfth Night*, "I'll be revenged on the whole pack of you!," and after-hours playing of a recording of Beethoven's famous Quartet in F Major, whose ignominious fate Marcus records as follows: "I rose screaming from my bunk to yank a phonograph record of his from the turntable and, in the most violent act I'd ever perpetrated, to smash it against the wall" (114). Fittingly enough for our purposes, that composition, Opus 135, was Beethoven's last substantial work,[27] meditated on by Adorno and Said, the one whose internal signpost for the finale, *der schwer gefasste entschluss* [the difficult or weighty resolution], Milan Kundera (in elective affinity with Roth) interprets as a joke turned into a metaphysical truth (*Unbearable* 195).

Might Marcus' smashing of the record accomplish something like the reverse, in possibly sly rebuke to studious accounts of Rothian late style? Probably not, but I let the question stand, anyway. As to *Nemesis*, is not Bucky Cantor's tragic self-enthrallment to guilty, monkish penance a perverse twist on lateness itself, in Said's words, the idea of surviving beyond what is acceptable and normal: "One cannot really go beyond lateness at all, cannot transcend or lift oneself out of lateness," he adds. One can only "deepen" it (13). Therein are Mr. Cantor's own trust and suspicion entwined, as if in grotesque parody of the caduceus, the common symbol of American medicine and healthcare, which, however, is itself erroneously (naïvely?) confused with the rod of Asclepius, with its single snake and staff embodying the uncanny paradox—like naïve twinned with sentimental—of the *pharmakon*: both remedy and contagion.

NOTES

1. Pierpont cites the March, 2011 interview for *Web of Stories* 158, www .webofstories.com/play/philip.roth/158.

2. Matthew Shipe, "*Exit Ghost* and the Politics of 'Late Style,'" *Philip Roth Studies* (Fall, 2009), 189–204, which reads the novella as all but allegorizing some of the attributes Said (and Updike) assign to the artist nearing his end, e.g., "as a figure for lateness itself, an untimely, scandalous, even catastrophic commentary on the present" (Said, 14), and the comparatively less ambitious essay by Alex Hobbs, "Resisting Conformity in Philip Roth's Late Writing," *EnterText* 12 (2014), 58–72.

3. Roth has wondered aloud publicly about this very question, citing the model of late Bellow (*The Actual, The Bellarosa Connection*): "when you're reducing and reducing, how do you do it?" See the online interview in multiple parts on *Web of Stories: Philip Roth* no. 30 www.webofstories.com/play/philip.roth/30 and no. 35 www.webofstories.com/play/ philip.roth/35.

4. Wyatt Mason, "I Buried a Novelist: Philip Roth and the End of Zuckerman" *Harpers* Vol 39, Num 1889 (October, 2007), 105–110 http://harpers.org /archive/2007/10/i-buried-a-novelist/; Bharat Tandon, "Philip Roth and the Consolations of Denouement," *TLS* (September 26, 2007), 21–22.

5. The pronouncement also appears as one of the epigraphs to Shipe's essay.

6. The title of his first book, *Pamiętnik z okresu dojrzewania* published in 1933, re-released with three more short stories as *Bakakaj* in 1957, and cited by the original title internally by the narrator of *Ferdydurke* (1937).

7. The phrase belongs to Lucien Lévy-Bruhl, as developed in *How Natives Think*, trans. Lilian A. Clare, London, 1926 (1912), and adapted by Jung in *Psychological Types, Collected Works, Volume 6* (Princeton: Princeton University Press, 1971).

8. In explaining a no-longer innocent relation to one's own authorship, Josipovici cites Kierkegaard's *The Book on Adler*: "For though it is indeed by writing that one justifies the claim to be an author, it is also, strangely enough, by writing that one virtually renounces this claim . . . To find the conclusion, it is quite necessary first of all to observe that it is lacking, and then to feel quite vividly the lack of it." Trans. Walter Lowrie (New York: Everyman, 1994), 114.

9. Both Schulz and Gombrowicz number among the Polish, Czech, Yugoslav, and Hungarian authors Roth recuperated in his capacity as general editor of the *Writers from the Other Europe* series 1974 though 1989.

10. The prosthesis as metaphor is the subject of Leona Toker, "Between Dystopia and Allohistory: The Ending of Roth's *The Plot Against America*," *Philip Roth Studies* Vol. 9, No. 1 (Spring 2013), 41–50. On wider critical implications of the prosthesis trope, see *Narrative Prosthesis: Disability and the Dependencies of Discourse*, ed. David T. Mitchell and Sharon L. Snyder (Ann Arbor: University of Michigan Press, 2001).

11. Marc Shell's *Polio and Its Aftermath: The Paralysis of Culture* (Cambridge: Harvard University Press, 2005) remains the authoritative source on the cultural context of illness and disability here. Although its framing dichotomy of historicist vs. allegorical readings of the novel unnecessarily flattens the complex overlap of these categories across the arc of Roth's fiction, Adam P. Newman, "Polio and the Body Politics of Assimilation in Philip Roth's "Nemesis," *Jahrbuch Literatur und Medizin* 6 (Spring 2014), Special Section on Posture, Literature and Culture edited by Sander Gilman, 177–190, also treats this topic.

12. On this thread, see John G. Rodwan Jr., "The Fighting Life: Boxing and Identity in Novels by Philip Roth and Norman Mailer," *Philip Roth Studies* Vol. 7, No 1 (Spring 2011), 83–96, Kasia Boddy, *Boxing: A Cultural History* (London: Reaktion books, 20008), and Patrick Hayes, *Philip Roth: Fiction and Power* (Oxford; Oxford University Press, 2014), 19–20. There's also Roth's own oft-quoted aside in an interview with Hermione Lee, "I knew what I was doing when I broke Zuckerman's jaw. For a Jew a broken jaw is a terrible tragedy. It was to avoid this that so many of us went into teaching rather than prizefighting." "The Art of Fiction No. 84," *The Paris Review* 93 (1984) www.theparisreview.org/ interviews/2957/the-art-of-fiction-no-84-philip-roth.

13. The diminution I want to isolate here differs from instances of adult infantilization in Roth's major characters that we can detect as early as in "Eli the Fanatic" and as late as *Everyman.*

14. On the Schulz connection, see Russell E. Brown, "Philip Roth and Bruno Schulz," *ANQ: A Quarterly Journal of Short Articles, Notes and Reviews* Volume 6, Issue 4 (1993), 211–214, and (with Gombrowicz and Kundera) Ross Posnock's *Philip Roth's Rude Truth: The Art of Immaturity* (Princeton: Princeton University Press, 2006), 61–66 and 80–81.

15. The phrase comes from Gombrowicz's *Diary.* See *Roth's Rude Truth*, 62 and 87.

16. In his review of *Nemesis*, Tim Parks observes of the novel's four heroes, "All were born around the same time as Roth, so that the novels of old age are set in the contemporary world and the novels of young adulthood in the 1940s and 1950s."

Tim Parks, "The Truth about Consuela," *London Review of Books*, Vol. 32 No. 21 (4 November 2010), 17–18 www.lrb.co.uk/v32/n21/tim-parks/the-truth-about-consuela.

17. They are Helen of Troy and Clytemnestra, and the Dioscuri (Castor and Pollux), according to source-texts like the *Bibliotheca* (Pseudo-Apollodorus, 1st-2nd century BCE) and the anonymous *Kypria* (7th century BCE).

18. Compare, for instance, the peach-eating scene in *Nemesis* with the famous Patimkin refrigerator in *Goodbye, Columbus* and their dual apotheosis of the "pit."

19. See Russell E. Brown, "Back to School in Poland: A Shared Motif of Witold Gombrowicz and Bruno Schulz," *The Polish Review* Vol. 32, No. 2 (1987), 175–179.

20. His eyesight is as poor as his stature is short. Moreover, as Deresiewicz sharply observes about the scene in which Bucky is compelled to dispatch a rat in the basement of his grandfather's grocery, "It is Homer in Newark again. The story of the rat is a working-class version of the celebrated story of Odysseus's scar."

21. See the review, "The Enemy Within" by Avi Steinberg in *Haaretz* (Nov. 5, 2010) www.haaretz.com/life/books/fiction-the-enemy-within-1.323129 which also correctly pinpoints the direct line from *The Plot Against America* to *Nemesis*: "By locating the conflict of self at an invisible, pathogenic starting point, *Nemesis* goes even further into the interior than the political horror imagined in *The Plot Against America*."

22. J. M. Coetzee makes a similar point about a subgenre of fiction associated with Defoe and Camus in his review of *Nemesis* in *The New York Review of Books*, "On the Moral Brink," October 28, 2010) www.nybooks.com/articles/ archives/2010/oct/28/moral-brink/?pagination=false.

23. The concept is analyzed at length in Andreas Schönle, *"Cinnamon Shops* by Bruno Schulz: The Apology of *Tandeta*," *The Polish Review* Vol. 36, No. 2 (1991), 127–144.

24. See *Web of Stories: Philip Roth* no. 41 http://www.webofstories.com/play/philip.roth/41 and also "Polio Breaks Out In Newark In Roth's *Nemesis*," NPR (5 October, 2010) www.npr.org/2010/10/05/ 130353198/polio-breaks-out-in-newark-in-roths-nemesis.

25. In a chapter on Roth and Kundera from *Modernist Futures: Innovation and Inheritance in the Contemporary Novel*, David James offers an excellent analysis of the intentionally "two-dimensional" timbre of narration here, "a register that renews the political force of a vital component in Conrad's aesthetic[,] Roth makes us see how stoicism operates ideologically when it becomes not so much an individual's trait as a mark of the cultural inscription and enslavement of individuality" (52).

26. Deresiewicz is acute on the mechanics of naming here where "a Flusser, a Cottler, a Ziegler, and a Spector" are not only "the names of agents, doers of action" but also "the names of occupations either working-class or Jewish . . . that evoke the world of Newark's Jewish fathers as Roth has built it up across his oeuvre, but especially in the nostalgic works of recent years."

27. On both compositions, one fundamentally "nostalgic" and the other always thwarting expectations, see K. M. Knittel "'Late', Last, and Least: On Being Beethoven's Quartet in F Major, op. 135," *Music & Letters* Vol. 87, No. 1 (Jan., 2006), 16–51.

WORKS CITED

Aarons, Victoria. "Expelled Once Again: The Failure of the Fantasized Self in Philip Roth's *Nemesis.*" *Philip Roth Studies* 9.1 (2013): 51–63.

Alpers, Paul. "Schiller's Naïve and Sentimental Poetry and the Modern Idea of Pastoral." *Cabinet of the Muses: Rosenmeyer Festschrift.* Ed. M. Griffith and D. J. Mastronarde. City: Scholars Press, 1990. 319–331.

Arnheim, Rudolf. "On the Late Style." *New Essays on the Psychology of Art.* Berkeley: University of California Press, 1986. 286–294.

Boddy, Kasia. *Boxing: A Cultural History.* London: Reaktion Books, 2008.

Boym, Svetlana. *The Future of Nostalgia.* New York: Basic Books, 2001.

Brauner, David. *Philip Roth.* Manchester: Manchester University Press, 2007.

Brown, Russell E. "Back to School in Poland: A Shared Motif of Witold Gombrowicz and Bruno Schulz." *The Polish Review* 32.2 (1987): 175–179.

———. "Philip Roth and Bruno Schulz." *ANQ: A Quarterly Journal of Short Articles, Notes and Reviews* 6.4 (1993): 211–214.

Chouard, Géraldine. "Fantasmes et fantômes dans *Sabbath's Theater* de Philip Roth." *Eros en Amérique*, 1 January 2003. https://erea.revues.org/142.

Coetzee, J. M. "On the Moral Brink." *The New York Review of Books*, 28 October 2010 www.nybooks.com/articles/ archives/2010/oct/28/moral-brink/? pagination=false.

Cohen, Leah Hager. "Summer of '44." *New York Times Sunday Book Review*, 8 October2010. http://www.nytimes.com/2010/10/10/books/review/Cohen-t.html? _r=0.

Deresiewicz, William. "Portnoy Agonistes: *Nemesis* by Philip Roth." *The New Republic*, 2 December 2010. 26–27 www.newrepublic.com/article/books-and-arts/ magazine/79073/portnoy-agonistes-philip-roth.

Gianopoulos, Panio. "Philip Roth: A Eulogy for a Living Man." *Salon*, 10 November 2012 http://www.salon.com/2012/11/10/philip_roth_a_eulogy_for_a_living_man/.

Głowacka, Dorota. "The Heresiarchs of Form: Gombrowicz and Schulz." Ewa Plonowska Ziarek, ed. *Gombrowicz's Grimaces: Modernism, Gender, Nationality.* Albany: SUNY Press, 1998. 65–88.

Goddard, Michael. *Gombrowicz, Polish Modernism, and the Subversion of Form.* West Lafayette: Purdue University Press, 2010.

Gombrowicz, Witold. *Bakakay.* Trans. Bill Johnston. New York; Archipelago, 2006.

———. *Diary.* Trans. Lillian Vallee. New Haven: Yale University Press, 2012.

———. *Polish Memories.* Trans. Bill Johnston. New Haven: Yale University Press, 2004.

Gooblar, David. *The Major Phases of Philip Roth.* London, New York: Continuum, 2011.

Hayes, Patrick. *Philip Roth: Fiction and Power.* Oxford: Oxford University Press, 2014.

Hobbs, Alex. "Resisting Conformity in Philip Roth's Late Writing." *EnterText* 12 (2014): 58–72.

James, David. *Modernist Futures: Innovation and Inheritance in the Contemporary Novel*. Cambridge: Cambridge University Press, 2012.

Jeffrey, Ben. "What's Next Isn't the Point: Philip Roth in Age." *The Quarterly Conversation* 25 (September 6, 2011) http://quarterlyconversation.com/whats-next-isnt-the-point-philip-roth-in-age.

Josipovici, Gabriel. *On Trust: Art and the Temptations of Suspicion*. New Haven: Yale University Press, 1999.

Jung. Carl. *Psychological Types*, Collected Works, Volume 6. Princeton: Princeton University Press, 1971.

Kaplan, Brett Ashley. *Jewish Anxiety and the Novels of Philip Roth*. New York: Bloomsbury, 2015.

Kierkegaard, Søren. *The Book on Adler*. Trans. Walter Lowrie. New York: Everyman, 1994.

Kimmage, Michael. *In History's Grip: Philip Roth's Newark Trilogy*. Stanford: Stanford University Press, 2012.

Knittel, K. M. "'Late,' Last, and Least: On Being Beethoven's Quartet in F Major, op. 135." *Music & Letters* 87.1 (January 2006): 16–51.

Kundera, Milan. *The Unbearable Lightness of Being*. Trans Michael Henry Heim. New York: Harper Collins,1984.

Mason, Wyatt. "I Buried a Novelist: Philip Roth and the End of Zuckerman." *Harpers* 39.1889 (October 2007): 105–110 http://harpers.org/archive/2007/10/i-buried-a-novelist/.

Mitchell, David T. and Sharon L. Snyder, eds. *Narrative Prosthesis: Disability and the Dependencies of Discourse*. Ann Arbor: University of Michigan Press, 2001.

Newman, Adam. "Polio and the Body Politics of Assimilation in Philip Roth's "Nemesis." *Jahrbuch Literatur und Medizin* 6 (Spring 2014): 177–190.

Parks, Tim. "The Truth about Consuela." *London Review of Books* 32.21 (4 November 2010): 17–18. http://www.lrb.co.uk/v32/n21/tim-parks/the-truth-about-consuela.

Parrish, Timothy. *The Cambridge Companion to Philip Roth*. Cambridge: Cambridge University Press, 2007.

Pierpont, Claudia Roth. *Roth Unbound: A Writer and His Books*. New York: Macmillan, 2013.

Pinsky, Robert. "Letting Go." *New York Times Book Review*. 6 January 1991. 1 www.nytimes.com/ books /98/10/11/specials/roth-patrimony.html

Posnock, Ross. *Philip Roth's Rude Truth: The Art of Immaturity*. Princeton: Princeton University Press, 2006.

Pozorski, Aimee. *Roth and Trauma: The Problem of History in the Later Works (1995–2010)*. New York: Continuum Press, 2012.

Rodwan Jr., John G. "The Fighting Life: Boxing and Identity in Novels by Philip Roth and Norman Mailer." *Philip Roth Studies* 7.1 (Spring 2011): 83–96.

Roth, Philip. *American Pastoral*. Boston: Houghton Mifflin, 1997.

———. "The Art of Fiction No. 84: Interview with Hermione Lee." *The Paris Review* 93 (1984) http://www.theparisreview.org/interviews/2957/the-art-of-fiction-no-84-philip-roth.

————. *Exit Ghost*. Boston: Houghton Mifflin, 2007.

————. *I Married a Communist*. Boston: Houghton Mifflin, 1998.

————. *Nemeses: Everyman / Indignation / The Humbling / Nemesis*. New York: Library of America, 2013.

————. *Operation Shylock: A Confession*. New York: Simon & Schuster, 1983.

————. *Sabbath's Theater*. Boston: Houghton Mifflin, 1995.

————. *The Plot Against America.* Boston: Houghton Mifflin, 2004.

Royal, Derek Parker. *Philip Roth: New Perspectives on an American Author.* Westport, CT: Greenwood-Praeger, 2005.

————."What to Make of Roth's *Indignation*; Or, Serious in the Fifties: Review Essay." *Philip Roth Studies* (Spring 2009): 129–137.

Safer, Elaine B. *Mocking the Age: The Later Novels of Philip Roth*. Albany: State University of New York Press, 2006.

Said, Edward. *On Late Style: Music and Literature Against the Grain*. New York: Pantheon, 2006.

Schiller, Friedrich. *Naive and Sentimental Poetry, and On the Sublime: Two Essays.* Trans. Julius A. Elias. New York: Frederick Ungar, 1967.

————. *Werke und Briefe*. Band 8. Frankfurt a Main: Deutscher Klassiker Verlag, 1992.

Schönle, Andreas. "*Cinnamon Shops* by Bruno Schulz: The Apology of *Tandeta*." *The Polish Review* 36. 2 (1991): 127–144.

Schulz, Bruno. *The Collected Works of Bruno Schulz*. Ed. Jerzy Ficowski. New York: Picador, 1998.

Shechner, Mark. *Up Society's Ass, Copper: Rereading Philip Roth*. Madison: University of Wisconsin, 2003.

Shell, Marc. *Polio and Its Aftermath: The Paralysis of Culture*. Cambridge: Harvard University Press, 2005.

Shipe, Matthew. "*Exit Ghost* and the Politics of 'Late Style.'" *Philip Roth Studies* (Fall 2009):189–204.

Showalter, Elaine. "Philip Roth, Albert Camus, and Plagues." *Readers' Almanac*, 10 October 2010 http://blog.loa.org/2010/10/philip-roth-albert-camus-and-plagues.html.

Steinberg, Avi. "The Enemy Within." *Haaretz*, 5 November 2010 http://www.haaretz.com/life/ books/fiction-the-enemy-within-1.323129.

Tandon, Bharat "Philip Roth and the Consolations of Denouement." *The Times Literary Supplement*, 26 September 2007. 21–22.

Toker, Leona. "Between Dystopia and Allohistory: The Ending of Roth's *The Plot Against America.*" *Philip Roth Studies* 9.1 (Spring 2013): 41–50.

Wood, James. "The Monk of Fornication: Philip Roth's Nihilism." *The Broken Estate: Essays on Literature and Belief*. New York: Modern Library, 1999. 216–228.

Updike, John. "Late Works: Writers and Artists Confronting the End." *The New Yorker*, 7 August 2006. 64–71. Collected in *Due Consideration: Essays and Criticism*. New York: Random House, 2007. 49–67. *Web of Stories: Philip Roth* http://www.webofstories.com/play/philip.roth/.

Chapter Ten

"[Sticking] to a plan completely"[1]

Performance, Affective Adaptation, Memory, Pretend Play and Suicide in Philip Roth's **The Humbling**[2]

Amy Gelbart

All the world is not, of course, a stage, but the crucial ways in which it isn't aren't easy to specify

—Erving Goffman, 1959[3]

Why do some people stick to their plans even when the results are unsatisfactory, disastrous, or clearly lead them away from the results they wish to attain, while others change direction, adjust and adapt to the changing circumstances that shape their existence? Why do authors relegate their fictional characters to similar fates? Some characters reinvent themselves while others bang their fictional heads against fictional walls. The present essay offers an interdisciplinary approach to the question: Why are we readers transfixed by these tensions? In so doing, it draws on methods from three very distinct disciplines: literary theory, performance theory, and cognitive science.[4]

Examining Philip Roth's *The Humbling* (2009) using these disciplines, I will elucidate the points of convergence between performance and improvisation, episodic and semantic memory, and affective adaptation and pretend play, and subsequently make plain the underlying roles of these components in propelling the novel to its seemingly avoidable conclusion. I posit that episodic remembering functions as a trigger that actuates Simon Axler's final deadly performance, and I demonstrate how this unlocks a process that leads to the acquisition of a new skill—pretend play—that temporarily restores and releases him, granting him the potential to change his dismal direction, or even to reinvent himself. Rather than availing himself of this opportunity, however, Axler utilizes the patently constructive tool of pretend play and sticks to his ruinous plan to bring about his own demise.

For the duration of this paper, I will ask you to join me on a cognitive-performative journey into *The Humbling*. From masterful improviser and "feeler" to paralyzed "observer" and "knower" who subsequently transforms into a pretend player, Axler traverses a performative continuum that is informed by performance theory, affective adaptation, episodic and semantic memory, and pretend play (Schechner 316). After a number of false starts, Axler succeeds in affectively adapting to his changed circumstances, setting a destructive plan in motion, and thereby attaining his goal. He imagines and then carries out his suicide. Author and pretender Roth initiates this trajectory, and we play along because it imitates familiar human behavior and stretches our imagination.

Cognitive literary theorists such as Alan Palmer claim that characters live in fictional worlds of their authors' and readers' creation, and have "fictional minds" that function in ways that resemble human minds (184).[5] These fictional minds emerge when humans use their "Theory of Mind" to understand and interpret other humans' and fictional characters' "thoughts, feelings, beliefs and desires" (Zunshine 6).[6] This offers an explanation of how, despite the limited amount of information readers acquire from the written text, they are able to interpret, draw conclusions, and understand the fictional worlds they encounter in texts. As Steven Pinker observes, "[c]haracters in a fictitious world do exactly what our intelligence allows us to do in the real world" (541). Authors often place their characters "in hypothetical situation[s] in an otherwise real world where ordinary facts and laws hold" (Pinker 541). Characters' minds function as human minds do, allowing the readers to relate and comprehend fictional narratives even when they possess very little information. Human beings are wired to fill in the gaps, identify inconsistencies and draw conclusions in everyday life, and literary characters (created by their human authors) do so as well.[7]

Philip Roth introduces the reader to Simon Axler without ceremony. A master of spontaneity and creativity, Axler has spent a lifetime transforming effortlessly from one character to the next as he acts and reacts to his ever-changing environment. The novel opens abruptly when one morning, this famous, aging stage actor wakes up to discover that his "magic" has deserted him (*Humbling* 1). An identity constructed from decades of virtuoso stage performances, scripted as well as improvised, has suddenly and without explanation been erased as if it never existed.

From a very young age, Axler is already developing into what performance theorists such as Richard Schechner consider a "skilled performer," who has "three halves" (295). Schechner's description evokes an image of people performing, acting out roles, and navigating the unsteady sea of interacting human minds: essential elements in defining the human experience. Schechner's project in his *Performance Theory* describes performances that transcend "culture" and "genre," that stretch along a continuum from ritual to everyday life to play performances, some that take only a moment and others that last a lifetime (256). Adapting Schechner's continuum for my own heuristic purposes, I appropriate his description of literary performers such as Simon Axler, according to his elucidation of the "skilled performer."[8]

> a skilled performer has "three halves," . . . the "center" of the performer, the "I," stands outside *observing* and to some degree controlling both the *knower* and the *feeler*. Clearly a complex operation engages both the cognitive and the affective systems simultaneously, without either one washing out the other. A similar "triple state" accompanies some kinds of trance, while in other kinds of trance the feelings may be so powerful that they blot out entirely both the "knowing half" and the *"observing/controlling"* half of the performer. (316, emphasis added)

The observer is a witness of sorts, peeking in from outside, watching and controlling, always aware of the performance; the knower is aware that he portrays something fictional and imaginary that might be considered a deception under other circumstances; and the feeler, who is fully present, is convinced that he is portraying a truth. These "three halves" can be configured in various proportions, creating a performative continuum, with the actor entering an improvisational zone or "trance-like state" when the feeler portion becomes so powerful that it nearly blots out both the knower and the observer, with the other extreme being when the knower and observer portions grow in size and virtually extinguish the feeler. Stated differently, at one extreme is the performer who is "fully taken in by his own act," while "[a]t the other extreme, we find . . . [that] the performer may not be taken in at all by his own routine" (Goffman 17). In the center of these two extremes lies a semblance of balance between the "three halves." This continuum informs Axler's performance.

From a young age, Axler acquires the abilities of—and portrays the skills of—a performer, transforming from role to role as if every performance both behind and in front of the curtain is his real life. Indeed, for decades his "everyday life is framed and performed" (Schechner 296). He has continually existed on the border between real and imagined: "It had started with people speaking to him. He couldn't have been more than three or four when he was already mesmerized by speaking and *being spoken to*. He had felt he was in a play from the outset. He could use *intensity of listening*, concentration, as lesser actors used fireworks" (*Humbling* 3, emphasis added).

Improvising involves entering a creative state, where profound listening and keen responding are critical, and active collaboration with whoever is participating leads to the creation of something new, unpredictable, and unexpected. This entails working without a plan or a script, living in the moment, being intuitive, and focusing on the process and not the product. Axler lives the art of improvisation, the "creation of an artifact and/or performance with aesthetic goals in real-time that is not completely prescribed in terms of functional and/ or content constraints" (Magerko et al. 117). Rather than function on content, improvisation utilizes tools of deep listening, empathy, awareness, collabora- tion, intuition, and the capacity instantly to transform into a character without a clear set of cues and sufficient information. Roth's description of Axler's development employs many of the tools of improvisation.

Before he loses his ability to act, Axler's performance is without thought or preparation. His acting is an experience of "wait[ing] for the freedom to begin and the moment to become *real*" as "he waited to forget who he was and to become the person doing it" (*Humbling* 3, emphasis added). Thus Roth reveals Axler's process of becoming the character and the construction of his identity. He is "sincerely convinced that the impression of reality which he stages is the real reality" (Goffman 17). Axler lives his life as if it is a perpetual performance. His identity is constructed on the basis of his repeat- edly successful improvisational performances.[9] He cannot recognize himself anymore (*Humbling* 16).

In addition, we are told that Axler continually redefines and reconstructs his narrative off the stage. He assists women in finding their own unique narrative, and helps them realize "that they had a story, a voice, and a style belonging to no other. They became actresses with Axler, they became the heroines of their own lives" (*Humbling* 4). Axler will enact this type of im- provisation later and briefly succeed with Pegeen, the middle-aged daughter of old actor friends with whom he has a relationship.

One day, Axler faces an existential crisis. He discovers that he can no longer inhabit the improvisational space between the real and imagined. He cannot act:

> All that had worked to *make him himself* now worked to make him look like a lunatic. He was *conscious* of every moment he was on the stage in the worst possible way. In the past when he was acting he wasn't *thinking* about anything. Now he was thinking about everything and everything *spontaneous* and vital was killed—he tried to control it with thinking and instead he destroyed it. (*Humbling* 2, emphasis added)

Axler has been accustomed to propelling himself forward from role to role, constructing and reconstructing his identity. Now, when acting and reacting is no longer an option, he is trapped in a self-conscious thought mode. The same actions and reactions lead to disastrous results. He does not believe anymore. He is no longer "sincere."[10] He flees to the world of thought, only to discover that thinking solves nothing.[11] He finds his life is "an act, a bad act" (*Humbling* 5). As his cue to come onstage approaches, he "*know[s]*" that he will fail and he observes himself having a mental breakdown (*Humbling* 3, 5, emphasis added). His thoughts terrify him: "When you're playing the role of somebody coming apart, it has organization and order; when you're *observing* yourself coming apart, playing the role of your own demise, that's something else, awash with terror and fear" (emphasis added). In "excruciating pain," unable to eat or sleep, he assiduously disbelieves the validity of his experience (5).

Axler has become the observer and the knower, the ineffectual "liar," the "fraud" (33). He has been banished from his trance-like state, and questions whether these new feelings and experiences are "genuine" (5). The actor who has spent his entire career making his performances real now doubts the authenticity of his breakdown. The only identity he has ever possessed is based primarily on the feeler portion of his psyche and it seems to have "melted . . . into thin air" (7).

In his desperation at this altered state of events, deep in thought, Axler contrives an alternative to his previous existence. He plans to commit suicide. He thinks about climbing the steps into his attic and shooting himself with his shotgun. Failed actor that he is, he observes himself from the side and finds himself unfit. He is caught up in the world of thought, "paralyzed" and suspended, all action inconceivable (14).

Unable to follow through with his plan, he checks into a psychiatric hospital. Axler is faced with "a self-relevant unexplained event": his inability to act (Wilson and Gilbert 371). At the age of 65, he has lost touch with the identity that he has constructed over a lifetime. Here, he reflects: "To cease so precipitously being the actor he was—it was *inexplicable*, as though he'd *been disarmed of the weight and substance of his professional existence one night while he slept*" (11, emphasis added). He has lost "[t]he ability to speak and be spoken to on a stage," and is bereft of his improvisational skills (11). No explanation is provided for this event, nor are the implications for his personal existence explored.

Cognitive psychologists Timothy Wilson and Daniel Gilbert suggest that humans respond to unexpected, unusual events by utilizing what they have dubbed "affective adaptation" skills (Wilson and Gilbert 370). The more unexpected and inexplicable the event, the more likely it will pack a large emotional punch. These types of events are also more liable to be remembered until they are "explained away" and understood (Wilson and Gilbert 370). Under ordinary circumstances, humans "attend" to the inexplicable, shocking event, "react" emotionally, search for a cause, and "explain" it. They then begin to "adapt" to the new situation (Wilson and Gilbert 371). Wilson and Gilbert have coined the acronym AREA: Attend, React, Explain, and Adapt (371). Ordinarily, once individuals have understood and internalized the event, they adapt it to their "self-concept" and can predict that it might happen again (373). When "self-relevant events" have been understood, the "extraordinary becomes commonplace and these events no longer elicit strong affective reactions" (370). Research shows that the individuals who recover most rapidly from traumatic events are those who find meaning. When such an occurrence is reintroduced, they do not respond with the same intensity of emotion. If humans are unable to understand or explain these events, the events cannot be reconciled and stored for further use, and the cycle is incomplete, which leaves the individual in a highly emotional state (Wilson and Gilbert 376, 374).

This explanation provides a cognitive account for Axler's "breakdown." Devastated and overwhelmed by the loss of his magic, he endeavors to "attend" to it. This is certainly the most unanticipated and incomprehensible incident that he has ever experienced, and so it remains prominent in his memory. He cannot follow the model of "affective adaptation" through to its conclusion. His affect remains high and he is incapable of reacting, explaining, and adapting; paralyzed, he cannot function.

Checking into a psychiatric hospital, Axler "remember[s] role after role that he ha[s] played with absolute assurance since he'd become a professional in his early twenties" (10). He uses his long-term memory to revisit events in his past and to explain and adapt himself to them. Searching for the cause during therapy with Dr. Farr should help him identify the reason, and move him toward healing. However, Farr and Axler fail. He has certainly attended to the inexplicable event, and has endeavored to react. He is struck by the "omnipotence of caprice," the causelessness of his circumstances (*Humbling* 17). He has failed abysmally at trying to explain and he certainly cannot resiliently adapt himself to the new situation. Cognitive theories of episodic and semantic long-term memory provide a way to understand why his attempts at rehabilitating himself prove unsuccessful at this point in the novel.

Cognitive neuroscientists have divided long-term memory into two categories, one of which subdivides into episodic and semantic memory.[12] With episodic memories, the "role of rememberer" is vital, and the rememberer functions as a time traveler of sorts (Baddeley 1348; Tulving, "From Mind to Brain" 3). This kind of remembering has been proven critically important not only for reliving the past, but also for imagining and simulating future events. The same portions of the brain that are involved with reviving past events help plan future events (Schacter et al. 657). In other words, episodic remembering allows the individual to travel back in time to feel and re-experience an event. The significance of episodic memory is in its cognitive capability to bring the "the past into the present" and thus influence the future (Tulving, "From Mind to Brain" 7, 14).

Semantic memories, on the other hand, are stored memories of scientific fact, "culturally shared knowledge," (Klein et al. 491) and "general" information about the world that remains unchallenged by the rememberer (Tulving, "Common Sense" 1506). To distinguish between semantic and episodic memory more clearly, semantic memory is used to recall that each day consists of a twenty-four hour period. It is unlikely that an individual will remember who taught her that, what she felt, or where or when she was when she learned it.[13] Endel Tulving states that "[t]he essential difference is between *knowing* that something is such and such, or occurs so and so, on the one hand, and *remembering* that one had a particular experience (witnessed, or felt, or thought something) in a particular place at a particular time" ("Autonoesis" 16, emphasis added).

We are faced here with a convergence of terminologies between episodic and semantic memory and the "skilled performer." During episodic remembering, the feeler actively re-experiences the event. Using semantic memory, the knower remembers the events without accessing the feelings and senses. Axler *knows* that he has played many different roles. Sitting alone in the psychiatric hospital, the first thing he does is remember briefly every role he has played. However, he does not *feel* or re-experience them. There is no reference to the time, place, or feelings evoked. His recollection resembles a "collated series of events in summary form."[14] As a result, though he searches for the cause, it is of no avail, and he dubs himself a "self-travesty," a warped, false, and absurd representation of himself (*Humbling* 10). During his sessions with Dr. Farr, they both search for a trigger or a cause. But Axler remains on a semantic level of remembering, not reliving the roles by "time traveling." Only later in the novel will he draw upon his episodic memory, and then it will be directly related to his ability to devise and complete future plans. Right now, he remains on the level of semantic remembering, *knowing* but not *feeling* the events, and he finds no cause for the loss of his magic.

Released from the psychiatric hospital, Axler immediately reverts back to his suicidal thoughts. A friendly visit from his agent, Jerry Oppenheim, leads Axler to revisit a very significant episodic memory that will eventually lead him to act in one final performance. During his visit, Oppenheim sets out to convince Axler that his predicament stems from a temporary loss of confidence. Axler is not convinced, for he perceives all of his successes and failures in acting as part of a meaningless life that's "a fluke from start to finish" (*Humbling* 33). Axler claims that the only thing that he can do on stage is "tell the audience, 'I am a liar. And I can't even lie well. I am a fraud'" (33). Axler knows that he can no longer act. "No, it's gone, Jerry. I can't do any of it again. You're either free or you aren't. You're either free and it's genuine, it's real, it's alive, or it's nothing. I'm not free anymore" (30). When Jerry presses him to reconsider, Axler recollects his beginnings as an actor. When he first commenced training, he discovered his acting abilities were limited:

> I remember that when I began taking class we'd have a *pretend* teacup and *pretend* to drink from it. How hot is it, how full is it, is there a saucer, is there a spoon, are you going to put sugar in it, how many lumps. And then you sip it, and others were transported by this stuff, *but I never found any of it helpful.* What's more, *I couldn't do it.* I was no good at the exercises, no good at all. (*Humbling* 37, emphasis added)

Axler travels back to visit this episodic memory. He remembers where the event took place, how it caused him to feel. He recalls this "past experience" with a "vivid and evocative description" (Boritz et al.). Precisely the tool that assists some actors to transform into their roles, that transports them into an alternate reality where they co-exist in both real and imagined worlds, Axler cannot use successfully.

His explanation for this inability is telling: "Everything I did well was coming out of *instinct*, and doing those exercises and *knowing* those things—were making me look like an actor. I would look ridiculous as I held my pretend teacup and pretended to drink from it. There was always a *sly voice* inside me saying, 'There is no teacup'" (*Humbling* 37–38, emphasis added). Revealing his speculation into his current state, Axler describes the disappearance of his "magic" to Oppenheim in light of his pretend play experience: "Well, that *sly voice* has now *taken over*. No matter how I prepare and what I attempt to do, once I am on the stage there is that *sly voice* all the time—'There is no teacup'" (38, emphasis added).

Games of pretend, exercises that free other actors, did not assist Axler at the beginning of his acting career, nor do they help him revive his "magic" now. Axler has not only revived a painful episodic memory, he has also provided himself with an explanation of his inexplicable event from the model of "affective adaptation." He has time-traveled back to his earlier life and discovered a cause for his downfall; the "sly voice" that prevented him in the past from using make-believe as a tool to transform his acting has reemerged, banishing him to the other side of the performative continuum where the feeler is shrunk to a minimum and the observer and knower expand to occupy the space in his head. He has become self-conscious. Not only has he "attended" and "reacted" to this inexplicable event by experiencing a mental breakdown and contemplating suicide, he has now "explained" it to himself. What remains of the process is for him to "adapt." Concurrently, revisiting this episodic memory begins to unlock his ability to plan for the future, leading to "the construction of new personal meanings in the context of important life events, in turn leading to new ways of viewing the self and identity reconstruction" (Boritz et al.).

As a result of the opening up of this episodic memory, in the final portion of the novel Axler adapts by pretending. Since he is no longer "free" to perform as in the past, as a last resort he tries twice to use the tool that has not served him well in the past. First, he fails when attempting to reconstruct his life through pretend play, and then is successful employing it to facilitate his death. While pretend play is regarded as one of the most constructive tools for children, and a significant milestone in human development, Axler uses it in remarkably destructive ways.

Developmental psychologists such as Angeline S. Lillard and Paul Harris define the fundamentals of pretend play as follows. When pretending, one, two, three, or more pretenders must be aware of the coexistence of a reality and "a mental representation of some alternate reality" existing within the "same space and time" and for which the pretenders create the rules (Lillard 357, 349). Children who pretend work on many cognitive strategies, such as "joint planning, negotiation, problem solving, and goal seeking" (Bergen 194). Pretend play fires emotional, cognitive, linguistic, sensory, and motor centers of the brain, as well as encouraging "perspective-taking, cooperativeness, and social competence" (Lillard 362). Children who imagine seem better able to infer what others are thinking or feeling (Jarrold et al. 455). This facilitates a gradual acquisition of Theory of Mind skills and more sophisticated pretend play (Whiten and Byrne 267).[15] Researchers hypothesize that pretenders function on two levels, both real and imagined, jumping inside and outside reality and having "one foot in the pretend world and the other in the real world, [while] masterfully existing in both" (Lillard 355). Humans have emotional reactions to imagined situations because they "have evolved a planning system in which felt emotion plays a critical role" (Harris 88). In the act of pretending, they can "trigger in an anticipatory fashion the emotions that [they] would feel were [they] to actually do it" (Harris 88). Children who pretend "deploy their understanding of the causal regularities of the real world to make sense of the novel possibilities that occur within that make-believe framework" (Harris 27).

To compare the skilled performer with the pretend player in light of the progression of Axler's experience, pretend play requires making space for all three categories of Schechner's "skilled performer." The feeler accepts the pretend role, the knower is mindful of the fact that he is lying, and the observer complies and is not distracted by his coexistence in the pretend and real worlds. With the loss of his acting, Axler's knower and observer become dominant. Feeling that he is no longer telling the truth, he cannot abandon the "real" world, nor can he forget himself for even a moment. He does not attempt to adopt the qualities of one who coexists with one foot in the pretend world and one foot in the real world. He knows from his previous experience that this is not an option.

I contend that because of his episodic recollection of pretend play from the past, Axler turns to this instrument when all else fails. Revitalized by his unexpected relationship with Pegeen, he invites a woman to fulfill their fantasies and transports her into their bedroom. First he enjoys the *ménage à trois*, but as the scene draws to a close, he realizes that Pegeen is interested in seeing this woman—without him.

Axler resorts to the mechanism that he has recently recalled episodically – pretend play. Sitting at the table, drinking a real cup of tea, he begins *imagining* quite extensively and vividly:

> He sat downstairs in the kitchen and had a cup of tea as if nothing had happened, as if another ordinary night had been passed at home. The tea, the cup, the saucer, the sugar, the cream—all answered a need for the matter-of-fact.
> "I want to have a child." He *imagined* Pegeen speaking those words. He *imagined* her telling him when she came into the kitchen after the shower, "I want to have a child." He was *imagining* the least likely thing that might happen, which was why he was *imagining* it; he was out to force his foolhardiness back into a domestic container. (115–116, emphasis added)

Until this point, Axler has been living within the realm of the knower and the observer, with the feeler banished. This pretend play exercise allows him to reintroduce the feeler, albeit in a limited capacity. Roth's choice of setting— Axler in the kitchen with his tea—is, of course, revealing, as it connects the reader directly to the pretend play scene from Axler's past. In case we have disregarded the other hints, the word "imagine" appears *eleven* times in this brief passage. His elaborate *imaginings* include Pegeen asking him to father a child, his successful return to the stage ("the lost magic returned"), and the recovery of his former confidence (119).

In this imaginary scenario, Axler places all of the initiative in Pegeen's hands. It is Pegeen who declares, "it's a matter of *adopting a plan* to end the uncertainty. A bold long-term *plan*" (117, emphasis added). Using pretend play as a method to pave his way toward a solution, he crowns Pegeen catalyst. In this invented scenario, she initiates a new era. With a sense of renewed "determination," he strides away from this game of make-believe, ready to render the alternative reality he has imagined real (120).

Wasting no time, he consults a New York specialist on the "genetic hazards of fathering a child at sixty-five" (120). Axler "felt ecstatic with the return of his force and his naturalness and the abandonment of his humiliation and the end of his disappearance from the world. This wasn't reverie any longer; the revitalization of Simon Axler was truly under way" (121–122). He has constructed an alternate world where he can re-create himself and Pegeen, bringing this game of pretend to life. However, he misses the essential significance of pretend play: its limited influence in the real world and its function as a learning tool to try on new scenarios. He has created a pretend world and established the rules without informing Pegeen. After the fact, he prepares to invite her to collaborate with him in this game. He is convinced that using pretend play has led to a cure with which he will achieve his goal—propelling his imaginary scenario with Pegeen into their "real" existence. However, the very nature of pretend play is in its co-existence in both an existing and an alternate reality. As in Axler's previous experience, he expects the feeler to prevail, and "make the imagined real" (139).

Notwithstanding Axler's reverie, Pegeen is uninterested in his companionship. When he is poised to reveal the product of his imaginings, she tells him directly, "This is the end" (126). She makes her exit, and the "process of collapse [takes] less than five minutes" (130). As when his "magic" fails him, and when he returns from his stay in the psychiatric hospital, just when he thinks he is on the verge of restoring the Feeler, Axler spends the day "preparing to pull the trigger" (130). For the fourth time in the novel, he cannot execute his plan. Even with the barrel of the gun in his mouth, he cannot do it. Axler has returned to his affective paralysis.

Paralyzed he does not remain. Trying to complete the fourth stage of affective adaptation, he has attended to his crisis, reacted, and explained the cause by identifying the dominance of the "sly voice." He can only adapt to his changed circumstances. He has endeavored to use pretend play and been unsuccessful, yet despite his earlier failures and in his desperation, he initiates an additional game. He is surprisingly determined to try again, but stops short of initiating a game that would lead to him recreating himself and changing direction. Instead, he employs the imaginary world to design a strategy for executing *the plan* he adopted earlier when he lost his magic. He will "pretend that he [is] committing suicide in a play" (*The Seagull)* (139).

"What could be more fitting" than recreating the scene of his first success as an actor in order to bring about his demise (139)? To realize his goal, Axler will be expected to coexist on two levels, real and imagined, maintaining awareness of the knower and the observer and the feeler simultaneously. He will need to locate himself in the center of the performative continuum. During his training as an actor and his one-sided collaboration with Pegeen, this has turned out badly. However, Roth has endowed Axler with persistence. He will now attempt to have all three portions coexist. This time, he seems to have learned from his earlier failures. He has chosen to play the game alone. He must construct and create the rules. Having attended, reacted, and explained, he will try to adapt.

He carefully sets the stage: the attic is his theater, and he is to make believe he is Chekhov's Konstantin Gavrilovich Treplev, committing suicide on the stage of his imagination.[16] Like a child playing a game of pretend, Axler banishes the "sly voice" and coexists with the observer, the knower and the feeler, creating a mental representation of himself as Konstantin on a stage, which becomes an alternate reality placed upon the reality of his attic. Once he has done so, like an actor or a child competent in pretend play, he uses this alternate reality as a lever, feels he is telling the truth, and, believing in this final performance, he ventures into the real world, pulls the actual trigger of his gun, and "make[s] the *imagined real*" (139, emphasis added). He has restored his "magic" and executed his destructive plan.

Let us examine Roth's performance as author and pretender, and our own willingness as readers to join him in this game of pretend play. He creates the rules. In effect, his job is to "make the imagined real" for us as we read.[17] By opening the book and reading, we agree to coexist in both worlds. We use what developmental psychologist Paul Harris theorizes as the continuation of pretend play in adults.

Fully grown men and women exercise an ability that they have developed as children to "imagine alternative possibilities and to work out their implications" (Harris xi). According to Harris, adult fascination with fiction, whether print, theater, film, or other non-factual media, is the natural continuation and extension of children's pretend play in grown-up life (Harris 6, 88). Adults use the ability they have developed as children to "imagine alternative possibilities and to work out their implications" (Harris xi). The advantages to be gained from skillful mind reading suggest an evolutionary explanation for adult fascination with fiction. Thus, reading about fictional characters offers readers similar learning experiences to those that imaginary play offers children, giving them practice in how "to plan ahead, to intend, and to decide between alternative actions" (Lillard 367).

By the nature of their creative work, authors build mental representations of an alternate reality that coexists with their everyday world. They venture back and forth, existing simultaneously, with one foot in the real world and the other in the imagined (Lillard 353). They suspend what they know about the world and "simulate a counter-factual, hypothetical reality" on their journey towards actualizing, in writing, a condition that does not exist (Jarrold et al. 455). This is the stuff of fiction. When it works, readers become feelers who are simultaneously observers and knowers.[18] They join the author in a game of pretend play for which he has set the rules, and created the characters, the plot, and the agenda.

In Philip Roth's navigation of Simon Axler's tale, we encounter a character with all the potential to redirect himself. Accustomed to improvising and feeling his way through his experience, Axler should be highly likely to bounce back. To make matters more likely to resolve successfully, we witness Axler turning a negative episodic memory into a potential breakthrough in his narrative. This clearly demonstrates his ability to learn, adjust, and even adapt. To convince us even further, we note Axler's temporary success with pretend play. And even though his first attempt at pretend play with Pegeen fails miserably, he uses the tool to make an additional attempt, and succeeds. With all of these opportunities at his main character's disposal, Roth encourages us, keeps us hoping, and sets us up to fall right along with Axler. With the flourish of a pen, he could have restored his magic, transformed him using pretend play, or left us with an ambiguous ending. Instead, he humbles Axler, who becomes yet another Rothian character who "[sticks] to a plan" and meets his death.[19]

Just as Roth's Axler ventures to convince Pegeen to collaborate in a game of imaginary play, Roth invites us to collaborate in creating an alternate reality that leads to Axler's suicide. By continuing to read, we place our trust in author and pretender, Roth. Once we have completed *The Humbling*, we close the book, and restore both feet to our real world. We readers are left considering whether there was "sufficient cause" for his suicide, whether "[anything] has a good reason for happening," whether a standing ovation is in order and whether we are interested in joining Roth for another game (15, 16–17).

NOTES

1. This quote is paraphrased from Philip Roth's *The Humbling* (Excerpts from *The Humbling*. Copyright 2009 by Philip Roth. Reprinted by permission of Houghton Mifflin Harcourt Publishing Company. All rights reserved) and *The Human Stain* (Excerpts from *The Human Stain: A Novel by Philip Roth*. Copyright 2000 by Philip Roth. Reprinted by permission of Houghton Mifflin Harcourt Publishing Company. All rights reserved); as well as Ralph Ellison's *Invisible Man* (Excerpts from *Invisible Man* by Ralph Ellison, copyright 1947, 1948, 1952 by Ralph Ellison. Copyright renewed 1975, 1976, 1980 by Ralph Ellison. Used by permission of Random House, an imprint and division of Penguin Random House LLC).

2. This chapter is based on a paper that I presented at the "Roth@80" conference in Newark, New Jersey in March 2013.

3. Excerpt from *The Presentation of Self in Everyday Life* by Erving Goffman, copyright 1959 by Erving Goffman. Used by permission of Doubleday, an imprint of the Knopf Doubleday Publishing Group, a division of Penguin Random House LLC. All rights reserved.

4. This is not my first effort at negotiating these fields. In my doctoral dissertation, *Mark Twain and Ralph Ellison: Passing Performances in America*, I discuss the significance of pretend play, performance and episodic and semantic memory upon the characters and authors of *Adventures of Huckleberry Finn* and *Invisible Man*.

5. I am indebted to the comprehensive work of cognitive literary theorists Alan Palmer and Lisa Zunshine, which successfully blends literary theory and cognitive studies. Their arguments thus lend legitimacy to my treatment of fictional characters' behavior as a representation of human behavior.

6. For a more comprehensive discussion of Theory of Mind and its implications, please see Simon Baron-Cohen's *Mindblindness* and "The Evolution of a Theory of Mind?" Alan Palmer's *Fictional Minds*, and Andrew Whiten and Richard W. Byrne's "The Emergence of Metarepresentation in Human Ontogeny and Primate Phylogeny."

7. For more information on this cognitive-literary connection, see the works of Ellen Spolsky, such as "Narrative as Nourishment," and Alan Richardson's "Studies in Cognition and Literature: A Field Map," to name a few resources.

8. Schechner delves deeply into the works of Erving Goffman, Victor Turner, Paul Ekman, Ray Birdwhistell, and others to firmly establish his argument.

9. According to Butler's discussion of gender and racial performativity, identity construction is an ongoing process, not a single performative utterance. What makes this identity seem fixed is when it is repeated by the individual and verified by others and by culture. Individuals are influenced by and identify with society's norms because their "formation of subject" has been influenced by the "identificatory processes" that every individual experiences, whether consciously or not. Axler's identity is likewise constructed over time and experience.

10. Goffman distinguishes between "sincere" and "cynical" performances in the following manner: "When the individual has no belief in his own act . . . we may call him cynical, reserving the term 'sincere' for individuals who believe in the impression fostered by their own performance" (18).

11. When referring to the death of his acting ability, describing his preparation for going out on stage, "he spent an entire day thinking thoughts he'd never thought before a performance in his life: I won't make it, I won't be able to do it, I'm playing the wrong roles, I'm overreaching, I'm faking . . ." (*Humbling* 2–3). Axler has transitioned from the world of creative improvisation to the world of self-conscious thought.

12. Long term memory has been divided into two categories: declarative (or explicit) and nondeclarative (or implicit) procedural memory. For my purposes, I will be focusing on the further subcategorization of declarative memory into episodic and semantic. For an extensive discussion of memory, see Larry R. Squire, Endel Tulving, Alan Baddeley, and Daniel L. Schacter.

13. As Lisa Zunshine aptly states in *Why We Read Fiction*, page 51, episodic memories are called up with some of the "source tags" ('who,' 'what,' 'where,' and 'how') still attached to them in an experiential manner.

14. Tali Boritz, et. al. refer to these types of "over-general, non-specific ABM (autobiographical memory) disclosure" as occurring in depressed patients and discusses the significance of "emotionally salient personal stories" that allow patients to experience a "therapeutic change process."

15. Andrew Whiten and Richard W. Byrne, 267. There is some disagreement among cognitive and developmental psychologists as to whether pretend play develops parallel to or precedes Theory of Mind skills. Since this chapter discusses

fictional characters and humans over the age of six, this disagreement does not affect my argument. Healthy children pretend in conjunction with ToM (Theory of Mind), and "with age, [they] become increasingly able to entertain multiple sets of dual representations," (Lillard 352). For more information about this discussion, see Alan M. Leslie, Chris Jarrold, et al., and Jennifer M. Jenkins and Janet Wilde Astington.

16. In Chekhov's play, Konstantin commits suicide offstage.

17. Roth, *The Humbling*, 139. Lisa Zunshine develops an extensive argument that adds to reader-response theory's focus on the reader's interpretation of the text, the importance of the "mind-reading mind of the writer" (161). This is a direction that I have developed in chapter four of my doctoral dissertation, "Nonfictional Passing Performers: Authors Caught in the Act."

18. Lisa Zunshine supports Paul Harris's theory: "The cognitive rewards of reading fiction might thus be aligned with the cognitive rewards of pretend play through a shared capacity to stimulate and develop the imagination. It may mean that our enjoyment of fiction is predicated—at least in part—upon our *awareness* of our 'trying on' mental states *potentially available* to us but at a given moment *differing* from our own" (17).

19. I have traced this intertextual echo to Coleman Silk's performance in *The Human Stain*. Philip Roth's Silk is another example of a character who constructs a plan and adheres to it. This is alluded to in my title. Roth chooses precisely the same words to describe Coleman's sister's description of his decision to remain silent as he uses to describe Axler's attempt to imagine an alternate reality with Pegeen. Both characters "stick to their plans." To demonstrate an alternative possibility to the one demonstrated by Roth, I refer you to "'Invisible Man': Misconstructing and Reconstructing an Invisible Self," where I explore Ellison's use of episodic memory to transform his main character, who also believes, "You have to stick to the plan." This treatment of episodic memory fosters his ability to alter his original plan and change his narrative. See my dissertation, *Mark Twain and Ralph Ellison: Passing Performances in America*.

WORKS CITED

Baddeley, Alan. "The Concept of Episodic Memory." *Philosophical Transactions: Biological Sciences* 356.1413 (Sept. 29, 2001): 1345–1350. Print.

Baron-Cohen, Simon. "The Evolution of a Theory of Mind?" *The Descent of Mind: Psychological Perspectives on Hominid Evolution*. Ed. Michael C. Corballis and Stephen E. G. Lea. New York: Oxford UP, 1999. 261–277. Print.

———. *Mindblindness: An Essay on Autism and Theory of Mind* (Cambridge: MIT P, 1995). Print.

Boritz, Tali Z, Emily Bryntwick, and Lynne E. Angus. "Working with Autobiographical Memory Narratives in Psychotherapy." *The Society for the Advancement of Psychotherapy*. American Psychological Association, June 1, 2008. Web. March 7, 2016.

Bergen, Doris. "The Role of Pretend Play in Children's Cognitive Development." *Early Years Education: Major Themes in Education.* Ed. Rod Parker-Rees and Jenny Willan. New York: Routledge, 2006. 193–204. Print.

Butler, Judith. *Bodies that Matter: On the Discursive Limits of "Sex."* London: Routledge, 1993. Print.

Ellison, Ralph *Invisible Man.* 2nd ed. New York: Random House, 1995. Print.

Gelbart, Amy. "Mark Twain and Ralph Ellison: Passing Performances in America." Diss. Bar Ilan University, 2008. Print.

Goffman, Erving. *The Presentation of Self in Everyday Life.* New York: Anchor, 1959. Print.

Harris, Paul. *The Work of the Imagination.* Oxford: Blackwell, 2000. Print.

Jarrold, Chris, Peter Carruthers, Peter K. Smith, and Jill Boucher. "Pretend Play: Is It Metarepresentational?" *Mind & Language* 9.4 (May 2007): 445–468. Print.

Jenkins, Jennifer M. and Janet Wilde Astington. "Theory of Mind and Social Behavior: Causal Models Tested in a Longitudinal Study." *Merrill-Palmer Quarterly.* 46.2 (April 2000): 203–220. Print.

Klein, Stanley B., Leda Cosmides, Kristi A. Costabile and Lisa Mei. "Is there something special about the self? A neuropsychological case study." *Journal of Research in Personality* 36 (2002): 490–506. Print.

Leslie, Alan M. "Pretense and Representation Revisited." *Representation, Memory, and Development.* Ed. Nancy L. Stein, Patricia J. Bauer, Mitchell Rabinowitz. London: Erlbaum, 2002. 103–114. Print.

Lillard, Angeline S. "Pretend Play Skills and the Child's Theory of Mind." *Child Development* 64 (1993): 348–371. Print.

Magerko, Brian and Waleed Manzoul, Mark Riedl, Allan Baumer, Daniel Fuller, Kurt Luther and Celia Pearce. "An Empirical Study of Cognition and Theatrical Improvisation." Proceedings at the Seventh ACM Conference on Creativity and Cognition Conference, University of Berkley, California, October 27–30, 2009. New York: ACM, 2009. 117–126. Print.

Palmer, Alan. *Fictional Minds.* Lincoln: U of Nebraska P, 2004. Print.

Pinker, Steven. *How the Mind Works.* Harmondsworth, England: Penguin, 1997. Print.

Richardson, Alan. "Studies in Cognition and Literature: A Field Map." *The Work of Fiction: Cognition, Culture and Complexity.* Ed. Alan Richardson and Ellen Spolsky. Hampshire, England: Ashgate, 2004. Print.

Roth, Philip. *The Human Stain.* New York: Houghton, 2000. Print.

———. *The Humbling.* New York: Houghton, 2009. Print.

Schacter, Daniel L., Donna Rose Addis, and Randy L. Buckner. "Remembering the Past to Imagine the Future: The Prospective Brain." *Nature* 8, 2007. Print.

Schechner, Richard. *Performance Theory.* New York: Routledge, 1988. Print.

Spolsky, Ellen. "Narrative as Nourishment." *Toward a Cognitive Approach Toward Literary Narratives.* Ed. Frederick Luis Aldama, Arturo J. Aldama, and Patrick Colm Hogan. Austin, Texas: U of Texas Press, 2010. Print.

Squire, Larry R. "Memory Systems of the Brain: A Brief History and Current Perspective." *Neurobiology of Learning and Memory* 82 (2004), 171–177. Print.

Tulving, Endel. "Episodic Memory and Autonoesis: Uniquely Human?" In *The Missing Link in Cognition: Origins of Self-Reflective Consciousness*, 3–56. Ed. Herbert S. Terrace and Janet Metcalfe. New York: Oxford UP, 2005. Print.

———. "Episodic Memory and Common Sense: How Far Apart?" *Philosophical Transactions: Biological Sciences* 356.1413 (Sept 29, 2001): 1505–1515. Print.

———. "Episodic Memory: From Mind to Brain." *Annual Review Psychology* 53 (2002): 1–25. Print.

Wilson, Timothy D. and Daniel T. Gilbert. "Explaining Away: A Model of Affective Adaptation." *Perspectives on Psychological Science* 3.5 (2008): 370–386. Print.

Whiten, Andrew and Richard W. Byrne. "The Emergence of Metarepresentation in Human Ontogeny and Primate Phylogeny." *Natural Theories of Mind: Evolution, Development and Simulation of Everyday Mindreading*. Ed. Andrew Whiten. Oxford: Basil Blackwell, 1991. 267–281. Print.

Zunshine, Lisa. *Why We Read Fiction: Theory of Mind and the Novel*. Columbus: Ohio State UP, 2006. Print.

Chapter Eleven

Newark

The Shtetl

Mark Shechner

I was born in Newark in 1940 at the Beth Israel Hospital on Lyons Avenue and lived in the Weequahic-Clinton Hill neighborhood until the age of 11, when family circumstances obliged me to move first to South Orange and, within a year, to Los Angeles, California. We lived over Galoff's grocery store at the corner of Hawthorne Avenue and Clinton Place, diagonally across the street from my grammar school, Hawthorne Avenue School, which also doubled as an annex to Weequahic High School.

Across Hawthorne Avenue was a bank, The West Side Trust Bank, which looked to be chiseled by stonemasons out of solid marble, while across Clinton Place was Chaplowitz's candy store. The firehouse was two blocks away on Clinton Place, and my nervous system was conditioned by sirens and bells that were as essential to my night's sleep as bedtime stories. When the hook and ladder fire truck had to make a left turn onto Hawthorne Avenue, I watched in wonder as the driver of the rear wheels had to turn his steering wheel to the right so that the long truck could negotiate a successful left turn.

That was my childhood introduction to paradox.

At night headlight reflections jitterbugged across the ceiling of my bedroom as cars with noisy mufflers and grinding gearboxes crossed the intersection. To this day, my friend N. wonders how I can nap through riotous sounds that have her on edge at all hours. She can't know. I had to be careful crossing streets and was given rules: 1. Look left. 2. Look right. 3. Look behind you. 4. Go. I had a badge to prove that I was a member of the 1-2-3 Go Club.

West Side Trust is no longer there, and my own building is now a gravel parking lot next door to the single story Pentecostal Church of God on Clinton Place. The school remains, and so does Chaplowitz's, which is now El Intocable Supermarket, whose awning advertises Hot and Cold Sandwiches, Frozen Foods, and an ATM machine. (*Intocable* means "untouchable" or

possibly "peerless." But it can also translate as "pricy" or "unaffordable.")
The neighborhood was one of the epicenters of the 1967 riots, and as of my
last drive down Hawthorne Avenue in 2008, some buildings, including the
Hawthorne movie theater, were still rubble. That's forty-one years after the
burning of Newark. My experience of Newark does not go deep nor is it
geographically very broad—how could it be?—but what remains are my own
imperishable building blocks which can't be torn down until I am.

I find that over the years my attention in reading Philip Roth has migrated
away from the ironies, soap operas, and pratfalls that first energized me
to the broad social panoramas and landscapes, and I wonder if that turn
comes from Roth or from me. Let's say for now that it is both, and that he
labored for some sixty years on his majestic diorama of the Jews of Jersey
as if it were to be installed along with other still-life *tableaus* in the Newark
Museum, alongside exhibits of the Leni Lenape Indians, Abner "Longie"
Zwillman, and workers at the G. Krueger Beer factory. In reading Roth
these days I feel like a Neanderthal who has been taken to a museum of
natural history and shown some imagined recreation of my own life including replicas of me and my family, brutish and unwashed, with thick ridges
of bone above the eye sockets, polishing off a haunch of bush meat (but
Hebrew National bush meat) around a woodland fire. Q: "Did the Jews
have a prayer for bush meat?" A: "We had a prayer for everything." Was
it that long ago?

But though Roth's attention and locales might wander now and then, to
London or Tel Aviv or Prague, Newark for Roth has been home base from
start to finish and is now securely torqued into his fiction, allowing him to
scout around confidently on a tensile bungee cord of imagination. Newark
itself, and its distinction from the suburb of Short Hills, is the locale of the
debut novella *Goodbye, Columbus* (1959), as well as the very last novel
Nemesis (2010). And in between them *American Pastoral* (1997), *I Married a Communist* (1998), *The Human Stain* (2000), and *The Plot Against
America* (2004) inhabit Newark and are inhabited by it. It is hard not to make
the comparison to Dickens's absorption with London, Dostoevsky's with St.
Petersburg, Balzac's with Paris, Joyce's with Dublin, and Faulkner's with
Mississippi, all layered and intricate symbols that not only contain the lives
in them but also create those lives. The cities and regions are virtually super-
organic beings possessing lives of their own.

And I want to say, before launching into my own Newark, that I find Philip
Roth's Newark entirely credible and faithful to the place. James Joyce once
said that if Dublin were destroyed, it could be rebuilt brick by brick from his
books. That can't quite be said of Roth's Newark, though like Joyce's Dublin
Newark is a landscape infused with moral purpose and social meaning.

Art historian Irwin Panofsky's *paysage moralisé*, or "moralized landscape," is an illuminating term that is sometimes applied to medieval landscapes and shows up as the title of a W. H. Auden poem. It applies in particular to allegorical art. Roth wrote his novel *Everyman* (2006) in homage to those medieval dramas in which allegorical characters named Faith and Trust and Death and Fellowship and Good Deeds lend moral guidance to Everyman in his pilgrim's progress toward death and salvation. Though Philip Roth does not believe in the medieval world's four last things: death, judgment, heaven, and hell, his Newark is a *paysage moralisé*. So is mine.

The Newark I grew up in was entirely Jewish. If there were Gentiles around me, they did not register at the time. I mean, they were there but also not there, if you know what I'm saying. There was a Polish guy, and of course we called him Polack, but I can call up no other memory of him than the name. Roth's Newark, from Brenda to Babalu and beyond, is Jewish also, but there were differences between the one I knew and the one he describes. They are subtle, but they account for my wanting to think of my Newark as a shtetl, as opposed to Roth's, whose links to the old world were mostly literary.

His series of publications by authors under the grip of the Soviet imperium, *Writers from the Other Europe*, was a stand-in for the Old World experience he never had. The series, which ran from 1974 through 1983, transformed Roth into one of America's most European-oriented writers.[1] No doubt my own exposure to the Old World is accidental; the differences were street-by-street, family-by-family. But on Hawthorne Avenue, at least some of the store front signage was in Yiddish, in particular the butcher shops and the delis. If I learned nothing else of Yiddish, at least I could recognize the *kaf*, the *shin*, and the *resh* of *kosher* spelled right to left, so that I didn't confuse the deli with the barber shop, where, by the way, I could get no haircut without first singing a Yiddish song: "*Sheyn vi di levone, likhtik vi di shtern*," I sang. The barber closed his eyes and placed his scissors and comb carefully in a jar of blue disinfectant until I had finished. I always got an extra dollop of Wildroot Cream Oil or Pinaud's Hair Tonic upon my crew-cut *keppele* for my performance upon leaving.

The original Tabatchnick's deli was there, with its signage in Yiddish. I know Bragman's deli, as of 2008, still was. (The Google street view has Bragman's still in place at 393 Hawthorne Avenue and, as of July 2015, its signage still announcing "Hot Corned Beef—Hot Pastrami.") Yiddish was also spoken, shouted, whispered, sung, and tossed about like Watson bagels, since my grandmother, my mother's mother, lived with us throughout those first eleven years and spoke to me pretty much entirely in Yiddish, which surprisingly I understood, though I never learned to speak it in return. Which I so regret now. There was also a steady stream of Yiddish radio from station

WEVB in New York, to which grandma sung along, songs about luck and grief and separation and Momma don't worry I'm coming home soon. "*Oy vey nit mama, ikh fuhr a heym,*" she sang along with the radio. It was *mama, mama, mama* all the time, 24/7 on that station.

Add to this the close-knit family ties we had in that neighborhood. Neighborhoods like that were described in the 19th century by the sociologist Ferdinand Tönnies as *Gemeinschaft* societies.[2] I had two aunts, two uncles, two grandparents, and four cousins in spitting distance. Indeed, before I was born, eight members of the family lived in the same building on Schley Street, about five blocks from the Roth home at 81 Summit Avenue (this information courtesy of the 1940 census). God, how they must have grown to loathe each other in such close quarters. They were my two grandparents, my mother and her two sisters, the husbands of two of them, and a son of one. I believe that some of that teeming household had moved intact into the Weequahic-Clinton Hill neighborhood from Newark's Third Ward, which centered on Prince Street, where Newark's Jewish community had first established itself, and where my mother's sisters and one brother all went to South Side High School together, which is now Malcolm X Shabazz High School. In addition they had migrated along with a group of other friends who constituted their inner circle, including some who were still known by their Yiddish names like Duddy and Moishe and Gitl (or Gittie) and Rebecca and Tziporah (or Tzipkeh). Oh yes, and there was one they called Shtuppy. I'm not making this up. That was his name among all of them, and for those of you who know no Yiddish, it is the equivalent of going around with the name Fucker.

My grandmother, who lived with us, maintained a sewing circle of perfumed and bejeweled friends from her sweatshop days who bought clothing off the racks in our living room and who vied with one another to let me know that I was a *shayne klayne* and that they wanted to eat me up. I should read to them from the newspaper, they said, and "*Oy,*" they *kvelled,* "*Sehr klig.*" The first acronym I knew by heart was ILGWU, the International Ladies' Garment Workers' Union.

Two of my cousins had elderly relatives on the other side of their family who owned a storefront business on Prince Street, in the center of the Third Ward, which was by then black and poor. In the store there was nothing but a cash register and bags of charcoal piled against the wall. In July and August it must have been in high demand for barbecues and mosquito repellant. They themselves were grimy with charcoal and bent with ancientness: walking in there you could imagine a thousand miserable *shtetlach* of Russia and Galicia where Jews for centuries performed the daily miracle of turning nothing into something in order to stay alive. Turning water into wine would have been nothing to such people; every day they turned dust into potatoes and charcoal into eggs. Oh yes, and numbers into savings accounts. I shouldn't forget that. The numbers were their Social Security. Theirs could have been faces out of Roman Vishniac photos. Prince Street might as well have been Sholom Aleichem's Yehupetz. Only as we left, these grandparents would reach into their pockets for $10 bills for each of the children. It was what, 1949, 1950 maybe, and these charcoal merchants dressed in *shmattes* were handing out $10 bills to the children. Said my aunt after we left, making spitting noises over her shoulder to ward off the evil eye: "What cheapskates. They're raking it in from the numbers." They were her husband's family.

I did not know for certain how far back everything went, except that both of my grandparents were from the same Polish shtetl of Czechenowitz and are buried next to each other in the Czechenowitzer burial site in the Mt. Lebanon Cemetery in Iselin, New Jersey. I may never know for certain just how this sense of community took root, but I think some of it went beyond the Third Ward and into the old country. Nobody in the family kept records, and the Mt. Lebanon Cemetery also has none on hand that would help me out.

So my mom knew about half the other mothers and fathers on the street and pretty much knew what I was doing and with whom without my having to tell her much. They were on the phone daily, from Waverly to Bigelow and from Bigelow to Waverly (these were the telephone exchanges), and did their neighborhood grocery shopping together. This was before supermarkets, when you got what you needed from Galoff downstairs or Kravitz on Renner Avenue or the produce man who came clop-clopping up the street in a horse-drawn cart and left green baseballs of horse shit at the corner of Hawthorne Avenue and Clinton Place.

But the telephone circuit was also a means of circling the wagons, for there were indeed threats from all sides. Weequahic/Clinton Hill was still, after all, a vulnerable Jewish enclave in a city with large populations of Irish, Italians, Ukrainians, Germans, and African-Americans, and sometimes those differences exploded into violence. You wanted to know whose son had been hit; whose brother was in the hospital; who was on crutches. I remember once an older cousin of mine lining up in the school playground across the street from my house with his friends waiting for an Italian gang to show up. The core of his friends were in a club that called itself "The Spartans, A.C." (A.C. for Athletic Club) but the whole neighborhood, including grown men, turned out for these things. It was an old-fashioned rumble. Some of the threats came from the Ironbound section (or "Down Neck," after Neck Avenue that ran through it), but I remember it as being Ukrainian as well. Now and then a gang would come up from there looking for Jews to beat up. The cousin who was poised for a rumble had his own Latin name, Tico; he wore his hair in a DA, or duck's ass, hairstyle and lifted weights. It was in Tico's coal bin that I saw my first York barbells. He was of the generation of Alex Portnoy's friend Babalu. (Tico was I guess, from Xavier Cugat's "*Oh tico, tico, tick, oh tico tock, he is the cuckoo cuckoo cuckoo in my clock.*")

There is a fine book by New Jersey historian Warren Grover titled *Nazis in Newark* (2003) that details the actual pitched battles fought between Jews and the pro-Nazi German-Americans from Irvington. The Jewish warriors called themselves "The Minutemen," and they consisted of former boxers, including one Alexander Portnoff, and perhaps a few Jewish gangsters under the leadership of Nat Arno, a boxer and a cigar-smoking patriot. These attacks began in 1933 and 1934, when pro-Nazi organizations were beginning to form under orders from Berlin and were meeting in Irvington. They were going to be a fifth column when the time came, and Roth's novel *The Plot Against America* is about the Nazi fifth column. In Roth's novel the Nazis win behind the presidential campaign of Charles Lindbergh, only according to Grover, in the real Essex County, the Jews won. Only in America.

In the Weequahic/Clinton Hill neighborhoods, there was a natural blending of the commercial sphere with the underworld. The mob life of Newark at the time was under the control of Jewish mobster Abner "Longie" Zwillman, whose mother lived on Hansbury Avenue, about six blocks from the Roth home on Summit Avenue, while Zwillman's sister lived on Clinton Place, just around the corner from Weequahic High School. Roth captures this presence ever so nicely in *The Plot Against America*, in which cousin Alvin comes home from the war a physical and emotional wreck and takes a series of jobs on the shady side of the economy. For me, that is one of the absolutely best parts of *The Plot Against America*: a book I find ruthlessly honest and honestly ruthless. That is where Roth really shines, in getting into the underlife of Jewish New Jersey without fake piety. We weren't all yeshiva *bukhers* or the children of rabbis. Yes, I had ten-year-old friends who played chess, collected stamps, and read Dostoevsky, but their fathers ran numbers, took bets, and maybe even went to Irvington to beat up on Nazis.

I had a good friend Izzy, who was one of my stamp and coin collecting buddies, and every weekend we'd go downtown to the stamp and coin store to buy something for our collections. I still have some of our prizes, like my "California Gold Centennial" stamp and my "These Immortal Chaplains" stamps for the chaplains that went down with their ships during the war, and I particularly prize the 1943–1944 "Overrun Nations" stamp set, with stamps in honor of Poland, Czechoslovakia, Norway, Korea, and so on. At that time it did not register but there was no stamp for the Jews. Luxembourg got its own stamp for being overrun but not the Jews. That's why we needed our own country: so that America would issue a stamp for us. Izzy was a serious collector; he was into it, and he collected First Day Covers, so that as each new stamp was issued, he received it in the mail attached to a commemorative envelope. His collection could have sent his children to college.

I recently went looking for my 1948 three-cent Mt. Palomar commemorative stamp, and there it was, a squarish stamp in aqua blue of the classic art deco dome that still houses the 200-inch Hale telescope, which remains in scientific use. It remains in my shopworn Scott's album, stuck to its page by the original hinge and flanked by Francis Scott Key to one side and the Oregon Trail Centennial to the other, stamps commemorating events or organizations in which I have no more interest than in the American Poultry Association, whose commemorative stamp closes out the page. A brown and white chicken against the rays of a brown and white sunrise (so it must be a rooster) defines the very term lackluster in a history of lackluster American commemorative stamps. Only the Palomar dome that protects the humongous Hale telescope has any mystique for me, and if it isn't exactly my Proustian madeleine, it is close enough in time to the actual madeleine that it did set off a lifetime's train of thought, lasting some sixty-plus years.

It was in Newark that I was introduced to the word *hustle*, only not in the sports sense that we use it mainly these days, as in "he hustled down to first base." It had to do with making a dollar any way you could, as in "everybody has a hustle." To be a *hustler* was a term of high praise, as high almost as being a *mentsch*. There was no higher praise than that: you were a *mentsch* if you did your duty, did right by your parents and your family and your community. You always had a dollar in your pocket for someone in need, and someone in the family was always in need. But just a notch below *mentsch* was *hustler*, and it meant someone who gets by on his wits and his energy and *mazel*. Without hustling you were destined to remain a *kabtsn*, a poor man. Worse, you were a *shlemiel*. And worse than that, a *pisher*. In the descending scale of Jewish unfortunates, there were even worse things than *pisher*, but that was the one you never wanted to be called. However, with a little *mazel*: "*Mazl, es shaynt a mol far yedn, far yedn nor nisht far mir.*" ("Good luck, it shines sometimes for someone; someone but never for me.")

That was one of my grandmother's favorite songs at the treadle as she sewed together dress after dress for the perfumed and bejeweled ladies whose hair was always meticulously permed to the texture of a wire-haired terrier's, and whose beaded necklaces clicked like metronomes as they walked, and whose breasts bustled out into fabulous points by God-knows what feats of cantilever engineering, and who would come to our apartment over the grocery store to rave over grandma's floral dresses that they swore cost an arm and a leg at Bam's (for Bamberger's), and who confided to me in private that if I were their child they would eat me up, *kenna hora*. Was I just imagining it or were those real beads of saliva lubricating their dentures?

Just down the hill from our apartment on Hawthorne Avenue, next door to the delicatessen, was the West Side Men's Club, just a storefront with men going in and out or, on nice days, hanging out outside and smoking. There was nothing furtive about it; they were bookies and some of them were the fathers of my grammar school friends. No doubt they operated with the full *proteksia* of Longie Zwillman, which meant also the full protection of the local police.

One summer, when money was tight, my mother rented out my bedroom to the bookies for day use, and they took bets on baseball as I recall, in the morning, right up until one p.m. game time. I'd wake up to cigar smoke and "Browns six to five over the Red Sox, Garver against Parnell. Dodgers seven to five against the Giants, Erskine against Maglie." When I was sick one day and had to stay home from school, the bookies brought me juice from the fridge and steaming matzo ball soup from Tabatchnick, with a generous half inch of real chicken fat at the top. It was family; they took care of us and we took care of them. Once I learned from my colleague, the literary critic Leslie Fiedler (who grew up in Newark), that certain Jewish toughs used to beat him up on the way home from school, and when he told me their names I recognized them as my mother's friends, the bookies who used to work out of my bedroom. I have since learned from reading that they were among Nat Arno's gang of prizefighters and *shtarkes* that used to beat the heil out of the German Bund members when they gathered at the Schwabenhalle on Springfield Avenue in Irvington before the war.

Maybe it was the Southside High School connection or the bookie connection or connections I knew nothing about—maybe it was Duddy or Gittie or Shtuppy—but around the time we had bookies in the house my mother began working as a receptionist at Sam Teiger's Tavern Restaurant on Elizabeth Avenue and also picked up a gig either there or elsewhere as a torch singer in Yiddish and English and Yinglish. A typical Yinglish song went, "*Ikh vil a hussin oy a shrek! For some real love starb ikh avek*." The Tavern was Newark's premier white tablecloth restaurant, and I don't think you just walked into The Tavern and asked for a job as hostess; someone had to speak for you. I never knew much about this; I was 9 or 10 and a lot of mother's life was off limits to me, thank goodness, but the songs she rehearsed around the house were all variations on "Blues in the Night," in whichever language they were sung. You could see how she might fit the role. She had red hair and high Tartar cheekbones: a walking argument for those who believe that some Jews are descended from the Khazars, the "red Jews," from the steppes of Central Asia.

She was a vivid character: everything about her was 3-D, high color: her speech, her talk, the dresses that she had sewn on the treadle sewing machine in the kitchen. She lived an octave higher than the rest of us. She told the butcher, "Mister Bragman, these chops were fresh when Jonah's *tuchas* was inside the whale." "So sorry Missus. Come back tomorrow and I'll slaughter a lamb on the spot for you. You can have the wool for a coat." Around the house, while doing housework in her undergarments, she would sing songs from Yiddish theater that she picked up as a child, and from American radio: from her favorite program, "The Make-Believe Ballroom" with Martin Block on WNEW. Block was an inspired DJ who played something old, something new, something borrowed, and something blue, ranging freely from pop to jazz to roots, and featuring a Saturday night in Harlem. I'm nine and I'm listening to the likes of Cab Calloway (Hi De Hi De Hi) and Duke Ellington, while my mother irons shirts and grandma throws yellow vulturish chicken feet into a pot of furiously boiling water. (Izzy has kindly reminded me in a recent conversation that I used to have him over to listen over and over again to Frankie Laine singing "Mule Train" and "The Cry of the Wild Goose." Yes, I liked Frankie Laine too.)

But lest life grow too modern too fast, Old World touches were all around. I can still remember the coal trucks rattling their way up the hill on Hawthorne Avenue, the chains on their drive wheels jingle-jangling in winter, and their coal chutes extending into our basement so that the shiny anthracite coal could get into the coal bin. Every basement had a coal bin that was filled through a transom window. When the heat didn't come on, we banged on the radiators until Mr. Schneider, the super, went down to shovel coal into the furnace and bring up the heat. The excess hissed out through a release valve on the side. "*I got psss, steam heat,*" went the song, "*I got psss steam heat, I got psss steam heat, but I need your love to keep away the cold*" (Adler and Ross). We also had Yiddish language radio, mainly on WEVD, where I might hear Shtumer's Pumpernickel Program or Life is Funny with Harry Hirshfield, sponsored by Edelshtein's Tuxedo Brand Cheese.

Mom was a part-time torch singer, and her songs were aimed right at the solar plexus of anyone in the audience who had ever been spurned in love. She knew the broken heart—it was to love what gravity was to falling bodies from high buildings. Frequently they had something to do with each other. I know this from hours of being the audience at her recitals, intoxicated by her pungent essence. She could do it with that catch in her throat, that gasp of breath that said, "I'll never be the same after that man." She was a master of that catch and I've listened for it from dozens of other female torch singers over the years. Was it a professional touch or a confessional sigh?

She sobbed in Yiddish:

Ikh hob dich tsufil lib,
tsu zayn oyf dir gor beyz,

a nar ikh heyz, ikh veyz,
ikh hodkh tsufil lib.[3]

Her tonal color, a tragic contralto, was hard-wired for the blues. Generations of exile had bred such voices to sing "Stormy Weather." You couldn't
do "Sunny Side of the Street" in a voice like that. Leave your worries on the
doorstep? Who are you kidding? You were lucky to have a doorstep. With
advance warning you left lamb's blood on your lintel to ward off the *Moloch
ha Movitz*, the Angel of Death. Generations of exile had bred such voices to
sing "Stormy Weather" or "*Eli eli lama lama sabachthani,*" the cry of Jesus
Christ on the cross that had been revived as a Jewish lament to a god who
had forsaken them. Or:

Vi ahin zol ikh geyn?
Ver kon entfern mir?
Vi ahin zol ikh geyn?
Az farshlosn z'yede tir

This translates as:

Tell me where can I go
There's no place I can see.
Where to go where to go.
Every door is closed to me.

Though the song carried the meaning all too clearly on its own, some in
her audience might have known that the composer, Igor Korntayer, did not
find a way out and died in the gas chambers at Auschwitz.[4] Song for a supper
club? Neither more nor less than Billie Holiday's "Strange Fruit." In a Jewish
supper club in 1949 history followed you to your table. The Angel of Death
had spared you for now.

Since Roth's parents were American born, he had no direct access to these
outcroppings of nightclub music and 2nd Avenue Yiddish theater; in a way
he was advanced a generation from what I knew, and his most-used musical reference was to American bandstand music. Leading up to that odd and
wonderful moment in *The Human Stain* when Coleman Silk and Nathan
Zuckerman dance, Roth has Silk burst out, "Everything stoical within me
unclenches and the wish not to die, never to die, is almost too great to bear.
And all this . . . from listening to Vaughn Monroe" (14). I guess that was his
Frankie Laine. Roth's father was a regional manager for Metropolitan Life;
you didn't earn a position like that with a thick Yiddish accent or sitting
before a pile of paperwork in the office—the working man's version of the
sewing machine—humming "*Bei Mir Bist du Shayne.*"

I don't mean that Roth was closer to the suburb; only that he was farther from the shtetl. The two aren't to be equated; there was no express train from the shtetl to the suburb, but a jagged line that had its own density and elasticity; it could stretch or collapse; it could take one generation or two. Did it take three in some cases? What I seem to be calling up in this recollection is anything but a routine social picture of Newark as a staging ground for the collective Jewish leap into the middle class to be found in the Oranges, Maplewood, Short Hills, and beyond. Old Rimrock? Hollywood? Didn't Jerry Lewis (Jerome Levitch), an Irvington High School dropout, make it all the way to the top? Sure Newark wound up being that, but what erupts in my reveries is old world disorder and heat and transitions that were far more ambiguous and incomplete than a conventional poorhouse-to-penthouse sociology would tell you. It was its own world and not just a transitional stage. I remember Jewish Newark as a hothouse, as were all those American shtetlach, from Coney Island to Chicago's West Rogers Park. There is a line from Philip Roth in *The Facts* that brings it home for me. In the middle of a peroration on his Hebrew School education at the Talmud Torah he writes, "Despite all our taboos and prohibitions and our vaunted self-denial, a nervous forcefulness decidedly *irrepressible* pulsated though our daily life, converting even the most agonizing annoyances . . . into unpredictably paradoxical theater" (122, emphasis added). A novelist could write a lifetime of books about that nervous forcefulness and the unpredictably paradoxical theater of daily existence.

So Roth would have missed then the horseradish pungency of the Yiddish language, which was not spoken around him. He does get something of the pacing and agitation right, and some of the best passages in *Portnoy's Complaint* do capture the *Sturm und Drang* of spoken Yiddish in Jewish homes. Yiddish is a language spoken with the mouth and soul wide open. But the insistent, daily vulgarity does not translate reliably into English, and to this day my memories of Yiddish are marked by its fluent and zestful vocabulary of insult that has no English equivalent. English grows tongue-tied at the moment of invective, reducing too much of its vocabulary of contempt to variations on the word "fuck."

Yiddish was original and even Shakespearean about the curse. Invective unlocked its genius. Riding in my grandfather's scrap truck, with its chain-drive wheels and windshield that tilted outward for ventilation, I absorbed the full range of his tirade, as he let the other drivers know what he thought of them, punctuated with cigar spit. "*Geh kocken*" (go take a shit); "*Ikh hub dir in d'rerd*" (you should be dead and buried); "*Ver geharget*" (drop dead); "*kish mir in tukhes*" (kiss my ass); "*Ikh kock af dir*" (I shit on you); "*Ich hob dir in bod*" (I'll have you in the bath); and "*Geh kocken afn yam*" (go shit in the ocean). This is just a fraction of it: my sense of life was formed in a magical kingdom wherein also dwelt such real and mythical beasts as *yentas* and *gonifs* and *schmucks* and *putzes* and *shtunks* and *shnorrers* and *vantsen* (bedbugs) and *momsers* (bastards) and *paskudnyaks* (the lowest of the low) and *schticks d'reck* (pieces of shit) and *klutzes* and *unglicks* (unlucky ones) and *miskeyts* (ugly people) and *mishugeners, alter kockers* (old shitters), *pishers*, and *tuchas lekers* (ass lickers), and much much more.

In North Jersey, Grandpa would shout these out the window to drivers who cut him off or got too close and they would respond in kind, in Yiddish or some other language: Italian maybe or Polish. He spoke Polish too, but only out the window. Grandma couldn't shut up about him. She spoke his name and made spitting noises. He was the tramp, the *trumbenik*, the liar and the *goniff.* He had other women: "Them he gives golden earrings. Me he gave *tsuris.*" That was her story. Such a family was my Torah and my Talmud. It was also a place where I learned to appreciate language in all its registers, not just the elevated ones used to address *HaShem*. It was a boy's education in being Jewish in North Jersey, and a small window onto the world of the shtetl, which tugged at my Polish-born grandparents like a fierce undertow, dragging them in their dreams back to the raging European fire.

NOTES

1. The books published in that series were György Konrád, *The Case Worker* (1974); Milan Kundera, *Laughable Loves* (1975) and *The Book of Laughter and Forgetting* (1980); Ludvík Vaculík, *The Guinea Pigs* (1975); Tadeusz Borowski, *This Way for The Gas, Ladies and Gentlemen* (1976); Bruno Schulz, *The Street of Crocodiles* (1977) and *Sanatorium Under the Sign of the Hourglass* (1979); Danilo Kiš, *A Tomb for Boris Davidovich* (1989); Jerzy Andrzejewski, *Ashes and Diamonds* (1980); Tadeusz Konwicki *A Dreambook for Our Time* (1983); Bohumal Hrabal, *Closely Watched Trains* (1981); Witold Gombrowicz, *Ferdyduke* (1983); Géza Csáth, *Magician's Garden and Other Stories* (1983). It was a remarkable outpouring of books collected in a single series over nine years.

2. See Tönnies, *Gemeinschaft und Gesellschaft.*

3. According to *Zemerl*, the online database of Yiddish songs, the full song's lyrics in English are:

> Lovely as the moon
> Bright as the stars
> Heaven sent me the gift of you
> I got lucky when I found you,
> lovely as a thousand suns,
> you caused my heart to rejoice
> Your teeth white as pearls
> And your gorgeous eyes
> Your hands, your hair

send me out of my mind.

YouTube has a very fine rendition of this song by the Barry Sisters, who were the Andrews Sisters of Yiddish.

4. The version by Leo Fuld, in both Yiddish and English, is probably the model for her own version, and is available on YouTube.

WORKS CITED

Adler, Richard and Jerry Ross, "Steam Heat." *The Pajama Game—Original Broadway Cast Recording*. Columbia, 1954. LP.

The Barry Sisters. *"Ikh hob dikh tsi fil lib."* Online video clip. *YouTube*. YouTube, Feb. 19, 2009. Web. March 7, 2016.

Fuld, Leo. "Where Can I Go? (*Wo Ahin Soll Ich Geh'n?*)." Online video clip. *YouTube*. YouTube, Feb. 7, 2009. Web. March 7, 2016.

Grover, Warren. *Nazis in Newark*. New Brunswick, NJ: Transaction, 2003. Print.

Roth, Philip. *The Facts*. New York: Vintage, 1988. Print.

———. *The Human Stain*. Boston: Houghton, 2000. Print.

———. *The Plot Against America*. Boston: Houghton, 2004. Print.

Tönnies, Ferdinand. *Gemeinschaft und Gesellschaft*. Berlin: Curtius, 1921. Print.

Afterword

Mark Shechner's Legacy

David Gooblar

A Newark Jew flees the candy shops and stickball games of Weequahic for Berkeley, where he devotes himself to his twin passions of psychoanalytic theory and Joyce. He's then exiled to Buffalo, of all places, to launch his mischievous and sneakily subversive assaults on the culture from the *goyische* stronghold of the English department. All the while he keeps something of the Jewish hustler's spirit even as he becomes the distinguished senior academic. If Mark Shechner hadn't existed, Philip Roth might have had to invent him.

Mark died in October of 2015, while we were still putting this collection together, and this book is dedicated to his memory. His loss will be sharply felt for many years by those of us who knew him and his work. Mark was a giant in the now-established field of Philip Roth Studies; he did a lot of the establishing. Before most of the literary critical world caught on to the fact that Philip Roth was more than just a narcissistic celebrity author, Mark was writing about Roth's books with insight, humor, and seriousness. In book reviews, essays, and monographs, Mark's work on Jewish-American literature in general, and on Roth in particular, paved the way for nearly everyone who writes about Roth today, including all of the contributors to this volume. He personally supported the work of many scholars who looked to him for guidance, including the two who have edited these pages. "I hope that debts which go deep and are unpayable may nevertheless be acknowledged in brief," reads the first line of the first page of the first book Mark published; I hope that I can acknowledge our debts to Mark in these pages, even if they are ultimately unpayable (*Joyce* ix).

It is difficult to talk about Mark's writing without talking about Mark's voice. His voice on the page was something else: knowing, ironic, learned without being pretentious, unafraid of stretched metaphors and violent similes, seeing no contradiction—or rather seeing no *problem* with the contradiction—in combining the language of the Jewish candy store with the language of the (Jewish) graduate seminar. He was a virtuoso prose writer; high and low registers mix in his sentences without any seeming effort. You can hear, in those sentences, his youth among the toughs of Weequahic and his adulthood among the book-drunk denizens of the English department. Here he is on the experience of reading literature: "I know from long self-acquaintance that this experience is haphazard, inconsistent, and whimsical. I mean, if you are going to be consistent or rule bound about the business of reading, why do it? Where's the adventure?" (*Copper* 18).

On the crisis of intellectual culture that faced many Jewish writers in the 1940s, Mark wrote that "[Philip] Rahv and [William] Phillips recommended 'the tradition of critical conformism going back to Thoreau and Melville' as one might recommend the Junior league to a stymied housewife" (*Revolution* 5).

And here's Mark on the differing stipulations facing Roth when he decided to write a book about his father:

> It is well and good to take corrosive postmodern views of your own life, espe-
> cially after you have been through years of psychoanalysis . . . But in writing
> about your father you had better be all business. You're his Kaddish after all. And
> this is getting it right, is it not? The "self" may be something you put together
> afresh every day, or every book, but your father was *your father*. (*Copper* 27)

You can find throughout Mark's work evidence of a relentless drive to "get it right." Getting it right *mattered* to Mark. And if you were going to sign up to read something he wrote, it damn well was going to matter to you too.

Mark's writing was pushy. It advocated for its points and then pushed for them and then badgered you about them some more. In this sense, Mark's writing has always been Jewish, at least in the sense described by Roth in his *Paris Review* interview: "It isn't what it's talking about that makes a book Jewish—it's that the book won't shut up. The book won't leave you alone. Won't let up. Gets too close" (140–141). Mark's books won't leave you alone either.

His *Up Society's Ass, Copper* (2003), a collection of essays and book reviews on Roth written over the course of thirty years, exhibits this pushiness well. Not content to let the writing speak for itself, Mark equipped nearly all of the essays with paracommentary devised to shape your reading of it: prefaces that lay out the context of the essays, and "Second Thoughts" that offer up evaluations, reflections, revisions, and conclusions. Of course, the essays them-selves have already been revised for the collection, "substantially edited to the point of being new essays" to reflect Mark's "change[s] of heart and mind" (xii, 17). In addition, there's a thirteen-page "Third Thoughts" essay at—or, I should say, near—the end of the book, offering a conclusion of sorts to the lifetime of

Roth reading that the preceding essays represent. Of course this is followed by an epilogue, thirteen further pages of reflection prompted by the 2003 publication of Alan Lelchuk's *Ziff: A Life*, a *roman à Roth* that Mark couldn't help but ruminate on for a bit. Not quite ready to leave it at that, Mark really and truly closes the book with "Notes toward a Bibliography," an annotated list of writings on Roth adorned with enough interpretive prose that it really should qualify as another essay. Reading through this, you can almost hear the sound of Mark's editor putting her foot down. *Enough*, Mark, no? Never.

This continual self-revision and nearly endless demands of the reader reflect Mark's deeply held vision of the world as one of argument, conflict, transformation, and ambiguity. His two books on Jewish-American literature—*After the Revolution* (1987) and *The Conversion of the Jews and Other Essays* (1990)—both take as an organizing principle the idea that moments of *conversion*, of the casting off of old skins and the pursuit of new ones, connect the most prominent twentieth-century American Jewish writers. To properly understand this dynamic literature, Mark urges us to "pay close attention to the atmosphere of faction and scrimmage that has enveloped it from the start" (*Revolution* 4). It is on the uncertain ground where ideas, identities, and ideologies are fought over that lasting art is created.

Mark was by no means the only scholar to see conversion narratives as a central vein of midcentury American Jewish intellectual and literary life. Indeed, many other writers have made the point that the casting off of Marxist youth in favor of an ambiguous, modernist adulthood was perhaps the single biographical detail that defined so many of the most important Jewish writers and thinkers of those decades. But Shechner was more or less alone in focusing intently on the act of converting itself, on the psychology of saying: *that—that is not me anymore; now I'm this.* "It is the trials and exactions of becoming that Jewish writers in our time have excelled in expressing," Mark argued, and argued, and argued ("Conversion" 16). This may explain why he was such a good match—a foil, really—for Roth, who admitted that his protagonists began "in a state of vivid transformation or radical displacement. 'I am not what I am—I am, if anything, what I am not'" (142).

It seems not coincidental that Mark was drawn to the contentious, the unsettled, the paradoxical. He had the mind—and the pen—for it. He relished the stuff: not fights for their own sake, but arguments for the sake of the life found within them. I think that Mark found something essential, something essentially human, in the push and pull of intellectual argument; his writing is testament to the satisfaction it gave him. He was, as I have said, pushy on the page, getting up close to his readers to make sure they got his point. But he was never disagreeable, never desperate. It's so obvious that he *liked* writing, and for this reason, among others, it is rarely less than a pleasure to read him.

In his chapter in this book, Mark notes that the Newark of his childhood was too complex a place to fit into any single reductive narrative. It was full of "transitions that were far more ambiguous and incomplete than a conventional poorhouse-to-penthouse sociology would tell you." That refusal to simplify, to reduce the messiness of life and art to something facile and palatable, shares more than a little with the war against the pastoral waged in many of Roth's late novels. That Mark's chapter, summoning up the lost world of "Newark the Shtetl"—a world that might be said to have birthed much of the literature that he devoted his life to reading, thinking about, arguing about, writing about—that it concludes with both a glossary of Yiddish insults and a reminder of the Shoah's haunting legacy seems to us only right. The world is full of such wild juxtapositions.

Mark died before he could finish revising "Newark the Shtetl." We've done our best to publish the chapter as close as possible to the way Mark would have wanted it published, and we have changed almost none of Mark's words. It seems fitting, if no less sad, that the piece should come out in this form, nearly done, provisional, with the author still reserving the right to change something. Some thirty years ago, Mark wrote:

> A book is never really finished, it has been said, only abandoned, and only the author knows how much he has left unsaid, how many puzzles he's left unsolved and mysteries unexamined, and how many loose ends he's left untied. That is inevitable, especially if the personal agenda behind the book remains open and the author's ideas are still in flux, even as he is shipping the manuscript off to the publisher. (*Revolution* vii)

Mark's ideas were always "still in flux"; may they remain so even in his absence.

WORKS CITED

Roth, Philip. "Interview with the *Paris Review.*" *Reading Myself and Others*, 119–149. 1984. New York: Vintage, 2001. Print.

Shechner, Mark. *After the Revolution: Studies in the Contemporary Jewish American Imagination.* Bloomington: Indiana UP, 1987. Print.

———. "The Conversion of the Jews." *The Conversion of the Jews and Other Essays.* New York: St. Martin's, 1990. Print.

———. *Joyce in Nighttown: A Psychoanalytic Inquiry into* Ulysses. Berkeley: U of California P, 1974. Print.

———. *Up Society's Ass, Copper: Rereading Philip Roth.* Madison: U of Wisconsin P, 2003. Print.

Index

About the Contributors

David Brauner is Professor of Contemporary Literature at The University of Reading (UK), where he teaches courses in contemporary American fiction and the graphic novel, and the Executive Co-Editor of *Philip Roth Studies*. He is the author of three books—*Post-War Jewish Fiction: Ambivalence, Self-Explanation and Transatlantic Connections* (Palgrave/Macmillan, 2001), *Philip Roth* (Manchester University Press, 2007) and *Contemporary American Fiction* (Edinburgh University Press, 2010)—and the co-editor of *The Edinburgh Companion to Modern Jewish Fiction* (2015). His essays have appeared in a wide range of journals, including *The Journal of American Studies, The Yearbook of English Studies, Studies in the Novel, Modern Language Review, Canadian Literature, Studies in American Jewish Literature*, and *Studies in Comics*.

Claudia Franziska Brühwiler holds a PhD in Political Science and she is an Adjunct Lecturer and Project Coordinator at the School of Humanities and Social Sciences at the University of St. Gallen, Switzerland, where she teaches courses in American political culture. Her first book, *Political Initiation in the Novels of Philip Roth*, was published in 2013 by Bloomsbury, and she is currently working on a monograph on Ayn Rand's relationship with Europe.

Alex Calder is Associate Professor of English at the University of Auckland, New Zealand. He has written extensively on the literature of the cross-cultural frontier and the problems of settlement, as well as on the works of Herman Melville. He is the author of *The Settler's Plot: How Stories Take Place in New Zealand* and *The Writing of New Zealand: Inventions and Identities*, and co-editor of *Voyages and Beaches: Pacific Encounters, 1769–1840*.

189

Amy Gelbart is the founder and head of the English Department at Herzog Academic College in Israel. Gelbart holds a PhD in English Literature from Bar Ilan University and an MFA in Television Production from Brooklyn College. Her literary interests include cognitive and performative approaches to the writings of authors such as Mark Twain, Ralph Ellison, and Philip Roth, and she has presented various papers on these topics. A Playback Theater actress and conductor, her current research involves studying the impact that improvisational and playback theater training has on the self-efficacy and performance of student teachers.

David Gooblar is a Lecturer in the Rhetoric Department at the University of Iowa. He is the author of *The Major Phases of Philip Roth* (Continuum, 2011). Alongside Aimee Pozorski, he helped to organize Roth@80, the 2013 conference that celebrated Philip Roth's eightieth birthday. His writing on American literature has appeared in the *Journal of Modern Literature*, *Critique*, *Philip Roth Studies*, *Saul Bellow Journal*, *The Guardian*, and *Jewish Quarterly*. He writes a regular teaching column for the *Chronicle of Higher Education's Vitae* website, and edits the *Pedagogy Unbound* website.

Aurélie Guillain is a Professor of American Literature at the University of Toulouse, France. She is the French translator of a number of stories for the Gallimard edition of Henry James' *Short Stories*, vol. II and IV. She is the author of a forthcoming Gallimard critical edition and revised French translation of *My Life As A Man* by Philip Roth. She has published two books on William Faulkner: *On* The Sound and the Fury (in English), and *Faulkner: le roman de la détresse* (in French). She has published many articles on Faulkner as well as on other American authors (Nathaniel Hawthorne, Henry James, Willa Cather, Philip Roth).

Patrick Hayes is a Fellow of St. John's College, Oxford University, where he teaches literature in English from 1740 to the present day. He the author of *Philip Roth: Fiction and Power* (2014), a book that explores Roth's impact on longstanding assumptions about the relationship between aesthetics and ethics. Other work includes *J. M. Coetzee and the Novel: Writing and Politics After Beckett* (2010), an exploration of how Coetzee's fiction engages with classic debates on the relationship between aesthetics and politics, which took a particularly intense form in late twentieth-century South Africa. He is currently working on the *Oxford History of Life-Writing, 1940–Present Day*, a history of the major developments in autobiography, biography, and other related forms.

Catherine Morley is senior lecturer of American literature at the University of Leicester. She has published *The Quest For Epic in Contemporary American Fiction* (2009) and *Modern American Literature* (2012). She has co-edited *American Thought and Culture in the 21st Century* (2008) and *American Modernism: Cultural Transactions* (2009) and edited *American Literature After 9/11* (2016). She has written essays on twentieth-century American literature and post–9/11 literature and culture for journals such as *Journal of American Studies*, *Review of International American Studies*, *Modernist Cultures*, and *Philip Roth Studies*.

Ira Nadel is a Distinguished University Scholar at the University of British Columbia and Fellow of the Royal Society of Canada. He has most recently published *Philip Roth, A Critical Companion* and *Modernism's Second Act*. Previous books included biographies of Leonard Cohen, Tom Stoppard, David Mamet, and Leon Uris, as well as such critical books as *Biography: Fiction Fact and Form* and *Joyce and the Jews*. His recent essays include "White Rain: 9/11 and American Fiction" in the *Canadian Review of American Studies* 45.2 (2015). He is currently completing a literary biography of Philip Roth.

Adam Zachary Newton is the author of *Narrative Ethics*; *Facing Black and Jew*; *The Fence and the Neighbor*; *The Elsewhere: On Belonging at a Near Distance*; and *To Make the Hands Impure: Art, Ethical Adventure, the Difficult and the Holy*. His forthcoming project is *Jewish Studies as Counterlife: A Report to the Academy*. He has held positions as the Blumberg Centennial Professor of English at the University of Texas at Austin, and University Professor, Stanton Chair in Literature and Humanities at Yeshiva University. He will be the 2017 Distinguished Visiting Professor in the Fox Institute for Humanistic Inquiry at Emory University.

Aimee Pozorski is Professor of English and Director of English Graduate Studies at Central Connecticut State University. She is author of *Roth and Trauma: The Problem of History in the Later Works* (2011) and *Falling After 9/11: Crisis in American Art and Literature* (2014). She has edited *Roth and Celebrity* (2012) and the Critical Insights edition of *Philip Roth* (2013). Her current research focuses on AIDS, trauma, and politics in contemporary American literature.

Mark Shechner (June 22, 1940—Oct. 16, 2015) was Professor Emeritus of English at the State University of New York–Buffalo and was twice a Fulbright lecturer on American literature. He authored several books, including *The Conversion of Jews and Other Essays*, *After the Revolution: Studies in the Contemporary Jewish American Imagination*, and *Up Society's Ass Copper: Rereading Philip Roth*.

Debra Shostak is Mildred Foss Thompson Professor of English Language and Literature at The College of Wooster in Ohio and Executive Co-Editor, with David Brauner, of *Philip Roth Studies*. The author of *Philip Roth—Countertexts, Counterlives* and the editor of *Philip Roth—American Pastoral, The Human Stain, The Plot Against America*, she has published on contemporary American novelists, such as Paul Auster, Jeffrey Eugenides, John Irving, Maxine Hong Kingston, and John Updike, and on film, with a special focus on cinematic adaptations.